ADRIAN BLOOM

WINTER GARDEN GLORY

Adrian Bloom

Winter Garden Glory

How to get the Best from your Garden from Autumn through to Spring

HarperCollins*Publishers*

To my wife Rosemary, who has shared the twenty-five years of the development of Foggy Bottom and much else besides, for which I thank her.

ACKNOWLEDGEMENTS

I hope this book will please, inform and encourage others to consider autumn and winter interest in the garden. In addition to those involved in preparing the book for publication, I would like to thank the following people for their assistance: Yvonne Innes, manager of Bressingham Landscapes, for her professional interpretation of my garden plans; Jaime Blake, curator of the Dell garden at Bressingham, for his exhaustive records of late-flowering perennials; my father, Alan Bloom, for his original groundwork on the alpine and perennial plants directories; in *Bloom's of Bressingham Garden plants*; John Bond, MVO, VMH, Keeper of the Gardens, Savill Gardens, Windsor Great Park, for his advice on specific plants; and John Elsley for his expert assistance with the hardiness zoning in the Directories. I would also like to thank George and Angela Edens, Steve and Maggie Putt and Roy and Judy Johnson who, although they received a "free" garden, have been kind enough to put up with continual visits and photographic sessions – and may have to be equally patient following the publication of this book! Nor should I forget Michel Boutet, "head gardener", for all his hard work over many years at Foggy Bottom. Special thanks goes to my wife Rosemary, who not only typed most of the manuscript, but gave support through what was a very long autumn, winter and early spring for both of us as I struggled to finish the book!

First published in 1993 by
HarperCollins Publishers

© Text and photographs Adrian Bloom 1993

Adrian Bloom asserts the moral right to be identified as the author of this work.

A catalogue record for this book is available from the British Library

ISBN 0 00 412892 3

Editor: Jackie Matthews
Art Editor: Ruth Prentice
Photographs: Adrian Bloom
Colour illustrations: Richard Bonson
Planting plans: Yvonne Innes
Picture research: Julia Pashley
Index: Dorothy Frame

For HarperCollinsPublishers
Commissioning Editor: Polly Powell
Project Editor: Barbara Dixon
Art Editor: Caroline Hill

Set in Garamond
Colour origination in Great Britain, by Saxon
Printed and bound in Great Britain by Butler & Tanner Ltd,
Frome and London

Introduction 6

THE "QUIET" SEASONS 10

Foggy Bottom 12
Autumn 18
Winter 30
Spring 52

WINTER COLOUR 58

Winter Colour in the Smaller Garden 60
Containers for Winter Interest 64
Year-round Colour and Low Maintenance 66
Mixed Planting for Year-round Colour 70
A Garden Without a Lawn 74
Planting Associations for Seasonal Colour 78

DIRECTORY OF PLANTS 86

Zones and Planting 88
Trees Directory 89
Shrubs Directory 92
Conifers Directory 110
Perennials Directory 119
Ferns Directory 129
Grasses Directory 130
Heaths and Heathers Directory 133
Alpines Directory 136
Bulbs Directory 139

Bibliography 142
Index 142

Author's Introduction

Most gardeners, I suspect, look upon the onset of autumn with a mixture of relief and depression. Relief that the rush to keep on top of the chores of grass cutting and weeding will soon be over, and depression, perhaps, that the fresh colours of spring and the warmth of summer are so far away. For those living in northern latitudes, especially, the certain knowledge that they must endure long months of shortened days and deteriorating weather bringing rain, wind, frost and perhaps snow, is even more depressing. The temptation to close the door on the garden is very strong.

But surely this is just the time of year when we most need interest and colour in the garden. When anything is scarce, it always seems to be more appreciated than when it is readily available. And so it seems with nature. When walking in the countryside during winter, for instance, you notice the silhouettes of trees, the bright bark of silver birch, the red berries of hawthorn. If snowdrops, lovely as they are, flowered in summer, they would create less of a stir than they do in late winter, when they appear suddenly along with winter aconites. And yet strangely, in the average small garden you see so little of these delightful harbingers of spring.

There is in everyone, I think, a latent interest in and need to respond to nature and plants, particularly in winter. This was confirmed for me when, during a BBC *Gardener's World* visit to my garden at Foggy Bottom in January 1991, Stefan Buczacki and I looked at some colourful plants. Some of these, which included the hardy *Cyclamen coum* and *Cornus sanguinea* 'Winter Flame', were so striking that over 6000 visitors arrived the next weekend that the garden was open to the public. The power of television is quite amazing, but so is the lift that plants, in all their beauty and drama, can give.

There are so many things that plants can do for a garden in winter. They bring nature to your doorstep – foliage, flowers and fragrance – to be enjoyed, and even taken indoors. Trees with colourful barks, shrubs with brightly coloured stems, evergreens with flowers and fruit, deciduous shrubs with fragrant blossom, conifers providing shelter, foliage and form, perennials, late autumn and early spring-flowering bulbs, and ornamental grasses adding texture and movement.

For many people in northern latitudes winter seems to extend from the end of one summer to the beginning of the next! And in this book I have 'extended' winter to cover autumn and early spring. Fortunately, there is an amazing range and variety of plants that can be used to create interest and give enjoyment throughout these long, dull seasons in the many areas that are largely frost and snow free. Even where

I live in East Anglia, supposedly one of the coldest areas of England, we can go through the whole of January without a single frost. So why not make plans to brighten up winter days with plants that we can see and enjoy?

This book is part of my crusade to open people up to the magic of the numerous plants that can brighten our dreary winters. Whether or not you are a keen gardener, whether you have a small or large garden, a patio or even just a balcony or window box, there are lots of ways of bringing life and colour to an otherwise drab prospect.

My own interest in gardens for winter appreciation began a long time ago when I joined the family nursery business back in 1962. By then my father, Alan Bloom, had already created one of the finest hardy perennial gardens in the world – the Dell garden at Bressingham in Norfolk, England – and

LATE IN AUTUMN, a shaft of afternoon sunlight strikes a potted Juniperus × media *'Gold Sovereign' and the ripe fruits of a trained* Pyracantha *'Orange Glow'* (above)

EARLY ON A WINTER'S MORNING, sun gradually disperses mist and frost at Foggy Bottom, revealing a garden packed with colour and interest (left)

THE WINTER BED at Foggy Bottom is vibrant with colour. Silver birch, dogwood stems, heathers, conifers, perennials and bulbs all contribute to a lively but ever-changing scene (left)

MYSTERY PERVADES THE garden early on a frosty morning. Evergreen shrubs and conifers provide the structure on which the frost works its magic, and then the sun dispels it (right)

naturally I wanted to contribute a group of plants about which he knew relatively little. Conifers and heathers seemed to fit the bill, particularly the dwarf and slow-growing types. Ten years later the nursery was growing over 100,000 dwarf conifers a year. Also by then I had expanded my own garden, started in 1967 on a quarter of an acre, to nearly six acres with a collection of over 200 different varieties.

Interest in dwarf conifers and heathers, which were appreciated for their year-round appeal and easy maintenance, was spreading rapidly. In order to widen the appeal I wanted to show people what could be achieved in an average-sized, suburban garden using such plants, but as clearly my own garden was far too big the nursery agreed to 'give away' a front garden as a real example and incentive. Located in an accessible part of the neighbourhood, it proved to be a great success (pages 66-69). By the early 1980s, there were nearly one million conifers growing in the nursery, and nearly 1000 varieties at Foggy Bottom.

Although my garden began to develop and change as the years rolled by, as do all gardens, conifers remained the mainstay, providing structure and form to what was once a nearly flat meadow. The garden certainly had year-round colour because I had also planted many other types of trees and shrubs to provide a more varied aspect. I have always had a keen interest in all other hardy plants, and in recent years I have tried to assimilate a wider variety of types, adding ornamental grasses, perennials and bulbs, to create pleasing plant associations – always with the theme of year-round interest in mind.

To put some of these developing ideas into practice on a smaller scale, I recently persuaded the nursery to 'give away' two more front gardens, each planted rather dramatically in a single day. The first was planted in the middle of autumn, not only to create a garden with winter interest but also to demonstrate the advantages of planting before the onset of the coldest season (pages 70-73). The second garden, next door to the first and by contrast planted in late spring, was designed to be drought-resistant and to give a completely different style of interest during winter months (pages 74-77).

The greatest challenge and the greatest reward in gardening is in creating pleasing plant associations which together make more impact than do the individual plants, and this is no less so when planning effects for winter months. Drawing on my experience with all the gardens mentioned above, this book discusses the best plants for introducing winter interest and shows how to use them in all sizes of garden. It is not so much about gardening in winter – although that can be enjoyable – as about enjoying the winter garden.

Adrian Bloom

THE "QUIET" SEASONS

ABOUT FOGGY BOTTOM

At the age of 27, I was given the somewhat unique opportunity of creating a garden from an open meadow. Designing and developing Foggy Bottom for over a quarter of a century has been a fascinating and absorbing experience during which many mistakes have been made, but much has been learnt about the art of gardening and the diversity and habits of garden plants.

The experience of collecting, trying out (and in many cases losing or discarding) over 5000 different species and varieties of plants has been enormously rewarding. But probably even more satisfying has been the opportunity to create a garden that has year-round interest and to watch it grow, develop and change over the years.

Perhaps by briefly running through the history of the garden's development, some useful tips and ideas will suggest themselves to readers.

Back in 1966, when our ranch-style house was being built, the thought of turning a meadow into a huge garden had not occurred to me. In fact, my wife Rosemary and I started with about a quarter of an acre surrounding the house. Fortunately, the soil was mostly good heavy loam with a pH of 5.5, ideally acid enough to grow summer-flowering heathers, rhododendrons and other ericaceous plants.

As I was already very involved with conifers and heathers, having started to develop production of both groups of plants for the family nursery business, it seemed logical to plant a mainly dwarf conifer and heather garden. The plan was to create a patchwork of colour using large groups of heaths and heathers, interspersed with an ever-widening selection of dwarf conifers that I was collecting both in Britain and from many other countries.

> "I first came across the name Foggy Bottom when working in the United States in 1959, and it rather caught my imagination. Located in Virginia, it is the site of many of the State Department offices. Apart from probably a lot of hot air, no doubt it gets foggy there, just as our garden does, when mist creeps up over it on cold nights."

My experience with these, however, was still limited, even though three years earlier I had pestered my father, Alan Bloom, into letting me create a small conifer and heather garden adjoining his five-acre Dell garden. So, I plunged in.

THE EARLY YEARS

Undoubtedly, most people become interested in gardening when they acquire their first garden, whether it is large or small. And so it was with me. Although the nursery business was then growing quickly, I found time in the evenings and at weekends (often working after nightfall with the headlights of the car switched on) to thoroughly prepare the beds and borders surrounding the house, constructing some semblance of undulation on what was a fairly flat piece of ground. I dug in a lot of soft sand which we had brought up from the lower meadows where the earth was more alluvial. With each plant I mixed in handfuls of peat to improve the aeration and moisture-retaining capacity of the soil. Finally, I mulched the small plants with peat or composted bark which, apart from visual appeal, also helped to retain valuable moisture in dry summer months and prevent annual weeds from germinating.

It took me nearly five years to create this first stage in the garden's development, taking on one bed at a time. But, it was surprising how quickly the plants that had been put in first started to grow. Being sheltered around the house, the plants grew well – almost too well! I soon began to wonder if these dwarf conifers I was learning about at first-hand really were quite as dwarf as the books and catalogues suggested. In many cases, they certainly were not.

Just six years after I had started, the garden was full, with no space left for any more plants. Coincidentally, at this time the conifer and heather department of *Blooms of Bressingham*, as the nursery was now called, was beginning to take off, and I desperately needed more room to trial and experiment with these plants. This was the argument that I used with my father and my brother Rob, who shared the joint managing director's responsibilities with me, as together we looked over the barbed wire fence to the five-acre meadow below my garden. To my delight both agreed that I should gradually take in the rest of the meadow. In 1974, the fence came down.

A NEW CHALLENGE

From a relatively small garden, designed around the house with a few undulations and limited views, I was now looking at the possibilities of much broader vistas. And with a flat open meadow to contend with, some forward vision was necessary. The strategy was to take in the meadow in manageable 1½-2-acre chunks, allowing the cattle to continue grazing until I was able to find the time to plant each newly prepared area.

Although the extended garden was to be primarily structured with conifers, I wanted to use a variety of deciduous trees and shrubs as well. Broad, winding pathways of grass would offer vistas and provide opportunities for creating distant focal points as well as interesting views round every corner. That, at least, was the theory.

First, I put out canes to mark the new borders, then I sprayed the grass inside the canes with a herbicide ready for soil preparation. At that time the nursery possessed a rather innovative, Dutch, machine spade digger, the revolving "spades" of which dug rather than ploughed the meadow. It was an imperfect job for a garden, but it certainly took a lot of the hard work out of the early preparation stage. The physical digging had still to be done, and I was fortunate at times to have help from the nursery to complement my own efforts.

With an open, very windswept field and little or no natural shade or shelter for most of the garden, many of the more tender conifers, shrubs and trees suffered, particularly after some severe winters. Foggy Bottom is a frost pocket. The lower part of the garden acts as a drain to cold air and is often a full degree centigrade lower in temperature than near the house, and two or three degrees lower than the slightly higher and well-sheltered Dell garden nearby.

In the first few years of the extended, unsheltered garden many Japanese maples, some magnolias and plants like eucalyptus and phormiums died. Even some of the hardy winter-flowering heathers were stunted as they tried to make new shoots after flowering.

Most gardens develop a microclimate of their own, and within each garden there are smaller microclimates. Those in Foggy Bottom were to change as the trees and conifers grew to provide shelter and shade to east- and west-facing beds. The soil, too, differs from place to

THE ORIGINAL GARDEN surrounding the house at Foggy Bottom in the summer of 1972, five years after the first planting. Soon afterwards, the fence between it and the five acres of meadow in front came down (left)

MANY NEW BEDS had been cut out by 1975 and prepared for planting. A few lonely conifers, planted in an open and windswept garden, were the first residents. Heaps of sand stand ready to be dug in to add undulation and to improve drainage (left)

THE SAME BEDS as above early on a late autumn morning, twenty years later and seen from a point a little closer to the house. The house is almost hidden from view and the original conifers have grown, packed around by heathers that were planted at about the same time (left)

place, with some low, poorly drained areas, and others which, being on a slight rise, dry out quickly. The soil in the lowest part of the garden, which was once part of a lake or valley bottom, is more alluvial than elsewhere and its pH rises to 7. Getting to know what to put where started to give the plants a better chance of success.

I did not want to create just a conifer and heather garden, but in the early years using mostly these plants did give me the opportunity to learn more about the large numbers of both that by the late 1970s I was collecting from all over the world. The garden was also an ideal vehicle for showing conifers and heathers in a garden setting, much as my father's Dell garden was used to show how to grow perennials successfully.

Foggy Bottom was first opened to the public after it was featured in a television programme in 1977. Several thousand visitors turned up to what was still a very undeveloped garden. Thus began an annual "open weekend" over the first Saturday and Sunday in September, but at least each year considerable growth and change could be seen by the regular visitors. Now the garden is open regularly from early spring to autumn.

A New Feature

A very large, flat garden, needs a special feature, and an informally shaped pond seemed appropriate for Foggy Bottom. The ideal spot was down at the lowest part of the garden, and in 1977 a bull-dozer scooped out a large depression, putting the soil between the pond to be and the old woodland beyond. This raised area was destined to be the woodland part of the garden.

Unfortunately, although the area where the pond was sited often flooded in the winter, it would never hold water

SPRING MAGIC in the winter bed from forsythia, ribes and daffodils (above)

THE POND MIRRORS fading rushes and distant conifers, adding to the atmosphere (opposite)

during the spring, summer and autumn. Two unsuccessful years later, we turned to the local aquatic expert who fitted a butyl liner to the contoured shape.

The pond added a new dimension to the garden: it was a feature to walk down to and around; it offered shifting reflections; it provided a habitat for fish and other aquatic wildlife; and in cold winters it became a skating rink.

Time for Reappraisal

With the help of two full-time gardeners, I reached the woodland planting at the bottom in 1980, but the garden was by no means finished!

It was planted primarily with conifers and heathers as well as a lot of ground cover plants. The latter consisted mostly of large groups of prostrate junipers, shrubs such as *Potentilla fruticosa* varieties, *Euonymus fortunei* and so on, but with a wide range within these. Other types of shrubs and some perennials added yet more variety.

Many of those plants that had been planted in the sun were now in shade as trees and conifers had grown, and many of the earliest beds around the house were becoming overcrowded. It was time to have another look at each completed section of the garden and consider change and improvement.

Like most keen gardeners who become avid collectors of plants, I wanted to broaden my knowledge. I felt Foggy Bottom offered an ideal opportunity to experiment with plants other than the conifers and heathers which hitherto had absorbed me on both personal and business levels. So the garden continued to be a trial garden not only for conifers but for a great many of the different shrubs and perennials I was by then introducing to Britain from Europe and further afield. I tried phormiums from New Zealand, weigelas from Holland and Canada, potentillas from everywhere, hostas and hemerocallis (day lilies) from the U.S.A., and many interesting and worthwhile plants from Japan and other countries.

Not all of these widely differing plants succeeded, but many have added immeasurably to my knowledge, even though, of course, the knowledge and experience of any individual plant in my garden alone is hardly exhaustive. A young plant killed in its first year by a severe winter, for instance, might have survived if it had experienced two or three milder winters giving it a chance

TRANSFORMATION OF A BED was brought about when three large × Cupressocyparis leylandii were removed along with some other shrubs and heathers to create space for a new planting using perennials, shrubs and ornamental grasses. When a garden has been planted for more than twenty years it is almost bound to be overcrowded and in need of some reorganization – particularly if fast-growing trees or conifers have been used (right)

to become fully established before being subjected to extremely cold weather. Now that there is more shelter and shade in the garden, many of the plants that have been tried and lost will be given another chance.

The opportunity for change should never be ignored – the challenge to create a more satisfying, diverse type of garden requires thought but gives a lot of pleasure, too, particularly when you feel something has worked well. Although we all like to see the instant garden effect, in truth I think it is much more fun to gradually build a scene, looking for the right plant, the right colour, shape or texture to create a satisfying or memorable plant association.

Redesigning parts of Foggy Bottom began in the early 1980s, and has contin-

ued ever since. Overgrown plants have been thinned out and, depending upon the soil and aspect, different features have been incorporated. Existing beds have been altered and extended and new ones have been created.

Although the whole garden has year-round interest, the border that we have dubbed "the winter bed" in particular has given a lot of pleasure, both in long view and close up. It was created in a way that one should approach most gardens, by structuring with trees, shrubs and conifers of year-round appeal, then filling in with lower-growing plants, shrubs, perennials and, lastly, adding many species of bulb, each with its own particular season of interest.

Now that the garden is getting quite mature, a lot of thought has to go into

not only what new plants to put in but which old plants must come out. For example, woody plants increase their dimensions in all directions as they grow, and so, even in a large garden, thinning out after some years have passed is likely to be essential. When creating a garden the ideal is to plant your choice plants wide enough apart, filling in between them with more disposable types. Then, when the time comes to thin, you can keep the best specimens. But, like many other things in life, such plans seldom seem to work out perfectly!

However, the "Leylandii bed", as I call it, did work out. In 1967, I had planted several 90cm/3ft high × *Cuppressocyparis leylandii* about 10m/30ft from the house to create a shelter from strong westerly winds. Twenty years later they were 15m/45ft high even though the tops had been cut out in 1978. Knowing that eventually they would have to come down, in 1980 I planted some slow-growing but choicer conifers behind, which were hidden from view from the house. Nearly ten years later we decided it was time to remove the Leylandii, thereby revealing a more attractive and less threatening background and making room in the foreground for a range of more interesting plants. One stump was left behind and is now covered with ivy. Despite there being no Leylandii left, the bed is still known as the Leylandii bed!

In developing Foggy Bottom I have closely observed many plants. Some I would never part with, others occasionally depart, without my blessing, and yet others must be discarded. Yes, even in a six-acre garden there is not room for plants that do not perform or have little to recommend them – there are too many others waiting in the wings for their turn to show what they can do!

THE FUTURE

For the present the garden has matured and the thinking behind the broad, grass pathways is only now becoming clear. As plants grow upwards they cut out more light, and had there been only narrow pathways at Foggy Bottom, the garden would soon have become one large woodland – and probably rather dark and dingy in winter.

While it is pleasing to get many kind comments from visitors, there is still much to be done because a garden must change to survive. Plenty of gardens planted over the last fifty years which have been subsequently neglected and are now completely overgrown bear witness to this reality.

I want Foggy Bottom to grow old gracefully. To do this, it will need to be constantly reassessed for new opportunities, such as creating plant associations and vistas that previously had not been envisaged or possible. Larger conifers and trees will need pruning, older, established perennials will need rejuvenating, shrubs and smaller conifers might need moving to new locations.

The garden is a place of peace and tranquillity (except when we are open to the public!) and gardening is a relaxing and enjoyable pastime. Unfortunately, business and writing commitments take up a lot of my time, preventing me at present from fulfilling the ideas and plans I have in mind. Right now, for instance, I can hardly wait to create a

GRASSES, HERE WITH PERENNIALS, seen two summers after replanting the bed shown opposite, will guarantee interest in winter as well (above)

stream running from near the house to the pond. Hopefully, the time will come soon. It is fascinating, meanwhile, to look ahead to the next twenty five years of change at Foggy Bottom.

The photographs that follow in the chapter called *The "Quiet" Seasons* are somewhat more eloquent than my words, but by progressing through the seasons at Foggy Bottom from autumn to early spring, they illustrate how a garden can offer interest the year round and, perhaps surprisingly, be full of colour and fragrance, too.

AUTUMN

For most gardeners the period from the middle of spring to the middle of summer is like life in the fast lane – a frenzy of activity as we prepare and plant, trim hedges, cut grass, water and weed, and generally try to keep up with events in the garden. It is a wonderful period, too, when perennials and bulbs break from the bare earth and trees and plants burst into blossom and growth, transforming themselves from a few shoots into verdant or colourful foliage and flowers that seemingly appear overnight. If our hearing were more acute, the sound of all this activity might be thunderous. And if we were to add the sound of birds singing, we could indeed imagine spring and early summer as the noisy season in the garden.

From mid-summer we begin to see the results of our endeavours and we can enjoy the peak of summer colour for annuals and many perennials, but still we must cut grass, trim, water and watch for drought, pests and diseases. It is a restless season but nevertheless a period when we can generally feel able to relax and even take time off for a well-earned holiday.

So, is that it? Is that the end of the main gardening season? The time when we can sit back and marvel at how long-lasting this or that plant is in flower this year, or how much a plant has grown. Once we have returned from holiday and the children are back at school, are we not likely to say: "The garden will have to wait until next year." Are we not, at this point, inclined to rest on our laurels and enjoy the last fine days of late summer and early autumn, watching the leaves turn and drop and looking for-ward to long cosy evenings in front of the fire and the television?

Perhaps, then, if we think of those months of activity as noisy, it may be

appropriate to call the long months of autumn, winter and early spring the quiet season for gardens and gardening. But while we all need a rest at this time of year, are we not missing something in the way of enjoyment and pleasure that the quiet season can give us by dismissing it so easily?

In my opinion, the period from early autumn to early spring is unfairly neglected by most gardeners, and when you think that, especially in the cooler temperate zones, these seasons comprise about half of the year, surely it is worth giving them more attention? Is this not just the time of year when we need *more* colour and interest in the garden than at any other? And, it is possible. There are hundreds of plants that you can include in your garden to lift your spirits at this time. In fact, so much is going on, that you will be amazed to discover just how much there is to see and enjoy.

One should plan to fill autumn, winter and early spring months with as much colour and variety as possible. The smaller the garden the more important that selection is. The crucial thing is to select plants that can be expected to give a good account of themselves in the particular conditions they are destined for and to be as versatile as possible.

The weather rules what we can grow in our gardens, and what we might grow well one year but perhaps not so well the next. Stipulating when a season ends

THIS SUPERB COLLECTION of conifers provides continuous colour, interest and structure throughout the year. Towards the end of autumn, as the days shorten and temperatures drop, the deciduous larch (Larix kaempferi 'Diana', centre), is turning golden, while the Pinus mugo 'Ophir' (foreground left) is on the point of swapping its bright summer green for winter gold (left)

SHRUBS AND CLIMBERS FOR AUTUMN

Of the many deciduous shrubs and climbers that I have found to be particularly reliable for providing good autumn colours, the following is but a selection. More information about these plants can be found in the directory section starting on page 86.

Acer palmatum 'Senkaki'. Golden autumn leaves, coral red winter stems.

A. p. 'Osakazuki'. Consistent, brilliant crimson autumn colour.

Aronia arbutifolia 'Erecta'. Rich red in autumn.

Berberis × carminea. Several selections offer coral fruits and pink and red autumn leaves.

B. thunbergii. Several of these have good autumn colour. 'Dart's Red Lady' is recommended.

B. × media 'Red Jewel'. Its glossy leaves acquire bronze and crimson shades in autumn.

Cornus alba 'Sibirica'. Bright red autumn leaves and red winter stems.

C. a. 'Kesselringii'. Crimson-purple leaves revealing black stems when they drop.

Cornus sanguinea 'Winter Flame'. Yellow, orange and gold autumn leaves with russet and orange-red stems.

Euonymus alatus 'Compactus'. Brilliant crimson autumn foliage in hotter climates, but duller in cooler ones.

E. europaeus 'Red Cascade'. Reddish purple leaves and scarlet fruits.

Aronia arbutifolia 'Erecta'

Hydrangea quercifolia 'Snow Queen'

Fothergilla gardenii. Spectacular yellow, orange and crimson leaves. Acid soil.

F. major. Spectacular yellow, orange and crimson leaves. Acid soil.

Hamamelis × intermedia 'Feuerzauber' (syn. 'Magic Fire'). Brilliant crimson autumn leaves, bronze-red winter flowers.

Hydrangea quercifolia. Bronze and purple autumn leaves.

Nandina domestica. Semi-evergreen with purple, red, pink and yellow shades.

Oxydendrum arboreum. Crimson leaves in autumn. Acid lover.

Parthenocissus henryana. Pink or bright red in autumn.

P. tricuspidata. Fiery crimson in autumn.

Prunus. Many to choose from. *P. incisa* 'Kojo-no-mai' has bronze to crimson colour in autumn.

Rhododendron, deciduous azaleas. Many turn yellow, crimson or red. Acid soil.

Rhus glabra 'Laciniata'. Orange and red.

R. typhina 'Dissecta'. Orange and red in autumn.

Spiraea betulifolia var. *aemeliana*. Good orange-red leaves in autumn.

S. prunifolia 'Plena'. Crimson autumn leaves.

Vaccinium corymbosum. Crimson-tinted leaves. Acid soil.

and when the next begins, however, is a somewhat inexact science. Each year the seasons roll into each other, often over several weeks depending upon location and climate, a little earlier or a little later than the previous year. And, as we know only too well, the climate can change from year to year, too.

Autumn begins at about the last time we can expect summery weather, which at Foggy Bottom is usually about the end of September. But the end of summer is not the end of colour and interest in our garden, nor need it be in any garden, no matter what its size.

Autumn foliage

In some parts of the world, especially in areas of the U.S.A. and Canada, autumn leaf colour can be breathtaking. In Britain, where it can be magnificent, it also can be disappointingly fleeting. There is, however, a wide choice of deciduous shrubs and trees, some more reliable than others, that sgive good autumn foliage colour. The North American sweet gums are a good example. Buy and plant a seedling of *Liquidambar styraciflua*, a native of eastern U.S.A., in Britain and you take a chance as to whether its leaves will colour when it matures. There is such a tree at Foggy Bottom, now nearly 10m/30ft high, growing in moist soil which it prefers and part shade, but in autumn its leaves make a poor attempt at being anything other than a dull green or purple. But *L.s.* 'Worplesdon', a splendid form which was selected in Surrey, England, for its brilliant crimson autumn leaves, is almost certain to colour each year. It is a clone or selection and so must be propagated by cuttings or grafting, making it a little more expensive than an ordinary seedling would be but worth every extra penny.

Whether you plant for autumn leaf colour alone is a matter of choice. With a larger garden you have more space for more variety. But if a tree or a shrub has another desirable attribute in addition to autumn colour this must be a bonus and have considerable bearing on your selection. Most of the silver birch family, for instance, have good, if brief, autumn leaf colour, but they also have the great advantage of silvery white, cream or pinkish bark. Nearly all the witch hazels (hamamelis) flower profusely in winter, but some are disappointing in their autumn leaf colour. While *Hamamelis × intermedia* 'Diane', does have attractive reddish purple autumn leaves, the most spectacular for autumn leaf colour in my experience is *H. × i.* 'Feuerzauber' (translated as 'Magic Fire').

The fothergillas, acid-loving relations of the witch hazels, have both pretty and

BRILLIANT AUTUMN FOLIAGE, distinguishes Fothergilla gardenii (above)

STUNNINGLY COLOURED LEAVES and deep crimson-red, late winter flowers are features of Hamamelis × intermedia *'Diane'* (below)

fragrant bottlebrush flowers in spring and wonderful foliage colours in autumn. Although *Fothergilla gardenii* 'Blue Mist', a recent introduction, goes one better by offering metallic blue leaves in summer, regrettably it does not have good autumn colour – a difficult choice if you have room for one only!

Evergreens, of course, retain their colour all year round, and are so much more desirable if they are prettily coloured like the dependable *Euonymus fortunei* 'Emerald 'n' Gold' and 'Emerald Gaiety'. Ivies, too, are there all year long and are often beautifully variegated.

Much smaller plants can have attractive foliage at this time of year, too. The marbled, silvery green leaves which accompany the autumn flowers of the hardy *Cyclamen hederifolium*, for instance, are delightful and last throughout winter. Some of the pulmonarias, such as *Pulmonaria saccharata* 'Leopard', which has hairy, spotted leaves, and *P. saccharata* 'Argentea', the bright, silver form, contrast beautifully when sited close to plants sporting brightly coloured autumn foliage or flowers.

BERRIES AND FRUITS

When shrubs shed their leaves, it is the time for colourful berries and fruits to come into their own – at least for as long as the birds leave them on the branches. All too soon we learn that the adjective "persistent" refers to those berries that, for some reason, the birds either do not like or like least and so leave until last. Judging by the speed

A YELLOW AND BLUE combination of Rudbekia deamii *and* Aster x frikartii *forms an early autumn association against the pond and a stand of* Miscanthus sinensis *'Purpurens'. As the pond is contained by a butyl liner, the soil is not as moist as one might think* (left)

Birds and berries

A great many trees and shrubs fruit regularly in late summer and autumn, adding another dimension of interest to the garden, which in some plants may last well into winter months. Birds, of course, take advantage of this bounty and can strip off berries in very little time, but there appears to be a pecking order for preference and some plants manage to keep their fruit through winter. Which fruits survive seems to vary according to location and, no doubt, type of bird and density of population (bird and human). In my experience the birds start on the sorbus, particularly the coloured rather than the white fruits. Then they work their way through the cotoneasters and hollies almost simultaneously, although the fruits of certain species or cultivars survive better than others. Finally, they attack the pyracanthas. But there is no real rule of thumb and I have found that the lower-growing plants, mostly cotoneasters and vaccineums seem to last well, too. The trick is to grow a selection of species and cultivars, according to the size of your garden, from low-growing shrubs to trees, in the

Rosa rugosa *in late autumn*

knowledge that not only are you going to derive enjoyment through the autumn, but that the birds are going to profit, too. You will be making a significant contribution to wildlife in your area!

with which some of the berries in my garden disappear – almost overnight – it seems the term should apply to the birds rather than to the berries!

Viburnum, malus, crataegus, holly, pyracantha, cotoneaster, vaccinium (blueberry) and many other berry-bearing shrubs give us pleasure for weeks, sometimes months, so perhaps we should not resent sharing them with the birds as winter weather approaches.

Flowers for autumn

Autumn colour does not depend only upon the changing foliage of trees and shrubs or the brightness of berries. The autumn-flowering plants give splashes of concentrated colour that foliage on its own cannot provide. Prime among these must be groups like the asters and dendranthemas, both members of the daisy family (the latter a recent and unfortunate name change from the better known chrysanthemums, but one which we will have to get used to). In these two enormous families alone there is a bewildering choice. The asters vary in colour and type, from plants growing less than 30cm/12in to over 2m/6ft, and add immeasurably to the autumn garden. Their small but abundant, daisy-like flowers can be white to pink, red and purple and there are yellow ones, too. The dendranthemas mostly originated in the Far East but have been greatly interbred in Europe and the U.S.A. as flowers for cutting, pot plants and garden plants. Single flowers, doubles and pompom types are all available

ORANGE BERRIES OF PYRACANTHA 'Orange Glow' and pretty blue flowers of the shrubby, sun-loving Ceratostigma willmottianum *achieve a cheerful autumn association on a sun-facing wall* (left)

to gardeners in almost all the colours of the rainbow. Many of the older varieties are too tall for today's gardens, but brilliant colour can be found that will provide cheerful autumn colours until severe frosts herald winter.

Among the perennials there are plenty of other stalwarts to choose from. The late-flowering, South African native kniphofia (red hot poker), for instance, adds colour and exotic brilliance. Schizostylis (Kaffir lily), which originated from the same part of the world, makes spreading clumps of spiky, iris-like foliage. Its flowering stems resemble miniature gladioli and come into flower when most perennials have finished. With a succession of delicate flowers in white, pink or red, they are excellent in the garden and for cutting.

Anemone japonica (syn. *A. × hybrida*), the Japanese anemone, has a totally different appeal. Its flat, open, single or double, rose to pink and white flowers with yellow stamens are resplendent on narrow stalks above leafy foliage. These are graceful plants ideal for mixing with other perennials or shrubs in sunny or partly shaded spots of the garden that are not too dry. The delightful *Liriope muscari* is a useful clump-forming, glossy evergreen which produces spikes which carry dense clusters of violet flowers in autumn.

If you have an acid soil, autumn-flowering gentians, make an unsurpassable show. I am referring primarily to the carpet-forming *Gentiana sino-ornata* types, the blue trumpets of which create sheets of colour in moist, acid soils, although there are also selections of paler hues and even whites now available. Sedums, both alpine and larger perennial types, add not only succulent foliage of various hues, but heads of colourful, pink and red flowers that are a

THE BRILLIANT BLUE of Gentiana sino-ornata *is hard to improve on for autumn colour. This acid-loving plant appreciates some moisture and full sun or part shade* (above)

SPECTACULAR FLOWERS from late summer into autumn are provided by Anemone × hybrida *'Alba'. Here they light up a shady corner. This plant does well on lime soils* (left)

WITH MUCH FLOWER still to come and plenty of fresh, green foliage in late autumn, this Hebe *'Great Orme', a slightly tender shrub, looks far from ready to accept winter* (top right)

PROVIDING A WELCOME DISPLAY in autumn, exotic, pink blooms of Nerine bowdenii *burst open on naked stems* (below right)

A HAPPY ASSOCIATION of autumn-flowering perennials is achieved by Dendranthema *(formerly* Chrysanthemum*)* rubella *'Apricot' and the taller* Astilbe chinensis (below)

drug for butterflies and some bees. The flat heads of *S. spectabile* and *S. telephium* have winter interest, too. Nerines have spherical, wavy-petalled, pink to red, occasionally white, flowers which may appear before or after the leaves. The list goes on and you will find many more mentioned on pages 118-127.

Compared with perennials there are relatively few late-flowering shrubs but there is still abundant choice, of which the following are but a few. The deciduous caryopteris has clusters of small but plentiful blue flowers in late summer and early autumn The hebes, all evergreen, include many species and cultivars whose spikes of white, pink, purple or blue often flower well into autumn. Even some of the lavandulas, mostly those with the species *L. latifolia* in them, continue to flower well into autumn and have a strong scent of camphor. Both 'Vera' and 'Fragrant Memories', with tall spikes and lavender-blue flowers can be relied on.

There are many other shrubs which bridge the gap between the summer- and winter-flowering types. Among these long-flowering, value-for-money shrubs are buddleias, fuchsias, many hydrangeas, hibiscus and potentillas, not forgetting autumn-flowering heathers like *Erica vagans* (Cornish heath) and *E. cinerea* (bell heather) or, indeed, many roses. Among the latter are not only bush roses (hybrid teas and floribundas) but shrub roses, which include the ground cover types and climbers. Good husbandry (pinching or removing dead flowers, for instance) will prolong flowering, and a great many roses can be a feature until late frosts.

Shrubs that flower into autumn meet up with some which, like the mahonia hybrids 'Charity' and 'Winter Sun' with lovely racemes of yellow flowers and the

BEES APPRECIATE the nectar of Caryopteris x clandonensis *'Heavenly Blue' well into autumn. Of some elegance, this sun-loving shrub is commonly called blue spiraea (above)*

A COLOURFUL contrast is struck by Potentilla fruticosa *'Red Robin' and the sun-loving, shrubby,* Ceratostigma willmottianum, *seen here in early autumn (left)*

FORM AND TEXTURE become more important as autumn runs its course. Here, silvery grey leaves of Artemesia stelleriana *set off the broad, flat heads of* Sedum 'Autumn Joy' *as they turn from bright pink to bronze. Sword-like foliage of crocosmia (top right) is outlasted by the evergreen leaves of* Yucca filamentosa 'Variegata' *(top left). Still in flower, as it has been for three months, is* Gaura lindheimeri *(left)*

evergreen *Viburnum tinus* and the deciduous *V.* × *bodnantense* 'Dawn', start in early autumn and continue into winter in favourable locations.

Many of the plants now available are exotic in relation to the British or European natives, but as I much prefer a "natural" look in the garden, whatever country plants originate from, overbred plants like most dahlias and many of the "chrysanths" which have been developed specifically for increased flower size and large number of petals would not find a place at Foggy Bottom. Nor would I include some of the brighter of the winter-flowering pansies, which I think do not look natural at all in the garden. There are more than enough plants for me to choose from to create a restful and natural-looking environment through the quiet season without having to resort to more splashy colour. I hasten to add, however, that the many people who do like the larger, brighter blooms have every right to use them as they think fit.

IN AN EYECATCHING early autumn combination, a five-year-old, fresh green Chamaecyparis lawsoniana 'Pygmy' *nestles between a bright yellow* Erica carnea 'Aurea' *and a* Calluna vulgaris 'Roma' *which has just finished flowering. The dwarf conifer will soon turn a deeper green and the erica will become golden-bronze and be smothered in pink flowers (right)*

LOBED LEAVES of the bulb Arisaema candidissimum, *has spectacular flowers in summer, and changes colour in autumn (above left)*

SILKY, SILVERY SEED heads of Clematis tangutica *make this a valuable long-interest plant (above right)*

SUNLIGHT FILTERS through an unkempt hedge of English yew (opposite)

WINTER

At Foggy Bottom, we know that when the westerly winds increase in strength and bring rain, interspersed with a few sharp frosts, we are on the verge of winter. The leaves start to tumble, the last to go being the oaks. The days get rapidly shorter and there are fewer fine ones to enjoy. Only the keenest gardeners are out at this blustery time, busying themselves with sweeping up the last of the leaves, making use of some as a protective mulch (oak leaves are particularly good for this) for the more tender plants and keeping them in place with a small branch or two. By now, the heavier soils may be too wet to work on, but planting and preparation can still continue on good days. Frost on well-dug garden soil does more good than anything garden tools can do to break down clay and heavy loam.

ONSET OF WINTER

Given the shorter days and inclement weather, it is hardly surprising that most people are not anxious to garden at this time of year. But, if winter features have already been planted there is much to look forward to and enjoy, either during forays outdoors on good days or from indoors on bad days. Even something as simple as a window box planted with a cheering array of colourful winter foliage and winter-flowering plants, or a terracotta container planted with a good

AN EARLY SNOWFALL TRANSFORMS a large group of pampas grass (Cortaderia selloana) *into a fairytale scene. In a sheltered position, the 3m/10ft stems, plumes and foliage all retain their grace in winter and show up well against a backdrop of dark pines. Buy named varieties, as, with the exception of C.s.'Pumila', all those grown from seed are generally inferior* (right)

FROST HAS A MAGICAL effect on the garden, altering the appearance of foliage, stems and fruits, especially when the sun shines. Often, the transformation is fleeting, lasting only until the warmth of the sun or wind destroys it. The photographs on these pages capture a few of those icy images. Lacy fronds of the hardy fern Polystichum setiferum *'Herrenhausen' are turned from green to silver (top right). Purple autumn leaves of* Rosa virginiana *are rimmed with hoarfrost (top far right). A spider's filament along with the needles and cones of* Abies procera *'Glauca', the noble fir, are delicately encased in ice (centre right). Crimson leaves of the oak leaf hydrangea,* H. quercifolia *'Snow Queen', appear as if dusted with sugar (centre far right). Mossy* Saxifraga *'Pixie' briefly takes on an ice-crystal camouflage (bottom right). A frosty edging emphasizes the frilled fronds of* Dryopteris borreri *'Pinderi' (bottom far right)*

TINGED PURPLE in winter, leaves of Mahonia aquifolium *'Smaragd', a form of the Oregon grape, are outlined with frost* (top far left). *Studded with bright red berries, the thorny, leafless stems of* Berberis thunbergii *'Atropurpurea Nana', a dwarf Barberry, are encased in glinting ice* (top left). *The leaves of a miniature, sun-loving, carpet-forming alpine* Sedum spathulifolium *'Purpureum' have been crystallized by a winter frost* (centre far left). *Silky strands of the seed heads of* Clematis tangutica *are thickened and whitened by frost* (centre left). *Papery petals of* Hydrangea paniculata *'Pink Diamond' are edged with ice crystals; the sterile flowers were white in summer before turning pink in early autumn and then fading to a parchment brown* (bottom far left). *Glossy leaves of the evergreen, dwarf shrub* Leucothoë *'Scarletta', purple in autumn and winter, are enhanced by a sparkling frost* (bottom left)

selection of differently shaded evergreens can be sufficient to brighten an aspect, however small. Ideas for these are given on pages 64 and 79.

The harshness of winter can come early or late and can affect different parts of the country at different times – some parts missing snow and frost almost completely. A wider range of plants can be grown outdoors in the warmer locations but when such areas do get severe frost it can be devastating. Urban areas, too, protected by the warmth of buildings, traffic, perhaps even people, often keep temperatures a degree or two warmer than the surrounding countryside.

Defining the hardiness of plants is an inexact science. With the much greater extremes of weather in the U.S.A., the gardening fraternity there relies on a set of "hardiness zones" to indicate how much cold (and heat) each garden plant will bear. Keen gardeners already know that this is only a guide and that given more shelter and some winter protection many plants can thrive in much colder zones or areas than is indicated in the United States Department of Agriculture zone map. A European zone map exists which shows most of Britain in zone 8, except for the coastal strip from Dorset, westwards and north to the tip of Scotland influenced by the Gulf Stream, which is zone 9. When you consider that zone 8 in the U.S.A. covers South Carolina, Georgia and Alabama, you will agree that this map needs a heat tolerance figure, too, to give the full picture. In the same way that less hardy plants will succumb to winter frosts, others which are native to cooler climates can struggle to survive prolonged spells of heat and humidity. So, although hardiness zones are used in the Directory section of this book (please

OVERWINTERING FROST-TENDER PLANTS

Keen gardeners everywhere will want to try in their gardens plants which may not always come through frosty winters. A good example of such frost-tender plants is Cosmos atrosanguineus *which has velvety, chocolate-scented, deep purple-red flowers (sounds nice doesn't it?). Planted in spring, it will flower for months until well into the autumn. At this time of the year you are faced with three choices: dig it up once the foliage has died down and dry it off in a frost-proof shed or room like a dahlia; leave it where it is and mulch it with leaves, bracken or straw to a depth of 6-10cm/2-3in until early spring; or leave it alone and let it take its chance. I did the latter last year and my plants withstood -10°C for several nights, and still grew away in the spring.*

But I was testing for hardiness in my garden and so had an incentive for taking the risk. Depending on where you live, some of the mostly perennial plants mentioned in this book that you might consider protecting for the winter are: agapanthus, cautleya, Commelina coelestis, *some crocosmias, some kniphofias, Melianthus major, nerine, penstemon hybrids, phormium, Salvia ambigens (and many other tender species not mentioned), schizostylis and zauscheneria. At the time of writing, recent mild winters have allowed most of the above plants to come through the winter without protection in my garden. Site and soil will make a considerable difference even in colder localities. Hardiness advice is given for each group in the directory that starts on page 86, but a basic rule might be to protect as for the cosmos above in the first winter at least.*

Cosmos atrosanguineus *(top) constrasts strikingly with* Commelina coelestis (below)

note that both cold and heat tolerance are indicated) do not take them as gospel! A key giving the temperature range for each zone appears on page 86.

The weather at the onset of winter can be pretty dull and depressing, but sometimes it can surprise us with magnificent sunny and frosty days. The magic of a brilliant hoarfrost on trees, shrubs and grasses makes one marvel at the beauty and simplicity of nature.

At Foggy Bottom, the winter sun comes up from well to the southeast and moves through a low trajectory. We could (but never seem to) sit in our lounge and watch the sparkle of frost disappear as the morning sun moves across the sky, striking the eastern side of stems and warming them. As the sun gradually moves round, the changing direction of the rays of light dramatically alters the appearance of many plants, none more so than the ornamental grasses. Shafts of sunlight flash and dazzle through the moving plumes of miscanthus and *Cortaderia selloana* 'Pumila' (pampas grass), the sun too low and too bright to be looked at directly. Dark evergreens absorb the sunlight, glossy leaves reflect it, the colours of the golden conifers and of the dogwood stems – especially *Cornus alba* 'Sibirica' and the magnificent *C. sanguinea* 'Winter Flame' – are intensified by it. On frosty days, as the sun begins its descent to the southwest, its strength declines rapidly and this seems to be the signal for the slowly swirling, ghostly mist and fog to draw in. Darkness soon falls, and another

HERE TRANSFORMED BY FROSTY weather in mid-winter, the beige stems of the ornamental grass Miscanthus sinensis *'Morning Light' create an interesting hummock shape and remain attractive until early spring (left)*

POTTED PLANTS BRING interest to a stepped patio in early winter. Three ornamental grasses, Carex comans *'Bronze Form' (front left),* Hakonechloa macra *'Alboaurea' (back) and* Imperata cylindrica *'Rubra' (front right) surround a* Bergenia *'Bressingham Ruby', the leaves of which turn ruby-purple in winter. The yellow-leaved* Choisya ternata *'Sundance' is susceptible to frost but can be placed in a conservatory, greenhouse or porch when at risk* (right)

A BLANKET OF SNOW heightens the bright colours of bare stems and their backdrop of conifers. The Foggy Bottom cat uses Betula costata *as a convenient resting place* (below right)

wonderful day is all too quickly gone. There is no other word to describe such a day but magical.

When snow comes, it transforms the garden, giving it an entirely new perspective. It may bury many of the lower-growing plants, but it can be quite dramatic to see some of the coloured-stemmed willows and dogwoods poking above the snow. Snow acts as a blanket of protection against frost, depending how deep it is of course, but it can also cause damage in the garden, especially to conifers and, to some extent, we have to be prepared for it. Heavy, wet snow can weigh down or even break branches and should be dealt with before it causes much damage.

Winter is certainly the time when we can appreciate the merits of the many different types of evergreens, which include conifers, many shrubs and a few trees. To my mind a garden needs a mixture of deciduous and evergreen plants. Evergreens can provide stability, structure, form and considerable colour in winter, as well as shelter from winter winds, whilst deciduous plants above ground offer a more evident change, reflecting the seasons with their succession of spring shoots, summer maturity, autumn ripeness and winter silhouette. One should remember the role that herbaceous plants and bulbs have to play in completing the seasonal picture. If you have a small garden it is well worth reflecting on these points for the selection you make.

The middle of winter is when evergreens, barks and stems really come into their own, although there is still some coloured foliage around. By the shortest day of the year, the birds have finally got to the *Pyracantha* 'Orange Glow' growing by our front door, the blackbird

cheekily darting in for a quick, wary look in case our cat is anywhere around, then off it flies with another orange lifesaver in its beak. In frosty weather, the pyracantha is stripped of its berries by the New Year.

Winter flowers

But there are flowers at this time, and how precious they are. I am sure many would agree with the plantswoman, Margery Fish, who in 1958 wrote: "we get as much pleasure from one tiny bloom on a winter's day as we do from a gardenful of roses in summer."

Almost wherever you live, winter flowers can enliven the dullest day. Of

HUGGING A SUN-FACING WALL, a heavily berried Pyracantha *'Orange Glow' sets off a collection of containerized conifers, mostly junipers, that will provide interest through winter. From left to right, these are:* Juniperus × media *'Gold Sovereign',* Juniperus communis *'Green Carpet',* Chamaecyparis obtusa *'Nana Gracilis',* Juniperus horizontalis *'Glauca',* Juniperus × media *'Sulphur Spray',* Thuja orientalis *'Aurea Nana'. Most of these are 4-5 years old or more* (below)

course, if you are snowbound and frozen all winter the options are limited, but for many cooler temperate climates winter can offer a varied choice. Perennials have much to offer. *Helleborus niger* (Christmas rose) is seldom in flower for the holiday itself, but the pure white blossoms arrive a few weeks later and continue until spring. *H. corsicus, H. foetidus* and *H. orientalis* each give weeks of flower colour from mid-winter to early spring. *Iris unguicularis*, which may already have borne a few fragrant, blue flowers in autumn, continues in succession through the winter. The golden-yellow flowers of *Adonis amurensis* are out in mid- or late winter along with the early bulbs, the delightfully simple snowdrops and golden winter aconites (*Eranthis hyemalis*), considered true harbingers of spring, but often premature. Many other bulbs soon start to appear.

There are plenty of winter-flowering shrubs to choose from as well, a few of which are mentioned here. *Hamamelis* × *intermedia* 'Jelena' is the first of the witch hazels to flower, its coppery-orange, strap-like petals a delight in the middle of winter. It is soon followed by others bearing fragrant, red, yellow or orange blossom. Mature examples of *Chimonanthus praecox* (wintersweet) bear unusual waxy, fragrant, purple-centred flowers in late winter. With golden-yellow flowers lasting from early winter to well into spring, few shrubs can surpass the inestimable winter jasmine (*Jasminum* × *nudiflorum*). Evergreen and bushy, *Viburnum tinus* and its cultivars are covered in blooms from autumn through to spring. Look out for the more compact 'Eve Price' whose pink buds open into heads of slightly fragrant, white flowers. Deciduous *V. × bodnantense* 'Dawn' is taller and has successive blooms which last throughout

SUN OR SHADE, the red-stemmed form of Helleborus foetidus *'Wester Flisk' gives a show throughout the winter months. Seedlings may vary in their colouring* (above)

OFTEN FLOWERING all winter, the witch hazel Hamamelis × intermedia *'Jelena', one of the earliest to bloom, shows up best against a dark background* (left)

*NOT QUITE ORANGE
perhaps but
resembling shredded
citrus peel extending
from crimson centres,
petals of* Hamamelis
× intermedia
*'Orange Beauty, drip
with moisture as the
sun strikes after an
overnight frost. This
cultivar is one of
many witch hazels
which offer flower
and fragrance
through the mid-
winter months* (left)

winter unless severe frosts spoil the fragrant pink buds and flowers. The bright yellow racemes of some of the evergreen, spiky-leaved mahonia hybrids such as 'Charity' and 'Winter Sun' start flowering in autumn and continue until late winter unless caught by heavy frosts, and are soon followed by the fragrant flowers of *M. japonica*.

There are many more flowering shrubs, particularly if you include catkins as flowers. Among these must be the often spectacular, evergreen *Garrya elliptica*, which has sombre, olive-green leaves, an eventually dense habit and produces a delightful show of catkins in mid-winter. The best selection is 'James Roof' whose grey-green tassels elongate from late autumn onwards, many reaching 30cm/1ft. *Corylus avellana* 'Contorta', a member of the hazel family, has light yellow catkins in addition to its interesting corkscrew stems. Where space permits, some of the alders are worth including, particularly those which have more than one desirable

attribute. Both *Alnus incana* 'Aurea' and *A. glutinosa* 'Aurea' have golden leaves in spring. The former produces pink to crimson catkins which turn yellow as they open and the latter has lovely, long yellow catkins in late winter. The catkins of some of the willows come later on in the season.

Some winter-flowering heathers are also in flower at this time, although the full flush of *Erica carnea*, *E. × darleyensis* and *E. erigena* is usually yet to come in early spring. For those who can grow them – almost any garden with reasonable soil and a sunny situation in Britain – they are a must for winter colour.

COLOURFUL EVERGREENS

Among evergreen shrubs there is considerable diversity that can be used to brighten up winter days. I have already mentioned the humble, common but invaluable *Euonymus fortunei* cultivars 'Emerald 'n' Gold' and 'Emerald Gaiety', the former perhaps having the edge as its gold and green variegations take

THESE NEW CATKINS *of* Garrya elliptica *'James Roof' will elongate to 30cm/1ft by late winter, to provide a spectacular display* (above)

WINTER-FLOWERING *heathers, with* Erica carnea *'Pink Spangles' in the foreground, dominate a colourful, twenty-year-old planting. Blue, green and gold conifers provide contrast in form and colour* (right)

FOR FOLIAGE, FLOWER *and fragrance some of the mahonias take some beating. Here,* Mahonia × media *'Underway' seems happy in a semi-shady, reasonably sheltered position, its prickly leaves forming an evergreen canopy above which contrasting clusters of fragrant, yellow flowers, which emerged in autumn, bring cheer into winter* (opposite)

Two evergreen shrubs successfully combine green and yellow. Still laden with rounded, yellow berries in early winter, this Ilex aquifolium *'Fructu Luteo' has so far escaped the attention of hungry birds which seem to strip red fruits first. Depending upon season and location, however, the yellow fruits are bound to follow, leaving the holly's glossy, green leaves for continued colour* (above)

Splashes of gold and green are the trademark of Elaeagnus pungens *'Maculata', which gives bright colour right through winter whether sited in sun or shade* (right)

on pretty, pink tinges in the severest of winters. These shrubs are useful as ground cover, can be allowed to scramble among other shrubs, and are able to climb walls and trees! There are many other varieties, all of which have small leaves and are very hardy. Less hardy, but of a more bushy, upright habit and with larger leaves are several attractive selections of the Japanese euonymus, some with green, some with gold and some with variegated leaves.

Golden variegated leaves are also found in several elaeagnus cultivars of *E. pungens* or *E. × ebbingei*, larger but adaptable evergreen shrubs. Most widely used, but not to be despised for that, is *E. pungens* 'Maculata' which has leathery, silver-backed leaves with a central splash of gold. Some defoliation may occur in severe winters, but these are good, useful evergreens which will tolerate shade.

The hollies, a large family of mostly dwarf and tall, evergreen shrubs and trees, can be placed in a similar category. There is ample choice, from *Ilex crenata* 'Golden Gem', which rarely exceeds 60cm/2ft even after many years and whose small, golden leaves are at their brightest in winter, to many selections of *Ilex aquifolium* (English holly) with silver- and gold-edged leaves and growing into small trees exceeding 10m/30ft. For the best berries a male form is needed near the female fruiting forms.

Both the large-leaved *Hedera colchica* (Persian ivy) and the smaller-leaved *H. helix* (common ivy) have selections with variegated leaves to provide winter colour for walls, fences, up trees and trunks or as ground cover. All are very well adapted for shade.

The spotted laurels, which are usually represented by *Aucuba japonica*, seem to arouse either favour or intense dislike.

They are mostly eventually large-growing shrubs with leathery, green, variegated or spotted leaves which can make quite a splash, as can the fruits of some. Much used by the Victorians, they are a little difficult to accommodate in a natural-looking garden.

Other evergreen shrubs for winter colour include fatsias, hebes, even the semi-evergreen (or evergreen, depending on climate) privets or ligustrum, osmanthus and pittosporums in addition to the rhododendrons and cherry laurels (*Prunus laurocerasus*).

There are two groups of interesting foliage plants from Australasia which can be useful in suitable gardens – both require milder climates to survive winters in cooler temperate zones. The spiky, sword-like foliage in colours ranging from cream to yellow, pink, maroon and purple of the phormiums (New Zealand flax) make them ideal for gravel gardens. (Of similar appeal are the variegated yuccas.) Most gardeners need to be aware of the vigour of eucalyptus, a group of fast-growing evergreens with mostly blue or bluish green foliage and attractive bark. Many of the species are much hardier than they were once thought to be, but they can be "stooled" – cut back to the ground every two or three years if they become too tall.

CONIFERS

There are many people who consider that conifers are pretty much the same the year round. Well all I can say is (and I constantly do) that such people do not know much about conifers! Many gardeners are not even aware that there are deciduous conifers. Some, admittedly, are very dull in winter and need additional colour from other plants to make them stand out, but mixed with other trees and shrubs, their wide range

of shades can create a wonderful backdrop to other plantings.

There are other conifers which respond dramatically to shorter days and lower temperatures by changing colour – from green to gold – just when such a colour is most needed. Such valuable conifers mostly belong to the pine family, and our only native, the Scots pine (*Pinus sylvestris*), has produced some variations or clones which do just this. As winter deepens, so the needles of *P. s.* 'Aurea' brighten, particularly if the tree is in a sunny, exposed position, eventually turning a light yellow. Such a tree can act as a shelter in the summer and a beacon in winter. It can be pruned to keep it more dwarf, the best time to do this is whilst it is still small and just as the new "candles" or growth begins in late spring. There are slower-growing forms such as *P. s.* 'Gold Coin' which are of a deeper golden-yellow, but these will

eventually get large so the same pruning suggestions apply. *Pinus mugo* 'Winter Gold', the Swiss mountain pine, is another of my favourites and will remain dwarfer, the green needles of summer changing to a clear golden-yellow for winter. The similar *P. m.* 'Ophir' is also delightful.

Many of the conifers that have gold or blue foliage are stunning in the winter sun. Others change from green or yellow to a distinctly bronze or even purplish tone as the days shorten and the weather gets colder. The carpeting, juniper-like *Microbiota decussata* whose bright green, lacy foliage turns bronze-

A STUNNING LINE-UP of conifers provides diversity of form and bright colour. From left to right they are Picea pungens *'Thomsen' (blue spruce), the dwarfer* Chamaecyparis obtusa *'Graciosa',* Pinus sylvestris *'Aurea' (golden Scots pine) and* Pinus leucodermis *(below)*

AN OVERNIGHT FROST gives this planting at Foggy Bottom a rather ghostly effect. The ice tones down the colours of the conifers and heathers but highlights the drooping stems of Stipa tenuifolia *(centre), an ornamental grass of some distinction. Grasses add both seasonal change and movement to static plantings of conifers and heathers* (right)

A SHAFT OF EARLY morning sun begins the melting process on a frosted Pinus parviflora 'Glauca' (opposite)

purple and the feathery-foliaged *Cryptomeria japonica* 'Elegans' which changes to a similar colour are two excellent examples. For the greatest effect they should be planted next to more brightly coloured plants such as golden or yellow-foliaged conifers or shrubs, or a silver-stemmed willow like *Salix irrorata* to highlight the contrast. I have an attractive grouping with *Microbiota decussata, Erica cinerea* 'Rock Pool' which has golden, almost bronze winter foliage, and *E. carnea* 'Myretoun Ruby' whose deep ruby-red flowers act as a catalyst against the gold and purple-bronze.

TWISTING BRANCHES

Choice there certainly is among evergreen shrubs and trees that give us colourful foliage through winter, but by a freak of nature, the branch configuration and habit of some deciduous plants have given them shapes and forms that create a picturesque and mature look when they have shed their leaves. These will provide an unusual winter feature in any size of garden, whether planted in the ground or in a container.

Most conifers retain their foliage all year but there are many that are deciduous. The larches, taxodium, pseudolarix and the ginkgo are the main types, although the latter, commonly known as the fossil tree, is not considered by many as a conifer. All of them have good autumn colour and attractive new shoots in spring. In winter the bare branches of the larches and *Taxodium*

distichum (swamp cypress) and its forms make an appealing shape against winter skies, especially when their twigs are adorned with a rimy frost or when drenched in dew, as they often are.

I am particularly struck with *Larix kaempferi* 'Diana', a cultivar of the Japanese larch. In spring it has delightful, paintbrush-like, bright green shoots which become needles in summer, turning to gold in autumn before they drop off to reveal a silhouette of snake-like branches. The way winter light shines through the curling, contorted branches and stems is indescribably sensuous. A grafted plant of relatively slow growth, this beautiful tree can be grown as a container or patio plant for many years, or as a plant top-grafted onto a stem to make an interesting shape with year-round appeal.

WONDERFULLY TWISTED BRANCHES of Salix × sepulcralis *'Erythroflexuosa' come into their own in winter, revealing orange to gold lower stems and crimson, pigtailed branchlets, an inspiring sight. This plant is trimmed to the ground annually in late spring* (above)

Attractive contortions and silhouettes are found in many other plants, too. Treated correctly these also can be useful in the small garden. Pruning opens up branches, rendering them less congested, improves the winter silhouette and keeps them dwarf.

Corylus avellana 'Contorta' (corkscrew hazel, but also known as Harry Lauder's walking stick) is much more interesting during its leafless winter months than in summer. Through winter its contorted, twisted, greyish branches resemble a sculpture which as spring approaches becomes covered with pendent, pale yellow catkins. Suckers at the base of this shrub must be removed each year.

Another of my favourites is *Salix × sepulcralis* 'Erythroflexuosa', a willow recently introduced from Argentina. In summer it is nothing much to look at but, if pruned to the ground in late spring, it will produce vigorous 2m/6ft or more shoots and twigs which twist and turn as though they were trying to escape from the name which the botanists have seen fit to give it! But when the burnished stems of maroon, gold and yellow glisten in the winter sun, what was a background shrub in summer becomes a star in winter. Prune this shrub to the ground each spring to keep it dwarf.

A shrub that epitomizes year-round value for all sizes of garden has to be *Prunus incisa* 'Kojo-no-mai', a slow-growing form of the Fuji cherry apparently found on the slopes of Mount Fuji in Japan. Translated, the name means 'Dance of the Butterflies' which is wonderfully descriptive of the myriads of small, white flowers produced in early spring. The branches of this remarkable shrub are twisted and angled to create a tangled mass of fascinating complexity in its winter nakedness. In addition it has attractive small, serrated, green leaves which usually, but according to situation, turn shades of bronze, purple and red in autumn. Attractive all year round and able to grow in a container, 'Kojo-no-mai' can earn a place even in the smallest garden. It is to my mind the best value for money.

COLOURED BARK AND STEMS

In addition to interestingly shaped branches and twigs, some trees and shrubs have yet another fine attribute

laid bare when stripped of their leaves – bark. The main stems of many trees such as the silver birches are visible throughout the year but the upper stems and branches remain hidden until the last leaves have fallen.

If you have room for a silver birch, depending on the species eventually it may require a width of 3-6m/10-20ft, which one should it be? Our own native *Betula pendula* (lady of the woods) or a more exotic selection, such as the creamy-barked *B. costata*, *B. utilis* and its forms such as 'Jermyns' all with white bark, or the slower-growing *B. jacque-montii*? There are several different species and selections at Foggy Bottom which create a spectacle in winter from both near to and far away.

Some of the maples have ornamental bark. *Acer griseum*, for example, slow though it is to develop its peeling, orange-brown bark, is well worth the wait. Some, such as *A. rufinerve*,

PRICKLY WITH ICE NEEDLES, the contorted branches of Larix × kaempferi *'Diana' are emphasized by a severe frost in early winter* (top far left)

FRESHLY FALLEN SNOW coats the snaking branches of Corylus avellana *'Contorta', the corkscrew hazel, dangling just-opened catkins in late winter* (top left)

GLOSSY, MAHOGANY-RED BARK of Prunus serrula *gleams in early winter sunshine* (bottom far left)

THE PEELING SKIN of Betula nigra *'Heritage', an improved selection of the sometimes dingy river birch, reveals delicate shrimp colouring. It may take four or five years before young plants mature to this stage* (bottom left)

Many shrubs are useful in the winter garden for the startlingly bright colours of their stems. These colours can usually be intensified by hard pruning each spring. The time for pruning is just as the new growth begins to show in mid-spring. Prune hard with secateurs to 10cm/4in above the ground, or in the case of Salix alba *varieties back to a stump (pollarding). Although this treatment guarantees abundant new shoots with the brightest colour, it will be at the expense of flowering in that year. The choice is yours! Some shrubs which benefit from this treatment are mentioned here.*

Dogwoods – red, yellow, orange and green stems

Cornus alba
Cornus sanguinea
Cornus stolonifera and their cultivars

Willows – orange-red and orange-yellow stems

Salix alba 'Britzensis'
Salix alba 'Vitellina'
Salix irrorata
Salix x *sepulcralis* 'Erythroflexuosa'
(syn. *S. erythroflexuosa*)

Brambles – white stems

Rubus biflorus
Rubus cockburnianus
Rubus thibetanus

YELLOW-GREEN STEMS *of* Cornus stolonifera *'Flaviramea'* (top right)

THE STEMS OF Salix irrorata *(foreground) and, from left to right,* Cornus alba *'Sibirica',* Pinus mugo *'Winter Gold' and* Cornus sanguinea *'Winter Flame'* (right)

A HAZE OF RED-TIPPED, *green-yellow twigs of* Cornus kelseyi *leads the eye to red-stemmed* Cornus alba *'Sibirica'* (opposite)

A. davidii, *A. capillipes* and *A. hersii* have stems that are striped green and silvery white. Most spectacular of all, if you can find one, is *A. pensylvanicum* 'Erythrocladum'. It is a slow grower and not always an easy doer, but winter shoots are coral pink and they stand out against any background. I am, of course, being very selective here, as there are many other worthy trees and shrubs with colourful winter stems and bark.

GRASSES

Ornamental grasses are becoming recognized as plants that have potential for giving great pleasure in winter and are now more appreciated by gardeners than ever before. This is largely due to the introduction of a great many new species and varieties, mostly from Germany and the U.S.A., where grasses have been used more widely in gardens and to greater effect than anywhere else. The low-growing, hummocky carex from New Zealand make their mark, too, being particularly adaptable to the smaller garden.

A few years ago, I brought back from Germany a group of *Miscanthus sinensis* cultivars bred by nurseryman and plantsman Ernst Pagels. I was impressed by seeing them in full flower at the height of summer during a visit to his nursery. At that time all the varieties available in Britain either flowered very late in autumn or not at all because British summers were too cool. This remarkable group offers British gardeners a whole new perspective. Their elegant plumes last right through winter, providing a ceaseless interaction of light and movement. They are totally hardy, and dwarf forms are available for use in the smaller garden.

It is gratifying to see the increasing appreciation that more and more gardeners have for ornamental grasses. Even so, it is mostly for their summer effect in association with more colourful perennials, and many gardeners have yet to explore the increased interest and value that grasses offer from autumn until early spring – even if most of the foliage above ground is dead. There are "evergreen" grasses such as the hummocky festucas and carex which provide colour contrasts to plantings of shrubs, conifers or heathers, and there are the deciduous types such as cortaderia, stripa, miscanthus and pennisetum, whose foliage and flowers give movement and light to plantings throughout winter. I have found them particularly effective when planted imaginatively among more static groups of heathers.

For giant plumes choose *Cortaderia selloana,* one of the pampas grasses, all of which have spikes topped by silvery white plumes in early autumn which last through most of the winter, even if the foliage turns brown. That said, the taller species or varieties such as 'Sunningdale Silver' will blow over or snap in high winds, so go for the more compact *C. s.* 'Pumila' which can have as many as 30-50 plumes on established clumps.

Miscanthus ranges in size from the 90cm/3ft *Miscanthus sinensis* 'Yaku Dwarf' to the 3m/10ft *M. sacchariflorus,* which is useful as a windbreak but seldom flowers in cooler, temperate climates. In between these extremes are forms like 'Little Fountain' ('Kleine Fontane') with pendulous, silver plumes which turn white, and 'Malepartus' with crimson-maroon summer flowers which turn silver then white as autumn becomes winter. The straight, brown stems of *Calamagrostis* × *acutiflora* 'Karl Foerster' or 'Overdam', the latter with pretty green, white and, in spring, striped leaves, add a lighter touch.

Stipa calamagrostis has arching stalks carrying rich brown autumn plumes that are still attractive in winter. One of my favourites is *Stipa tenuifolia* which grows to only 45cm/18in, its green, grassy spring and summer foliage producing delicate, feathery heads which blow about in the wind. These fade to beige in autumn, but the whole plant remains attractive throughout the winter. What matter if it seeds itself around since the seedlings seem natural in the most unlikely places.

The deschampsias, too, are worthwhile, particularly the one that goes by the name 'Golden Dew' ('Goldtau'). Its fine, fluffy heads attract dew in autumn and winter, which gives a quite magical effect if it freezes. I can never praise enough the virtues of a dwarf "deciduous" Japanese grass with the difficult

SHARPLY POINTED LEAVES of Yucca filamentosa *'Variegata' balance the flat heads of* Sedum *'Autumn Joy' and varieties of* Miscanthus sinensis, *an ornamental grass* (above)

ARCHING FRONDS of the ornamental grass Stipa tenuifolia *fill the space between conifers in a bed overshadowed by a leaning* Pinus parviflora *'Glauca' which has been pruned to accentuate its character* (opposite)

name of *Hakonechloa macra* 'Alboaurea'. Its narrow, wavy leaves are golden yellow and green in summer. Whilst it is undoubtedly a beautiful plant in the garden, its true beauty is revealed when it is used as a container plant on a patio. In autumn its colour gradually fades to gold or russet hues through to beige, but the "dead" leaves and stems remain to give pleasure through winter.

Lastly, I would like to mention two plants which fulfil the roles of grasses, although neither of them is one. The dwarf, rush-like *Acorus gramineus* 'Ogon' makes a bright hummock of arching, golden leaves throughout winter and contrasts well with *Ophiopogon planiscapus* 'Nigrescens' which is somewhat similar but creeping in habit with startling, black leaves. These two are valuable enough on their own, but in combination with each other or with different plants they can create a year-round feature in any garden.

FRAGRANCE

Among the treasures on offer for the winter garden, fragrance is arguably one of the most valuable. Deliciously scented plants can be dotted around the garden, filling it with pleasant smells to enjoy when you venture out on fine days. Position plants where you know that you are likely to walk regularly in winter – on the way to your shed, greenhouse or garage and certainly by the front and back doors. The waft of the heady scent from the tiny, white flowers of the humble *Sarcococca humilis* can be like nectar on a winter or spring day.

Not only do those plants that are scented last for a long period through the winter outdoors, but many hold on well when cut for indoors. The exception to this are the mahonias which, fragrant as they are in the garden, unfortunately drop their yellow petals quickly once brought inside. But *Lonicera fragrantissima,* a winter honeysuckle, the bewitching witch hazels (hamamelis), chimonanthus (wintersweet), sarcococca (sweet box, although it is not a box) and *Viburnum × bodnantense* all keep quite well, depending on how much heat there is in the room, gently releasing fragrance into the air.

SPRING

Hardly have we settled down to enjoy the pure delights of the cold season, than winter hovers on the verge of spring. In some parts of Britain, we can go through the middle few weeks of winter without a single frost, but we often pay for that oversight of nature, since seldom do we escape frosts entirely before the arrival of spring. Mild weather early on often gives a false message to the plants which consider that spring is just around the corner, if it has not already arrived. Snowdrops and aconites pop out, even the tightly rounded, purplish brown winter buds of the Japanese hardy perennial *Adonis amurensis* start pushing through the ground. Once they have raised their heads they are inclined to go the whole way to open their buttercup-like flowers, which are followed by ferny foliage. This handsome plant is a good example of how climate affects plants, appearing in January, February, March or even April depending upon the mildness or severity of the winter. So is it a winter-flowering plant? You see the difficulty we have when trying to categorize plants. They will not be put into firm boxes, they will not always conform to what experts say about them, but surely this is what makes plants and gardening such a challenge. There is always something different happening or about to happen. Nature likes to keep us guessing, and generally does a pretty good job of it.

A FEELING OF CHEER emanates from massed, early spring blooms at Foggy Bottom. Narcissus 'Mrs R. O. Backhouse' carpets the ground. To their left, two modern representatives of popular flowering shrubs, Forsythia 'Weekend' and Ribes sanguineum 'Red Pimpernel', front the developing leaves of Acer platanoides 'Princeton Gold', a useful spring foliage plant (right)

SPRING FLOWERS

Even if we do not know exactly when spring is going to begin, we do know that the days are getting longer, and that inevitably the quiet season will have a limited span from now on. As the days become longer, lighter and brighter, buds start to swell, catkins lengthen, and, on milder days, bees buzz around the winter-flowering heathers.

Although at Foggy Bottom, many of the *Erica × darleyensis* types have been in flower for a couple of months already, and some of the *Erica carnea* cultivars have been showing colour since before Christmas, most start to open fully as late winter slips into early spring and only then begin to make their mark.

In my opinion, the winter-flowering heathers offer so much that they are indispensable. They are impressive in large drifts, interesting as individual plants and fascinating at close quarters. Their massed flowers, in pink, white, purple, maroon and red, last for months. Invaluable to bees as an early source of nectar, useful as weed smotherers, generally trouble-free and long-lived, what more could a gardener want from a plant?

The winter-flowering types are lime tolerant, the summer-flowering types are not, but, in the gardens that can grow them, they can offer bright golden, yellow, pink, russet or crimson winter foliage, with the dead flower heads of *Erica cinerea* (bell heather) and *Erica vagans* (Cornish heath) being particularly attractive. Winter-flowering heathers seldom require any pruning, except perhaps to tidy them up, but summer-flowering types are best pruned in spring, just as new growth begins. Remember that summer-flowering heathers require an acid soil.

There is so much else to look forward to at this time as the pace of life in the garden begins to quicken. The fewer the plants in bloom, the more they are appreciated. Each tree, shrub, perennial, alpine or bulb is eagerly watched as it prepares to do its stuff. One of my own favourites is *Cyclamen coum*. Its pretty flowers open tentatively in winter, testing the weather then, as winter turns into early spring, they gradually break into full flower one or two months later. The small flowers are bright crimson and stand out against the heart-shaped, dark green leaves. There are also forms with pink or white flowers and many that have silver or silver and green patterned leaves. Hardy cyclamens are much more readily available as young, pot-grown plants these days and they are considerably easier to establish than dried corms. Place them in a sunny or sheltered spot where they are unlikely to get disturbed or trampled, and they will reward you with years of pleasure.

By the time the cyclamen flowers have emerged, other bulbs are beginning to show themselves – *Iris danfordiae, I. histrioïdes*, various narcissi, scillas, crocuses and others. In my garden, the first two alpine plants to bloom are the creeping *Saxifraga oppositifolia* 'Florissa', with minute, bright pink flowers, and *Saxifraga juniperifolia*, its bright yellow flowers resplendent above green mats. Also among the first harbingers of spring are such plants as pulmonarias, helleborus, euphorbias, dentarias, epimediums, primulas, violas and forms of *Ranunculus ficaria*.

LATE FROSTS

Camellias, early rhododendrons, stachyurus, magnolias and wisterias are but a few of the spring flowers which can be totally lost to spring frosts. When

FROST DAMAGE

As spring weather prompts more plants into early bloom, so there is an increasing danger from damaging frosts. No garden is perfect, and for all the benefits of site and situation at Foggy Bottom, one distinct disadvantage is that it lies in a frost pocket. Exposed, hilly sites have their problems, too, but valley bottoms, particularly if water exists at the floor, are notorious for collecting frost which literally drains down from surrounding slopes. This means that overnight spring frosts settle on plants, but if the frost is not severe it may do little damage unless the morning sun strikes shoots, buds or flowers before the temperature rises above freezing. The sun striking frozen soft plant tissue can maim and kill – and, in fact, can do far more damage than much more severe frosts in the fully dormant season. To minimize the effects of serious frost damage, it makes good sense, obviously, to avoid planting frost-susceptible plants on easterly facing beds or walls – go west facing or even north for shade-lovers where sun will not reach until later in the day.

all new developing buds and shoots are caught by a hard frost in late spring it can kill a plant outright, too. Then, not only some of those mentioned, but Japanese maples, stewartias – even hamamelis – can be lost, as I know only too well from my experience over the years at Foggy Bottom. In May 1991, I measured fourteen successive nights of frost in the garden, which did considerable damage.

Fortunately, the trees and conifers at Foggy Bottom have grown to a stature where they offer shade and shelter, so I am able to find microclimates that are protected as much as possible from the dangers of frost.

PURE YELLOW FLOWERS of Epimedium pinnatum colchicum, *one of the best evergreen types, are caught by a shaft of spring light. Epimediums are often underrated spring-flowering plants, partly because they often hide their delicate blooms among masses of evergreen foliage* (top)

PULMONARIAS, THE LUNGWORTS, are among the most hardy and versatile of the late-winter and spring-flowering perennials. Pulmonaria 'Highdown', also known as 'Lewis Palmer', flowers for over two months as winter turns into spring then follows with good-looking, spotted foliage (above)

MOTTLED FOLIAGE AND creamy flowers of Erythronium californicum, *a woodland plant which grows quite well in the open, show up well against surrounding* Muscari armeniacum *in early spring* (top)

A SMALL GROUP of Helleborus orientalis *have a background of* Magnolia stellata *enhancing their flowers which have been blooming for several weeks. Cut away their leaves in mid-winter, if they are unsightly* (above)

THE VIVID, DEEP pink flowers of the hardy, glossy-leaved Cyclamen coum *are a welcome sight in late winter and early spring. Here, a fine example is on excellent terms with a gold-needled* Pinus sylvestris *'Gold Coin'* (left)

Trees and shrubs are not the only plants that can have flowers and foliage ruined if frost comes at the wrong time in spring. Some early developing perennials can have their living cells destroyed by frost, making them look like lifeless compost. The flowers and foliage of some bergenias and the tender new leaves of hostas are just two examples of susceptible plants, but, fortunately, they are likely to shoot up again once the danger has passed.

Given the right selection of plants, all gardens can be given a new lease of life if the perspective of autumn, winter and spring colour and interest is studied with greater attention. Foggy Bottom is an example of a garden that has consciously developed the quiet season theme. Many of the beds, groupings and plant associations in it could be used in other gardens. I have always enjoyed the challenge of creating plant associations

IN EARLY SPRING, Ribes sanguineum 'White Icicle' makes a pleasant change from the more common red or pink flowering currants (above left)

PINK, DOUBLE BLOOMS of Camellia 'Donation' are out by early spring in a sheltered position. Euonymus fortunei *'Emerald 'n' Gold' provides foreground contrast* (above)

which can be adapted to smaller gardens, and in those that are featured in the next chapter I have been able to suggest ideas on what can be done on a small scale.

Of course, there are a lot of recipes available to meet individual tastes. Designing a garden is much like decorating a room – selecting and moving the furniture around to fit. The same can be done in a garden. But, to my mind, garden designs these days so often seem to concentrate more on the design principle, whether it be shape, form or colour scheming, than on the plants themselves. Hard landscaping, although necessary in a living environment for patios or terraces, is in danger of becoming an end in itself, with the plants looked upon as merely ingredients of secondary value to help create a certain effect. My belief is that you can have no better materials than plants themselves to use in a garden to create year-round effect, beauty, life and pleasure. Such designing, of course, calls for constant change and adaption as plants grow, and as such a garden becomes a living, breathing entity, a life unto itself. Learning about plants leads to a desire to widen knowledge, which in turn leads to yet more changes, and, hopefully, to more self fulfilment and a better quality of life connected to nature.

These are some thoughts as I write on a late winter evening, before the sun's warmth releases the energy of plants to produce an unstoppable burst of growth which will herald the onset of the noisy season once again. We need these quiet times to take stock, to prepare and to plan. Whether planting in spring, summer or autumn I hope this book makes you think about bringing more colour and pleasure to your garden and your life in the quieter time of the year.

A CALENDAR FOR FRAGRANCE

Anything that can introduce colour and fragrance into our lives is doubly valuable. So why not plan to have fragrant plants near your front or back door, along the path to the street, garage, washing line, shed or greenhouse. The evergreen foliage and delightfully smelling winter flowers of the sarcococcas *(Christmas or sweet box) make them ideal for this job. Their fragrance can knock you out at several metres distance and they will grow happily in shady spots. Mahonias, viburnums, chimonanthus, hamamelis and loniceras are other large-growing, winter-fragrant shrubs to plant.*

AUTUMN
Perennials and bulbs
Cosmos atrosanguineus
Cyclamen hederifolium
Cyclamen purpurascens
Iris unguicularis

Shrubs
Abelia
Akebia quinata
Clerodendrum
Elaeagnus × ebbingei
Elaeagnus pungens
Heptacodium jasminoïdes
Jasminum officinale
Mahonia × media
Pittosporum tenuifolium
Roses (some)
Viburnum × bodnantense
Viburnum farreri
Viburnum tinus (some)

WINTER
Perennials and bulbs
Galanthus 'S. Arnott'
Iris reticulata
Iris unguicularis
Leucojum vernum

Shrubs
Chimonanthus
Cornus mas
Erica arborea
Erica erigena
Hamamelis (most)
Lonicera fragantissima
Lonicera × purpusii
Mahonia japonica
Mahonia × media
Prunus mume
Rhododendron moupinense
Sarcococca
Viburnum × bodnantense
Viburnum farreri
Viburnum tinus (some)

EARLY SPRING
Perennials and bulbs
Iris foetidissima
Iris reticulata
Narcissus (some)
Muscari (some)
Viola odorata

Shrubs
Abeliophyllum distichum
Choisya ternata
Clematis armandii
Cornus mas
Corylopsis (some)
Daphnes (some)
Mahonia aquifolium
Mahonia japonica
Osmanthus × burkwoodii
Osmanthus delavayi
Pieris (some)
Rhododendron *(some)*
Ribes odoratum
Skimmia × confusa
Skimmia japonica
Viburnum × bodnantense
Viburnum × burkwoodii
and hybrids
Viburnum farreri
Viburnum tinus (some)

USEFUL FOR COVERING sheltered walls or pergolas, the strong-growing evergreen Clematis armandii *usually flowers in mid-spring* (left)

WINTER
COLOUR

Foggy Bottom is much larger than the average-sized garden, of course, yet there are a great many wonderful gardens that make our six acres look relatively small in comparison. However large a garden is, it has its own individual style which results from a unique combination of ideas and designs. Naturally, the larger the garden is, the more opportunity there is to experiment. And large gardens that are open to the public can be used by ordinary gardeners as sources of inspiration, full of ideas to be taken away, adapted and tried out in smaller situations.

Being a keen gardener and plantsman as well as nurseryman, I have been only too well aware of the comments that many gardeners might make as they walk around my own "large" garden, the most obvious perhaps being: "well of course, anyone can create a good garden in six acres." So I have tried to show in practical terms how to create interest and colour the year round in more modestly sized gardens.

To put some of these ideas into practice, over the years I have adopted three typical, suburban front gardens near to my home and, with the help of some of our nursery and garden staff, I have completely replanted them, subsequently recording their growth and development at regular intervals.

Naturally, these three situations cannot possibly represent all the different types of smaller gardens in the country. To do that would require at least twenty gardens, covering categories such as town gardens, shade and dry shade gardens, gardens on slopes, seaside, chalk and limestone gardens and many more, all with their own peculiarities as to shape and restrictions. But these three gardens (shown on pages 66-69, 70-73, 74-77) do, none the less, represent a great many plots and will, I hope, provide inspiration and plenty of practical ideas for those readers seeking to introduce year-round beauty and colour on their own doorsteps.

In addition to the planting plans for these three gardens, this chapter also contains a selection of planting associations (pages 78-85). These are designed for specific situations and will be useful for creating isolated areas of winter interest within an already established garden. Small sections taken from the planting plans for the three new gardens already mentioned would also serve this purpose.

The personal touch

No matter what its size, every garden generally reflects a different approach, a different aspect according to its age, history and surrounding topography, and, of course, an individuality derived from the imagination, skill and objectives of its designer and/or owners. The common denominator of all gardens is the interaction of plants and people.

While a garden can express the individuality of the person or people who own and tend it, not everyone has the time, inclination, or, perhaps, knowledge or confidence to achieve something enduringly interesting on their own. To help in just such situations was the prime motivation for adopting the three front gardens that are described later. Even though I was doing the initial work and supplying the plants, the three families concerned all had their own likes and dislikes about their gardens, their favourite plants or associations, and they are free to develop some of their ideas further in their back gardens if they wish.

By the same token, anyone can create their own plant associations, using their own artistic flair, whether in a garden, own artistic flair, whether in a garden, patio, window box or simply in a container or two. Each of the gardens and planting associations featured in this chapter gives ideas from which readers can start to influence their own gardens by introducing aspects to turn them into something that will be a pleasure to see and watch the whole year through. Thus each of us can become an aspiring artist in our own garden!

Adding winter interest to an established garden

If your garden is already well established it will probably contain some plants that fit the category of "quiet season" plant. You can build on these by adding appropriate bulbs, perennials or shrubs to existing beds or borders. Alternatively, you could extend one of these to give more space for developing winter-interest plantings. This book contains plenty of ideas for creating more autumn, winter and early spring interest, including walls, fences, containers or window boxes in addition to beds or borders.

For those with larger gardens, the ideas for creating new beds or plant associations illustrated later in this chapter may be limited in scope. If this is the case, you may wish to make an even larger, bolder winter interest feature. Take time to select plants carefully according to their rates of growth and suitability to your soil conditions. A larger garden allows you scope to select more vigorous and larger-growing plants if you wish. You can use the information contained in this book as a basis for planning your own feature according to the size of your garden and your own interests in particular types of plant.

The principal players

Plants are wonderful material for artistic use. They flow and ebb with the seasons, becoming a living, expanding canvas, unlike the dry, inanimate, one-dimensional material of the painter's work. Not that I wish to denigrate this form of art, for it captures a moment, an impression, but the artist once finished with his or her painting has it under control, finished. Not so the gardener, who has a much more difficult task looking after all the diverse, living plants in his care at the same time as orchestrating an artistic creation that changes with the seasons.

Such is the range of shapes, forms and colours of garden plants that I have always maintained that one needs little else with which to create a garden, although I am not against the odd humanizing feature or two! Nor am I too much against those who wish to colour scheme their garden, but this does not always lead to the best results, and in the smaller garden it can limit the selection of plant material.

The smaller the garden the more important the selection of plants, partic-

STARTLING SCARLET TWIGS of Cornus alba *'Sibirica', contrasting brightly with green grass and a darker background of conifers, give a winter-long show at Foggy Bottom* (below)

ularly if you want colour all the year. Whilst the bold architectural look might be dramatic, it will call for relatively few, but large specimens – certainly not generally suitable for the smaller garden. My own preference, which I have used in the three gardens shown on the following pages, is for a wide range of plants. With careful planting and subsequent management this makes possible an ever-changing scene of sustained interest throughout the year and a reasonably easily maintained garden. As one plant goes past its peak it will always be followed by another at its best, and another just about to come into flower.

Gardening is about observation and learning how plants grow and how to make them grow better. Part of the fun is comparing your plants' performances with what the books say about them! It is always good to have at least one reliable reference book to pore over – even better to have two – although it can be somewhat confusing if they give conflicting advice! But whilst you can learn from books, you can never learn better than from your own experience.

TIME VERSUS COST

Something I had to face with both my own garden and the three adopted small ones was the time factor, that is, how long are people prepared to wait for results. I suspect that along with wanting a garden that looks attractive for most of the year without much looking after, most people also wish for an instant, semi-mature garden where one does not already exist. But as anyone who spends any time at all browsing around garden centres will know, the larger plants and specimens which can help to achieve this cost money.

When talking about specimen plants we can certainly use the time-honoured

phrase "time costs money" in a literal sense. But, if money is not too much of a problem, the choice is the customer's. A dwarf or slow-growing conifer, something like *Picea glauca albertiana* 'Conica' which has a narrow, cone-like habit, is a good example. A two-or three-year old plant will be 20-30cm/8-12in tall at the most. It may take at least ten years to reach 90-120cm/3-4ft and will need to be sold in quite a large container. Needless to say, a ten-year old specimen of the *Picea*, even if it is smaller than a two-or three-year old × *Cupressocyparis leylandii* (which once established grows 90cm/3ft per year!), will cost considerably more to buy. You are buying a bigger plant, of course, but what you are really paying for is seven years of growing and caring time at the nursery which enables you to install an instant, established effect in the garden. The decision is yours to make.

Conversely, and hopefully not to confuse, while purchasing fast-growing plants might save a lot of money, in the small garden this strategy can lead to problems early on as these plants will soon become unmanageable without constant, severe pruning.

On the whole, I think that most people would consider a wait of three years before seeing some positive results when developing a new garden – with plants

FOR YEAR-ROUND APPEAL in a limited space, few deciduous plants can claim as many pleasing attributes as Prunus incisa *'Kojo-no-mai', seen here with its naked, twisted branches encased in ice on a frosty mid-winter morning. Pink buds will soon swell to open at the beginning of spring as a mass of white flowers which will fade to pink as serrated, fresh green leaves emerge. In autumn the foliage turns bronze and crimson. This specimen, at 1.5m/5ft, is about ten years old* (opposite)

beginning to meet together and associations starting to work – as reasonable.

Depending upon the style of garden or the type of plants installed, after three years is usually the time when the faster-growing plants will need to start being pruned. This is the beginning of the "management" phase. Some plants will have succeeded only too well, and may either have to be pruned or even moved to another part of the garden. Others will have spread or become overgrown, some will not have done well and may want trying somewhere else.

THE FRONT GARDEN

Although the front garden is not used for recreation, it is passed or crossed by the average house-dweller at least twice a day, every day, totalling a conservative minimum of 700 times a year – and the figure is likely to be much higher. And that is just for one member of the family!

In view of its frequent use, and the fact that it is constantly on show to neighbours and passers-by as well as from the house itself, it has always amazed me that people do not do more with their front plot. With all the possibilities and opportunities it holds for enjoyment and pleasure, the front garden is arguably a more important area than the back garden.

There are large front gardens, small ones and even minuscule ones, some have even been covered with concrete and turned into car parking areas. For many people they can be a bit of a nuisance, perhaps consisting of a patch of lawn which has to be cut once or twice each week during spring, summer and autumn. Or they might be ugly, unimaginatively planted with an uninspired selection of a few shrubs, conifers, roses, bulbs or annuals in formal borders.

CHOOSING PLANTS FOR THE SMALL GARDEN

1. Think about what you would like your garden to look like and how it can be achieved.

2. Look at books to get ideas and be prepared to ask for advice from your local garden centre or nursery, or consult a garden designer.

3. Find out about the habits and requirements of the plants you choose, especially their rates of growth and eventual size.

4. Consider the garden's aspect and its soil. If necessary get a soil test taken. Seek advice from a reputable local garden centre or expert who will advise as to what will grow successfully in your locality.

5. Select plants that are in scale with each other – this applies particularly to smaller plants such as dwarf conifers, shrubs and alpines.

But it does not have to be like this. It is so easy to turn this "nuisance" into an asset by planting it up to create a living garden, a tapestry of colour and interest for year-round enjoyment. Even a front yard that has been paved over can be enlivened with pots and containers carefully planted to spice up drab winter days, or have planting holes gouged through the hard surface. And do not be put off by thinking that to create a small paradise on your front doorstep is all labour, for it can be done in easy stages.

So there is nothing to stop you creating a garden with colour and interest that you can enjoy every day of the year.

GOLD AND RUSSET for autumn but otherwise with dark green leaves, Acer palmatum *'Shishigashira' is just one of the slow-growing Japanese maples that have good winter shape and are ideal for growing in containers. This magnificent example is about eight years old* (above)

Terraces, patios, balconies or window boxes, whether located in sun or shade, can all be planted to give a full six months of interest during the autumn, winter and spring – a period often neglected by books on the subject of patio or container plants. So anyone with little garden, or even none at all, need not be denied the pleasure of an attractive winter display to be enjoyed through the quiet season. Whether you have room for one or many containers, large or small, there are plants to suit, the most valuable being those that will give year-round interest. These could be conifers or evergreen shrubs but for something different some ornamental grasses, perennials or deciduous shrubs or trees could be used. I have used all at Foggy Bottom.

Containers planted with individual plants can be moved around, if you have the space, to form containerized plant associations. Alternatively you can create interesting planting associations from whatever plants take your fancy at the garden centre.

Plants in containers must have suitable composts, with plants such as camellias, rhododendrons or pieris requiring acid soil. Most make do with a general container compost supplied by your local garden centre. Containerized plants require regular watering, especially in the summer to sustain growth, and feeding, either by using a slow-release fertilizer or a regular liquid feed. You can choose containers to suit your taste and pocket, but remember that glazed or ceramic ones retain moisture better than terracotta ones and so require less watering. Recently there have been some very good plastic imitation terracotta pots on the market and these will require a different watering regime. Good drainage is essential in winter, and the plastic pots require far less watering in summer.

In countries where severe frost is a regular feature, container plants are often wrapped in hessian or even plunged into the ground. This is the ultimate way to protect pots from cracking and roots from freezing, but for most Zone 8-9 hardiness areas (page 88), which includes the British Isles, this is probably extreme. A good idea for wetter areas is to lift the containers on blocks of wood or special terracotta "legs" to allow free drainage in winter.

The ideal time to plant up containers and window boxes for a winter display is in early autumn, planting any acid-loving specimens in ericaceous compost. Such a plant grouping can look good all year if it is fed, watered and trimmed regularly. But if you want to change your plants in spring, ready for a summer show, you can leave the plants in their pots and place these in the larger container in the autumn instead of planting them out. Simply remove these plants, in their pots, in the spring and place them elsewhere. Keep them watered, fed and trimmed through the summer, potting on into a larger pot if required, ready to be reinstalled in the container the following autumn.

If you do have a garden where you can plant your winter window box plants in spring, plan for the space to plant them before purchasing your selection in autumn. Plants such as some dwarf conifers, the evergreen euonymus, skimmias, heathers, *Viburnum tinus*, even colourfully stemmed dogwoods can all be used to good effect in window boxes and other containers in autumn, winter or early spring before planting out in the garden. It is a way of bringing the garden closer to your house during the quiet months.

SOME PLANTS FOR AUTUMN, WINTER AND SPRING WINDOW BOXES AND TUBS

SOME OF THE PLANTS put in the window box at Foggy Bottom are ultimately destined for the garden, but in their first winter they will make more impact close to the window (far left)

AN INSPIRED USE for this evergreen sedge makes the most of long threads which gradually sweep downwards (left)

In recent years, we in Britain have been catching on to the idea of using a wider range of plants for pots and containers for patio or terrace gardening as well as for window boxes. But by and large, these are for late spring, summer and early autumn use. So what about winter, when a cheery planting of foliage and flowering plants can brighten any aspect? With a window box winter garden you can bring nature closer to you and this is where variety is the key. Dwarf shrubs, perennials and bulbs can all play a part depending on the size and aspect of your window boxes. If you plan to plant some shrubs in your garden in spring that are suitable for window boxes, too, why not order them early and put them in your window box, still in their pots, over winter? Dwarf conifers can be selected from garden centres in mid-autumn, as can winter-flowering heathers, the best value perhaps being in Erica x darleyensis *types which flower from late autumn until late spring. Mix in a few yellow and gold* Calluna vulgaris *to brighten things up. Dwarf shrubs with good winter foliage colour have to*

include Euonymus fortunei *'Emerald 'n' Gold' and 'Emerald Gaiety',* and perhaps Hebe *'Red Edge'* which is red-tipped in winter. Skimmias are good for their evergreen foliage and their flowers and fruits. Larger-growing shrubs like Elaeagnus pungens *'Maculata',* variegated holly or aucuba will provide splashes of colour, and one of the dogwoods – Cornus alba *or* C. sanguinea *cultivars – will give colourful stem colour. You also can create a miniature garden. Why not use perennials like* Iris unguicularis, Bergenia *'Bressingham Ruby',* Ophiopogon planiscapus *'Nigrescens',* Helleborus niger *or* Acorus gramineus *'Ogon'* to give a combination of scented flowers, ruby red leaves, black foliage, classic white flowers and bright golden leaves. If you mix winter- and early spring-flowering bulbs in with some of the above, you should have a joyous winter! When making room for summer colour, some of the plants can be removed to a sheltered spot and fed and watered for one or two years, others can be planted in the garden, but even if there is no space for some, what price months of pleasure?*

Year-round Colour and low-maintenance
The Edens' Conifer, Heather and Shrub Garden

'I let it be known through the local newspapers that our nursery would give away a "free garden"....Sifting through the applications, I finally selected a garden that had been established for eight years. It belonged to George and Angela Edens and became known as (you have guessed it) the Garden of Edens!'

Visitors to Foggy Bottom often said how much they admired the combination of conifers and heathers, but that "obviously these plants were suitable only for the large garden". This prompted me to prove that dwarf conifers and heathers could be used together successfully, perhaps with a few appropriate dwarf shrubs, to create an attractive, low-maintenance, trouble-free garden in a limited space.

The Edens were quite happy for me and my helpers to dig up their small, unprepossessing front garden of shrubs and none-too-healthy roses around a rather tired looking lawn. The soil, which had been imported some years before, was a mixture of clay and sandy loam. Luckily we were able to add many bags of peat and compost to improve aeration and add some acidity to the soil. Because most plants are grown in peat or organic compost, it was helpful to add a generous handful in with each plant when it was put in. Finally, the soil's surface was covered with a heavy mulch of coarse-grade composted bark to help retain moisture during dry weather and keep down weeds.

Once established, the new garden took the Edens less than half an hour a week to maintain – with the exception of the lawn – and an eye had to be kept open for potential pests or disease.

A WORD ABOUT WEEDS AND MULCHING

Weeding is therapeutic to some, a real bore to others, but it has to be done if you are to stay in control of your garden, rather than the other way round. But anything you can do to minimize the spread of weeds in the first place is always worthwhile. You must give yourself a fair chance by first eliminating perennial weeds, but annual, seeding weeds are easier to control by mulching. Planting ground covers or whatever selection of plants is desired takes up space that would otherwise be colonized by weeds but if the space between the plants is covered by a mulch it will have many benefits. A mulch refers to a covering of material over the surface of the soil. It will generally be considered as organic material such as composted bark or leaf mould and should be put on to a depth of 2.5-5cm/1-2in. Mulching helps considerably to conserve water loss, benefiting both gardener and plants. Where weeds do grow, weeding "little and often" is the catch phrase to bear in mind, and if you can get to the young weeds well before they seed, you will save yourself a lot of time and frustration later. Easier said than done, as we know all too well at Foggy Bottom.

THE LOW-MAINTENANCE GARDEN *looks good in spring, just a few months after being planted in autumn* (opposite top)

NINE YEARS LATER, *the same garden has filled out and is looking mature* (opposite below)

A GROUP OF VERY DWARF *conifers six years after planting* (left top)

CONSISTING MOSTLY OF DWARF *conifers and heathers, the garden, seen here in spring six years after planting, is relatively easy to maintain, requiring occasional pruning* (left)

Design for year-round colour

THE EDENS' LOW-MAINTENANCE GARDEN
is made up of conifers, heathers and dwarf
shrubs. It shows how easily an average-
sized, square or rectangular-shaped,
suburban front garden can be transformed
into an informal garden, allowing the
plants to form a tapestry of colour, the
structure being provided by upright
conifers. Some non-flowering and
carpeting alpines have been included to
add variety. The number of these could be
increased and bulbs could be added as well
to give yet more colour at certain times of
the year. Even though the garden is quite
small (20x10m/60x30ft), a number of
vistas and focal points have been possible,
making it look much larger while
imparting a feeling of intimacy to anyone
strolling into the central area. Summer-
and winter-flowering heathers, planted in
groups of three to five of the same type,
make use of different foliage and flower
colours to create a pleasing patchwork
effect. The conifers are integral to this
patchwork scheme, their various shapes,
forms and colours perfectly
complementing the ground-covering
heathers, which in turn set off the conifers.
The plants are not difficult to grow. They
tolerate most soils and should not require
the addition of fertilizers unless the soil is
impoverished. Remember, though, that
summer-flowering heathers dislike lime.
They can be substituted by dwarf shrubs
or more winter-flowering heathers, many
of which have coloured foliage.

BED A

1 *Abies balsamea* 'Hudsonia'
2 *Juniperus squamata* 'Pygmaea'
3 *Thuja plicata* 'Rogersii'
4 *Chamaecyparis lawsoniana* 'Pygmaea Argentea'
5 *Picea mariana* 'Nana'
6 *Chamaecyparis pisifera* 'Nana Aureovariegata'
7 *Chamaecyparis obtusa* 'Nana'
8 *Picea abies* 'Little Gem'
9 *Juniperus squamata* 'Blue Star'
10 *Thuja occidentalis* 'Danica'
11 *Chamaecyparis pisifera* 'Nana'
12 *Chamaecyparis obtusa* 'Nana Lutea'
13 *Cryptomeria japonica* 'Vilmoriniana'
14 *Juniperus communis* 'Compressa'
15 *Chamaecyparis lawsoniana* 'Minima Aurea'
16 *Chamaecyparis obtusa* 'Kosteri'
17 *Chamaecyparis obtusa mariesii*
18 *Thuja orientalis* 'Aurea Nana'
19 *Chamaecyparis lawsoniana* 'Minima Glauca'

BED B section A

1 *Juniperus × media* 'Gold Sovereign'
2 *Erica carnea* 'Pink Spangles'
3 *Arabis ferdinand-coburgii* 'Variegata'
4 *Thuja occidentalis* 'Rheingold'
5 *Erica cinerea* 'C.D. Eason'
6 *Juniperus horizontalis* 'Hughes'
7 *Erica × darleyensis* 'Darley Dale'
8 *Picea glauca* 'Albertiana Conica'
9 *Calluna vulgaris* 'Robert Chapman'
10 *Calluna vulgaris* 'Silver Queen'
11 *Calluna vulgaris* 'Darkness'
12 *Chamaecyparis lawsoniana* 'Ellwood's Gold'
13 *Dianthus* 'Garland'
14 *Ajuga reptans* 'Purpurea'
15 *Chamaecyparis pisifera* 'Boulevard'
16 *Juniperus squamata* 'Holger'

BED B section B

17 *Erica erigena* 'W.T. Rackliff'
18 *Acaena buchananii*
19 *Chamaecyparis pisifera* 'Plumosa Aurea Nana'
20 *Euonymus fortunei* 'Emerald Gaiety'
21 *Chamaecyparis pisifera* 'Filifera Nana'
22 *Erica carnea* 'King George'
23 *Thuja orientalis* 'Aurea Nana'
24 *Juniperus horizontalis* 'Glauca'
25 *Erica cinerea* 'Pink Ice'

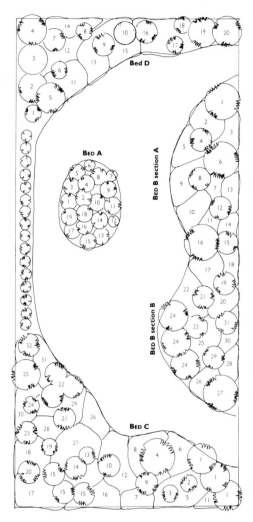

26 *Calluna vulgaris* 'Golden Carpet'
27 *Juniperus conferta* 'Blue Pacific'
28 *Sempervivum* 'Othello'
29 *Juniperus chinensis* 'Pyramidalis'
30 *Phlox subulata* 'Daniel's Cushion'
31 *Thuja occidentalis* 'Holmstrup'

BED C

1 *Juniperus sabina* 'Tamariscifolia'
2 *Thuja orientalis* 'Conspicua'
3 *Thuja occidentalis* 'Smaragd'
4 *Taxus baccata* 'Repens Aurea'
5 *Hebe pinguifolia* 'Pagei'
6 *Erica vagans* 'Mrs D.F. Maxwell'

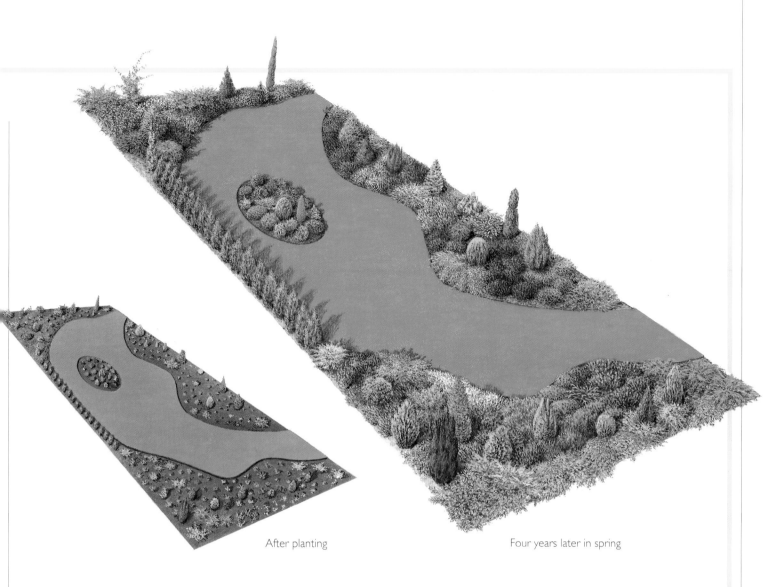

After planting

Four years later in spring

7 *Hedera helix* 'Chicago'
8 *Erica carnea* 'Myretoun Ruby'
9 *Chamaecyparis lawsoniana* 'Golden Pot'
10 *Chamaecyparis lawsoniana* 'Chilworth Silver'
11 *Hedera helix* 'Silver Queen'
12 *Erica carnea* 'Foxhollow'
13 *Chamaecyparis obtusa* 'Nana Gracilis'
14 *Thuja occidentalis* 'Sunkist'
15 *Juniperus horizontalis* 'Plumosa Youngstown'
16 *Potentilla fruticosa* 'Red Ace'
17 *Euonymus fortunei* 'Emerald 'n' Gold'
18 *Berberis thunbergii* 'Atropurpurea Nana'
19 *Juniperus scopulorum* 'Wichita Blue'
20 *Chamaecyparis lawsoniana* 'Little Spire'
21 *Chamaecyparis pisifera* 'Filifera Aurea'
22 *Juniperus squamata* 'Blue Carpet'
23 *Chamaecyparis lawsoniana* 'Moonshine'

24 *Cryptomeria japonica* 'Lobbii Nana'
25 *Taxus baccata* 'Semperaurea'
26 *Erica carnea* 'Springwood White'
27 *Erica* × *darleyensis* 'Furzey' (syn. 'Cherry Stevens')
28 *Calluna vulgaris* 'H.E. Beale'
29 *Erica vagans* 'Lyonesse'
30 *Erica* × *darleyensis* 'Arthur Johnson'
31 *Erica carnea* 'Vivellii'
32 *Juniperus* × *media* 'Sulphur Spray'

Bed D

1 *Taxus baccata* 'Standishii'
2 *Taxus baccata* 'Repandens'
3 *Elaeagnus pungens* 'Maculata'
4 *Juniperus* × *media* 'Old Gold'
5 *Tsuga canadensis* 'Jeddeloh'
6 *Chamaecyparis pisifera* 'Squarrosa Sulphurea'

7 *Juniperus scopulorum* 'Blue Heaven'
8 *Chamaecyparis pisifera* 'Filifera Aureovariegata'
9 *Juniperus squamata* 'Blue Swede'
10 *Choisya ternata* 'Sundance'
11 *Erica cinerea* 'Purple Beauty'
12 *Erica* × *darleyensis* 'Silberschmelze'
13 *Erica* × *darleyensis* 'Jack H. Brummage'
14 *Hedera helix* 'Silver Queen'
15 *Erica carnea* 'Myretoun Ruby'
16 *Thuja occidentalis* 'Smaragd'
17 *Thuja plicata* 'Stoneham Gold'
18 *Juniperus scopulorum* 'Skyrocket'
19 *Juniperus procumbens* 'Nana'
20 *Juniperus* × *media* 'Sulphur Spray'
21 *Erica carnea* 'Springwood Pink'
22 Hedge: *Thuja occidentalis* 'Smaragd'

Mixed Planting for Year-round Colour
The Putts' Winter Interest Garden

'I had had my eye on the small front garden belonging to No. 2 Copeman Road for some time prior to my knocking on the front door late one dark October evening. It seemed the ideal size and it was in the perfect location for me to watch its progress, once, if I were allowed to, I had planted it for year-round interest – especially for colour in autumn and winter.'

My scheme for the Putts' garden, a very small plot, was to provide year-round interest using a wide range of plants. Maggie Putt was probably no different from many gardeners in cooler climates in not wanting too many large trees or shrubs in the front garden because they would block out too much light from the house.

The original garden was mainly laid down to grass, with a small central border containing a few conifers and heathers, and another narrow border just in front of the window. When we started digging, I left a small strip of grass in the centre of the plot, curving away from the front step. This feature divided the small area into two separate entities, immediately giving it a lot more interest. A pH test of the light, slightly sandy soil showed it to be neutral, so it probably would not suit most acid-loving subjects. I was to find out later, that it was also rather prone to drying out. We dug it over and prepared it by mixing in some planting compost.

We finished the two small beds with contrasting types of decorative mulch or surfacing. The larger, mixed bed received a 5-8cm/2-3in layer of composted bark that would help retain moisture in dry weather. The alpine, scree bed, appropriately enough, was finished with a 2.5-5cm/1-2in layer of fine shingle.

ONE YEAR AFTER planting, the bed in the foreground contains conifers interplanted with spring-flowering bulbs and alpines. The bed beyond is replete with flowers, fruits, stems and evergreen foliage (left)

WINTER MAGIC goes right up to the front window on a frosty, mid-winter morning (opposite)

THREE YEARS ON, the tiny garden is transformed and full of interest in autumn (below)

DESIGN FOR YEAR-ROUND INTEREST WITH WINTER HIGHLIGHTS

THE MIXED PLANTING for this 6x6m/20x20ft garden consists of over seventy species and varieties of hardy plants. The fairly dense planting allows the inclusion of a wide variety of carefully selected plants to ensure continuous colour, shape and interesting plant associations throughout the year. It manages without annuals, roses and trees for which there was just not enough space.

The smaller bed has been turned into a little scree garden, planted up with a selection of dwarf conifers, shrubs, alpines and dwarf bulbs, all more or less in proportion with one another. The larger bed, which nudges up against the similarly sized front garden next door, is crammed with a wide selection of mixed dwarf conifers, low-growing perennials, dwarf shrubs, a few larger shrubs and bulbs.

The few larger shrubs in the selection can all tolerate the fairly severe annual spring pruning that will be required to keep them in proportion with the limited size of the planting area. Few people, perhaps, would risk planting three dogwoods close together in such a restricted area, but they are included here for their year-round virtuosity. One has variegated summer leaves, the others green ones, but in winter they show stems of deep red, scarlet or orange-red. To ensure the best stem colour as well as to control their size, they must be pruned each late spring to within a few centimetres of the ground. Cultivated in this way, they seldom grow to more than 1.2m/4ft in a year. The other shrubs and the conifers will first need pruning in two or three years' time.

BED A

1 Picea pungens 'Globosa'
2. Chamaecyparis lawsoniana 'Pygmaea Argentea'
3. Juniperus × media 'Gold Sovereign'
4. Chamaecyparis obtusa 'Nana Gracilis'
5. Chamaecyparis thyoides 'Rubicon'
6. Chamaecyparis pisifera 'Nana'
7. Abies balsamea 'Hudsonia'
8. Juniperus communis 'Compressa'
9. Juniperus communis 'Green Carpet'
10. Chamaecyparis lawsoniana 'Minima Aurea'
11. Berberis thunbergii 'Bagatelle'
12. Hebe ochracea 'James Stirling'
13. Geranium sanguineum 'Alan Bloom'
14. Sempervivum arachnoideum 'Laggeri'
15. Campanula garganica 'Dickson's Gold'
16. Ajuga reptans 'Braunherz'
17. Raoulia australis
18. Campanula carpatica 'Bressingham White'
19. Sedum spathulifolium 'Capo Blanco'
20. Thymus 'Anderson's Gold'
21. Campanula turbinata 'Wheatley Violet'
22. Sisyrinchium 'May Snow'
23. Saxifraga oppositifolia
24. Saxifraga 'Winifred Bevington'
25. Geranium cinereum 'Laurence Flatman'
26. Thymus doerfleri 'Bressingham Pink'
27. Arabis ferdinandi-coburgii 'Variegata'
28. Armeria juniperifolia 'Bevan's Variety'
29. Viola 'Rebecca'

BED B

1 Viburnum tinus 'Eve Price'
2 Mahonia aquifolium 'Smaragd'
3 Viburnum davidii
4 Skimmia × confusa 'Kew Green'
5 Camellia 'Donation'
6 Hosta 'Ground Master'
7 Caryopteris × clandonensis 'Heavenly Blue'
8 Dicentra 'Snowflakes'
9 Pulmonaria saccharata 'Highdown'
10 Euonymus fortunei 'Emerald 'n' Gold'
11 Helleborus orientalis
12 Santolina incana
13 Thuja occidentalis 'Smaragd'
14 Juniperis squamata 'Blue Star'
15 Thymus 'Anderson's Gold'
16 Lamium galeobdolon 'Hermann's Pride'
17 Erica carnea 'Myretoun Ruby'

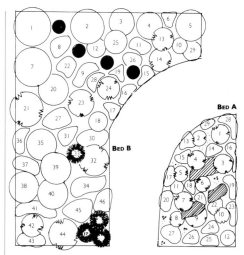

18 Hebe 'Emerald Green'
19 Lamium maculatum 'White Nancy'
20 Berberis thunbergii 'Dart's Red Lady'
21 Juniperus × media 'Sulphur Spray'
22 Bergenia 'Bressingham White'
23 Thuja occidentalis 'Rheingold'
24 Juniperus horizontalis 'Grey Pearl'
25 Spiraea japonica 'Golden Princess'
26 Primula 'Sue Jervis'
27 Iris pallida 'Argentea'
28 Fragaria 'Pink Panda'
29 Hebe 'Quicksilver'
30 Ophiopogon planiscapus 'Nigrescens'
31 Viola 'Clementina'
32 Microbiota decussata
33 Festuca glauca 'Blue Glow'
34 Coreopsis verticillata 'Golden Gain'
35 Cornus alba 'Sibirica Variegata'
36 Helleborus foetidus
37 Euonymus fortunei 'Sunspot'
38 Cornus alba 'Sibirica'
39 Cornus sanguinea 'Winter Flame'
40 Lavandula 'Hidcote Blue'
41 Bergenia 'Bressingham Ruby'
42 Thuja occidentalis 'Sunkist'
43 Erica carnea 'Pink Spangles'
44 Abies procera 'Glauca Prostrata'
45 Euphorbia myrsinites
46 Erica carnea 'Springwood White'
47 Acorus gramineus 'Ogon'

'To dramatize the advantages of a winter-interest garden, and to some extent autumn planting, I decided to add a bit of excitement by creating an instant garden – and, with the help of two other gardeners, planted it in one day.'

After planting

Two years later

Today

A garden Without a Lawn

The Johnsons' Drought-resistant Garden

Bearing in mind that the soil in the Johnsons' tiny front garden was fairly well-drained and that water restrictions were regularly in force throughout the country, it seemed appropriate to consider a "drought-resistant" theme for this new venture. Since the Johnsons had already said how much they liked the small, shingle-covered scree bed, that I had incorporated in their neighbours' front garden, I knew they would not object to a more Mediterranean look on their own patch.

I decided to completely strip off the grass and plant the entire garden with a blend of alpines, perennials and a few select trees, shrubs and conifers, covering up the earth with different shingles and small pebbles. This distinctive, interestingly patterned surface would enhance the dry theme and act as a mulch helping to retain valuable moisture during dry weather.

Colour, foliage, form and flower were to form the basis of this garden. The plan was to allow the plants freedom by not overcrowding them, although in some cases growth during the first couple of years was much more rapid than I had expected. The garden was also designed to illustrate how attractive plant associations can be made to work in a small area. If anything, perhaps because it was so different from most other front gardens, it excited more comment and interest from visitors and passers-by than the one I had already planted next door.

After removing the turf, we dug over the soil, adding some planting compost. Being dry and littered with builder's rubble the work was quite hard going in places. Before planting, I fashioned a curving "dry stream bed" through the centre of the garden simply by throwing some of the soil from the centre to the sides. This provided some slight undulation on the otherwise flat surface. Large flint stones, readily available in the locality, placed on the surface imitated rocks or pebbles, enhancing the dry stream bed effect.

When all is taken into consideration, this garden should take very little more time than would a grass lawn with a few shrubs scattered around it, if any, to keep it looking good. You have the cost of the plants, but you do not have the cost of the mower. And, if you choose carefully, the investment in the plants will pay great dividends in terms of interest and pleasure for many years to come, throughout both summer and winter months.

'I wanted to plant a completely different type of garden, something that, in view of all the dry summers we seemed to be getting, would be somewhat drought-resistant with a shingle surfacing. Next door to the Putts, the Johnsons 6×6m/20×20ft plot seemed ideal. It would give a direct comparison of styles and would save me making two separate journeys to record and photograph the gardens' developments. It was to be planted in one day in early May, just two and a half years after we had planted the Putts garden.'

PERENNIALS AND GRASSES, planted in late spring, have already achieved results by the beginning of autumn. Geranium x riversleaianum *'Russell Prichard' and* Carex comans *'Bronze Form', with* Agapanthus *'Lilliput' to the right, create a pleasing association* (below)

LESS THAN A YEAR after being planted, the pulmonaria, (back left), and Chrysanthemopsis hosmariense *(syn.* Chrysanthemum hosmariense*) (back right), are in flower in early spring. Bulbs planted in the autumn will heighten spring interest* (left)

FORM AND TEXTURE provided by grasses and perennials in mid-autumn will last through most of the winter, as will the foliage interest of conifers and shrubs to the left of the bed, creating an arresting alternative to the common lawn (left)

DESIGN FOR HOT DRY SEASONS

THIS GARDEN IS PACKED with colour in summer. But in winter, apart from the brightly variegated leaves of *Elaeagnus pungen*s 'Maculata' and one or two conifers, the interest is sustained more in form and foliage. The wind and the frost on the grasses give movement and beauty and the contrast of light and shadow are more important because they are so much more noticeable during the duller months of the year.

Ornamental grasses, attractive the year round, add an architectural quality and look very natural on gravel, as do many of the sun-loving perennials such as the kniphofias and crocosmias. The perennials have been chosen to give as long a period of flowering as possible; plants such as *Geranium* 'Russell Prichard' and South African diascias fit the bill admirably. The few trees used in this garden are grown as shrubs; regular pruning – every year or every other year – keeps them small without making them look too stunted. *Acer negundo* 'Flamingo' will grow on most soils, providing a long period of interest with its attractively variegated summer leaves brightly splashed with pink. The area near the front of the garden is planted with dwarf alpine plants, their small size allowing a wider selection of interesting plants.

1 *Pulmonaria saccharata* 'Highdown'
2 *Stachys byzantina* (syn. *olympica*) 'Primrose Heron'·
3 *Platanus × acerifolia* 'Mirkovec'
4 *Miscanthus yakushimensis*
5 *Ajuga reptans* 'Burgundy Glow'
6 *Agapanthus campanulatus* 'Isis'
7 *Rosmarinus* 'Jessop's Upright'
8 *Chrysanthemopsis hosmariense*
9 *Crocosmia* 'Jenny Bloom'
10 *Festuca glauca* 'Blue Glow'
11 *Eryngium variifolium*
12 *Miscanthus sinensis* 'Kleine Silberspinne'
13 *Sempervivum arachnoideum* 'Laggeri'
14 *Heuchera* 'Bressingham Bronze'
15 *Hebe albicans* 'Red Edge'
16 *Diascia elegans*
17 *Molina caerulea* 'Variegata'
18 *Gaura lindheimeri*
19 *Geranium cinereum* 'Ballerina'
20 *Artemisia nutans* (*splendens*)
21 *Lysimachia nummularia* 'Aurea'
22 *Sisyrinchium macrodenum* 'May Snow'
23 *Ophiopogon planiscapus* 'Nigrescens'
24 *Crocosmia* 'Spitfire'
25 *Acer negundo* 'Flamingo'
26 *Carex testacea*
27 *Acorus gramineus* 'Ogon'
28 *Agapanthus campanulatus* 'Albus'
29 *Hakonechloa macra* 'Alboaurea'
30 *Kniphofia* 'Little Maid'
31 *Euphorbia wulfenii* 'Humpty Dumpty'
32 *Festuca cinerea* 'Blue Seas'
33 *Geranium* 'Russell Prichard'
34 *Artemisia schmidtiana* 'Nana'
35 *Lavandula stoechas* 'Pedunculata'
36 *Rhodiola rosea* (syn. *Sedum rosea*)
37 *Campanula carpatica* 'Chewton Joy'
38 *Sempervivum* 'Royal Ruby'
39 *Agapanthus* 'Lilliput'
40 *Geranium* 'Russell Prichard'
41 *Campanula turbinata* 'Karl Foerster'
42 *Geranium* 'Ann Folkard'
43 *Gypsophila* 'Rose Beauty'
44 *Mertensia asiatica*
45 *Hakonechloa macra* 'Alboaurea'
46 *Sagina subulata* 'Aurea'
47 *Origanum laevigatum* 'Hopleys'

48 *Campanula carpatica* 'Chewton Joy'
49 *Festuca cinerea* 'Blue Seas'
50 *Morisia monanthos* 'Fred Hemmingway'
51 *Hebe ochracea* 'James Stirling'
52 *Armeria maritima* 'Dusseldorf Pride'
53 *Sempervivum* 'Cleveland Morgan'
54 *Scabiosa graminifolia*
55 *Viola* 'Molly Sanderson'
56 *Campanula* 'Dickson's Gold'
57 *Hebe* 'Caledonia'
58 *Sisyrinchium macrodenum* 'May Snow'
59 *Eryngium bourgatii*
60 *Sempervivum* 'Wollcott's Variety'
61 *Pulsatilla vulgaris* 'Rubra'
62 *Pinus mugo* 'Ophir'
63 *Miscanthus sinensis* 'Morning Light'
64 *Carex buchananii*
65 *Geranium lancastrense* 'Shepherd's Warning'
66 *Scabiosa graminifolia* 'Pincushion'
67 *Euphorbia amygdaloides* 'Rubra'
68 *Dicentra* 'Snowflakes'
69 *Acorus gramineus* 'Ogon'
70 *Geranium* 'Alan Bloom'
71 *Artemisia lanata*
72 *Aster thompsonii* 'Nanus'
73 *Geranium × cantabrigiense* 'Biokovo'
74 *Kniphofia* 'Bressingham Comet'
75 *Stipa tenuifolia*
76 *Bergenia* 'Bressingham Ruby'
77 *Campanula poscharskyana* 'Blauranke'
78 *Lamium maculatum* 'White Nancy'
79 *Juniperus scopulorum* 'Moonglow'
80 *Deschampsia caespitosa* 'Golden Dew'
81 *Pulmonaria saccharata* 'Leopard'
82 *Elaeagnus pungens* 'Maculata'
83 *Ajuga reptans* 'Burgundy Glow'
84 *Carex* 'Frosted Curls'
85 *Hemerocallis* 'Stella de Oro'

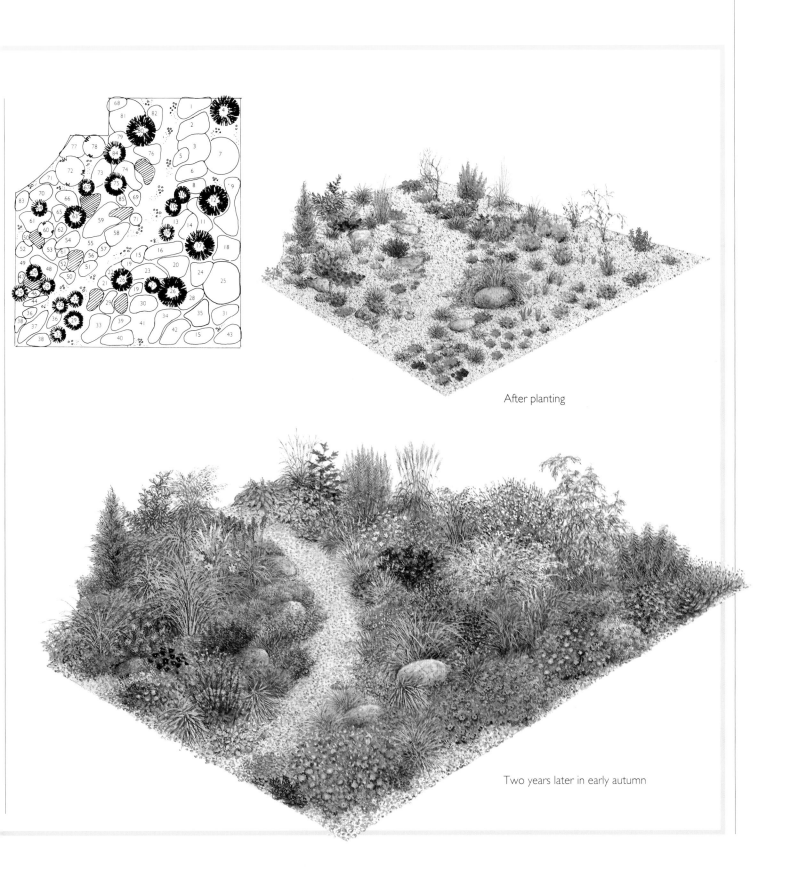

After planting

Two years later in early autumn

Perhaps the least understood or appreciated of plant associations are those that are most successful. One plant can
make a striking specimen or show on its own, but if used in
association with certain other plants it can produce some
pleasing and often stunning scenes. The first thing to do when
attempting a planting group is to decide in general terms what
your require *before* you start planting.

Choice of plants and arrangements are very personal and
the ideas shown on the next few pages can be used a guides as
to what should work, but in fact the choice can be wider.
There is undoubtedly less choice for winter than summer, so
even if you wanted to, it would be difficult to create one-
colour beds, although a white or silver winter arrangement
using, for instance, a white-stemmed silver birch, *Rubus cockburnianus* or other with *Helleborus niger* and snowdrops could
be quite stunning, particularly if given a light dusting of snow!
But I think that most people like the idea of colour, and as
some of the illustrations show, colour there is.

The seven plant associations shown here are for particular
situations. There are associations for sun or shade, for walls
and open beds, shrubs, trees, perennials, grasses, ferns, alpines
and bulbs. Heathers, too, but no conifers, a conscious decision
since they are featured so strongly elsewhere in the book,
particularly in the Edens' garden (page 66). There are two
illustrations each for autumn, winter and spring highlight,
plus one featuring container-grown plants.

Each planting association has a note about when it would
be best to plant for success. Climate, aspect and soil all have a
bearing on what can safely be planted and the notes accompa-
nying the illustrations are given as guidelines only.

All the plants have been grown in my own garden, and
some of these associations used, too. I hope they will be a
useful guide, but they also can be improved on. It is a good
discipline to keep looking at new plants, new ideas, new associations to see how they might fit into your garden. Learn
from both failures and successes!

AGAINST A DRAMATIC
backdrop of
Cortaderia selloana
'Pumila', the so-
called dwarf pampas
grass, and Stipa
calamagrostis, *a*
group of plants
provides plenty of
colour just outside the
back door at Foggy
Bottom on a sunny
day in late winter.
Blue Chamaecyparis
lawsonia *and fiery*
Cornus sanguinea
'Winter Flame' front
a prostrate, light
yellow cedar (right)

CONTAINERS FOR THE "QUIET" SEASON

For patios, terraces, courtyards or even balconies there are innumerable plants which can give autumn, winter or early spring interest. The selection in this group of containers offers year-round diversity and colour by including deciduous and evergreen shrubs and a few perennials and grasses. Of the plants illustrated here, the following will all do well in shady or semi-shady positions: *Hedera colchica* 'Dentata Variegata', *Acer palmatum* 'Senkaki', *Viburnum tinus* 'Eve Price', *Camellia* 'Donation' and the mixed planting of *Skimmia reevesiana*, *Euonymus fortunei* 'Emerald 'n' Gold' and *Sarcococca* x *confusa*. The remainder all prefer sun. Although all of these plants, except *Choisya ternata* 'Sundance' which must be put under

cover during frosty periods, can stand light autumn frosts, the camellia, viburnum and prunus require protection during prolonged winter frost in exposed situations (see page 34). Other plants such as dwarf conifers and a wide range of evergreen shrubs, including heaths and heathers, can be equally successful and attractive, even more so when used in combinations.

Best potted from spring to late summer are: *Carex comans* 'Bronze Form', *Choisya ternata* 'Sundance', *Prunus incisa* 'Kojo-no-mai and *Camellia* 'Donation'. But all could be potted in early autumn if given the protection of a cold greenhouse. Advice for protecting containerized plants over winter is given on page 65.

1 *Acer palmatum* 'Senkaki'
2 *Bergenia* 'Bressingham Ruby'
3 *Camellia* 'Donation'
4 *Carex comans* 'Bronze Form'
5 *Chamaecyparis pisifera* 'Filfera Nana'
6 *Choisya ternata* 'Sundance'
7 *Cornus sanguinea* 'Winter Flame'
8 *Erica carnea* or *E.* x *darleyensis*
9 *Euonymus fortunei* 'Emerald 'n' Gold'
10 *Hakonechloa macra* 'Alboaurea'
11 *Hedera colchica* 'Dentata Variegata'
12 *Juniperus* x *media* 'Gold Sovereign'
13 *Juniperus* x *media* 'Sulphur Spray'
14 *Prunus incisa* 'Kojo-no-mai'
15 *Salix* x *sepulcralis* 'Erythroflexuosa'
16 *Sarcococca* x *confusa*
17 *Skimmia reevesiana*
18 *Viburnum tinus* 'Eve Price'

SCENTED COLOUR FOR A SUNNY WALL

Offering year-round variety, this packed planting for a sun-facing wall is particularly colourful from late summer to early spring. The wall is covered by a thick mantle of lush evergreen foliage. At the base, the linear, silver-backed, dark green leaves of the rosemary contrast with the grey of *Santolina incana,* whose yellow summer flowers will have just finished, and the rush-like foliage of *Iris unguicularis.* With autumn come the beautiful pink flower heads of *Nerine bowdenii,* and the iris may produce a few of its charming and fragrant, light blue blooms although most appear in the middle of winter. Most visually striking is the free-fruiting pyracantha. Catkins decorate the garrya for weeks from early winter until early spring and are followed by the fragrant flowers of *Abelio-*

phyllum distichum (white forsythia) and of *Prunus mume* 'Beni-shidare', which are pink.

In summer the wall is less interesting but the evergreens show well and the rosemary has blue flowers in late spring, the pyracantha bears white flowers in early summer and the santolina yellow ones in late summer.

Apart from the self-clinging hedera, the taller shrubs may need tying to wall supports or brackets as well as pruning regularly to keep them neat. Widening the 1m/3ft bed would allow for finer touches to be added.

With the exception of the pyracantha, hedera and abeliophyllum, these plants are best planted from spring to early autumn. Use container-grown plants.

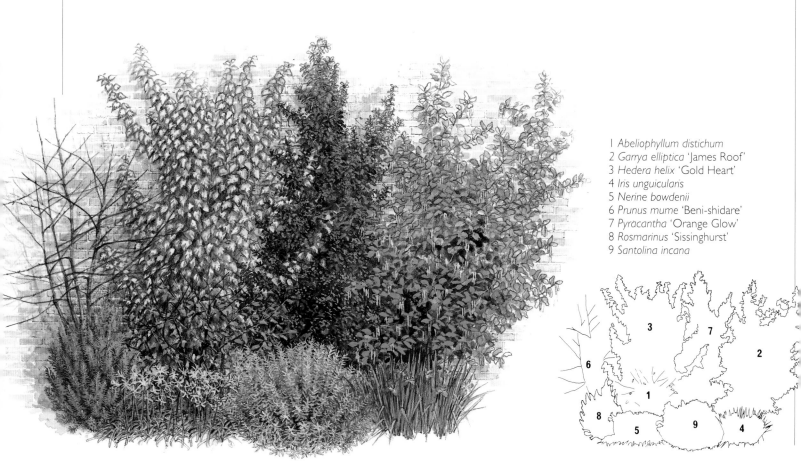

1 *Abeliophyllum distichum*
2 *Garrya elliptica* 'James Roof'
3 *Hedera helix* 'Gold Heart'
4 *Iris unguicularis*
5 *Nerine bowdenii*
6 *Prunus mume* 'Beni-shidare'
7 *Pyracantha* 'Orange Glow'
8 *Rosmarinus* 'Sissinghurst'
9 *Santolina incana*

A MIXED BED FOR AUTUMN, WINTER AND SPRING

This simple planting, shown here in mid-autumn, guarantees startling colour throughout autumn, winter and spring. It centres on one of the shrubby dogwoods, *Cornus sanguinea* 'Winter Flame', which is surrounded by a mixture of heaths, perennials and two types of bulb (snowdrop and winter aconite) that will play an important role in late winter and early spring. The bed should be sited in full sun, or at least in a position that receives sun for no less than half of the day and the plants will do best on any reasonable soil that becomes neither too wet nor too dry.

In autumn, the violet flowers of *Liriope muscari* and the bright blue foliage of *Festuca glauca* 'Blue Glow' contrast superbly with the startling transformation taking place in the dying leaves of the dogwood. Slower to change than most other dogwoods, these turn from pale green to pale yellow then gold, often finishing with russet hues. The naked, upright stems – yellow-orange at the base with fiery crimson tips – retain their striking colour, which deepens with frost, through the quiet season. They should be pruned almost to the ground in mid-spring. The pulmonaria's silver-spotted leaves will die away in winter to be renewed in early spring along with deep blue flowers which contrast with the bronze-green foliage and carmine blooms of *Erica carnea* 'Vivellii' which will flower until late spring. The snowdrops will have their perfect foil in the narrow, strap-like, black leaves of the evergreen ophiopogon which in turn contrast all year round with the silver-blue grassy foliage of the *Festuca glauca* 'Blue Glow'. It is against these that the bright, cheery yellow of the winter aconites will show up. In summer the grouping will be primarily sober shades of green. More summer colour could be introduced, perhaps by using a hardy geranium such as 'Russell Prichard' which flowers from early summer until well into autumn.

All the plants mentioned here can be planted from pots from spring to late autumn. Snowdrops can be planted "in the green" as divisions after winter flowers have finished, or as bulbs in late summer.

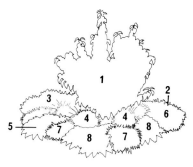

1 *Cornus sanguinea* 'Winter Flame'
2 *Eranthus hyemalis* (not in flower)
3 *Erica carnea* 'Vivellii'
4 *Festuca glauca* 'Blue Glow'
5 *Galanthus nivalis* (not in flower)
6 *Liriope muscari*
7 *Ophiopogon planiscapus* 'Nigrescens'
8 *Pulmonaria* 'Lewis Palmer'

CHEERING UP A SEMI-SHADY WALL

Based on foliage plants this planting, shown here in late winter/early spring, remains attractive all year, but it has particular appeal for autumn, winter and early spring. It consists of deciduous and evergreen shrubs and herbaceous perennials, including one evergreen fern, which represents an often neglected group of plants that adapt well to shade. The recommended width of the bed at the base of the wall is 1.2m/4ft, which allows for root development of the shrubs and space for the lower-growing plants.

The large-leaved hederas are invaluable for such a situation, and *Hedera colchica* 'Dentata Variegata' has year-round appeal. It may need some help to cling in its first year or two and tones well with the mahonia's dark green, behind which it may eventually grow, and in autumn, when 'Charity' opens it fragrant light yellow flowers, this will make a pleasing association.

The winter-flowering deciduous chimonanthus is a much treasured plant in winter once established. It usually bears enough waxy pendulous flowers for cutting. Climbing among its branches, but possibly also requiring supports on the wall, is the evergreen *Clematis cirrhosa* which has crimson-purple spotted flowers during mild periods from autumn to early spring. Classed as tender, it often seems hardy in well-sheltered spots.

Closer to the ground, the spreading dwarf evergreen *Sarcococca humilis* has shiny, dark green, box-like leaves and a profusion of small but delicately fragrant flowers in late winter. The pointed, dark green marbled leaves of the *Arum italicum pictum* emerge in autumn to last until spring. The mass of white flowers of *Pulmonaria* 'Sissinghurst White' last for weeks from early spring, while in summer it has hairy silver-spotted mid-green leaves. Arching above is *Dryopteris erythrosora* (Japanese wild fern), one of the most attractive of the hardy ferns. Its bronze-tinged fronds have a metallic sheen and are likely to be damaged only in severe winters. The rounded leathery leaves and sugar-pink spring flowers of *Bergenia* 'Baby Doll' complete the base planting.

The *Clematis cirrhosa* and possibly the *Dryopteris erythrosora* are best planted in the spring to late summer period, the remainder of the plants from spring to late autumn.

1 *Hedera colchica* 'Dentata Variegata'
2 *Mahonia* × *media* 'Charity'
3 *Chimonanthus praecox*
4 *Clematis cirrhosa* 'Freckles'
5 *Dryopteris erythrosora*
6 *Bergenia* 'Baby Doll'
7 *Pulmonaria* 'Sissinghurst White'
8 *Arum italicum pictum*
9 *Sarcococca humilis*

FOLIAGE AND BARK FOR WINTER

Silver and white are the predominant colours in this startling winter foliage combination. *Betula utilis* 'Jacquemontii' is one of the smallest of the silver birches, but will grow, perhaps over fifteen years, to over 10m/30ft. Its even branching habit and the bright silvery bark on its main stems and branches make it a superb specimen. Pruning away the lower branches reveals more of the trunk and lets light onto the plants growing beneath. The ones used here will thrive in all but the driest situations, but are best planted before the tree becomes large and competes for food and moisture. Mix in plenty of compost when you plant them and mulch well.

The black-leaved *Ophiopogon planiscapus* 'Nigrescens' contrasts impressively with the silver birch's trunk and the *Lamium maculatum* 'White Nancy'. Nestling against the trunk, *Epimedium pinnatum colchicum* provides evergreen cover for the summer and winter and bears yellow flowers in spring. There are a few other bergenias with red winter foliage, but 'Bressingham Ruby' appears to be tougher than most and turns from green to ruby-red in autumn reverting to green as the deep crimson flowers arrive in spring. Evergreen *Iris foetidissima* 'Variegata' reinforces the white-silver theme whilst sun-loving *Euphorbia myrsinites* with its long, prostrate, segmented blue stems contributes year-round foliage and large yellow spring flowers. Yet more colour could be added by planting crocus, snowdrops and other spring-flowering bulbs. All items can be planted from spring until autumn, particularly if they are pot grown.

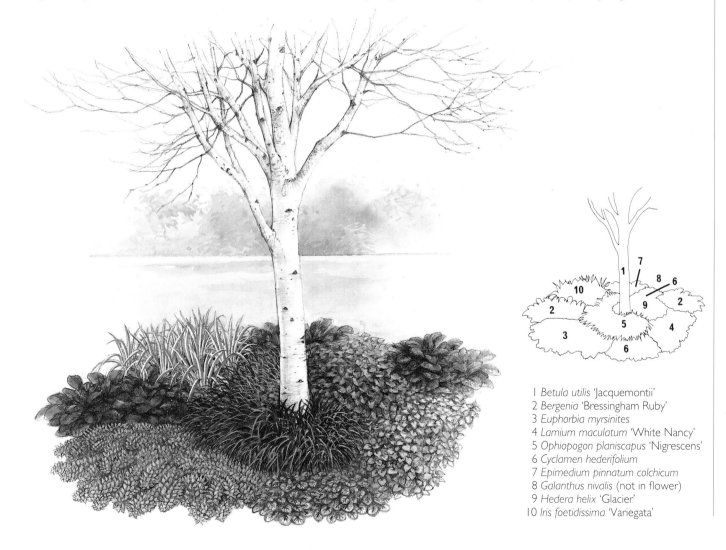

1 *Betula utilis* 'Jacquemontii'
2 *Bergenia* 'Bressingham Ruby'
3 *Euphorbia myrsinites*
4 *Lamium maculatum* 'White Nancy'
5 *Ophiopogon planiscapus* 'Nigrescens'
6 *Cyclamen hederifolium*
7 *Epimedium pinnatum colchicum*
8 *Galanthus nivalis* (not in flower)
9 *Hedera helix* 'Glacier'
10 *Iris foetidissima* 'Variegata'

WINTER STEMS, SUMMER COLOUR

This planting features a fast-growing willow – *Salix × sepulcralis* 'Erythroflexuosa' – as its centrepiece. None too remarkable in summer it can become a striking feature in winter if pruned to the ground each spring. It will take quite a few frosts to dislodge the last of the willow's leaves, but eventually these will all go, exposing spectacular curling, twisted, orange, brown and maroon stems. It grows well on all soils that are not too dry as do the other two shrubs. *Cornus alba* 'Kesselringii' is a black-stemmed dogwood which bears purplish black and green leaves in spring, summer and autumn. Quite different is the bramble *Rubus cockburnianus* 'Golden Vale' with arching stems that carry bright yellow leaves in summer which show up as ghostly white in winter. If this is placed on the shady side of the willow it is less likely to get scorched in very hot weather.

Winter aconites, snowdrops and the Christmas rose contrast well with the black stems of the dogwood. Additional colour for spring could be easily provided by a blue-flowered pulmonaria or *Muscari armeniacum.*

Pruning back the stems of the willow, dogwood and bramble should be done when shoots start to develop in mid-spring, the willow being a little earlier than the others. The later you prune the shorter the year's growth will be, but the willow will have grown to between 1.2-1.5m/4-5ft by midsummer and will be creating some shade. Summer foliage colour will be provided by the bramble and the dogwood, the pink flowers of the ground cover *Fragaria* 'Pink Panda', which last all summer, looking particularly good against the bramble. Additional summer colour could be added by planting something like a shrubby potentilla such as 'Goldfinger' or 'Kobold', yellow-flowered varieties, which could be placed close to the dogwood, but which would also complement the yellow of the bramble. The blue flowers of an *Aster amellus* would also set the bramble off.

All these plants can be planted from spring through autumn if they are purchased in containers. If available, snowdrops and aconites are best planted "in the green" as divisions after flowering, or they can go in as bulbs in autumn.

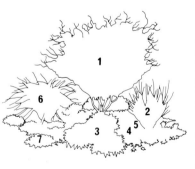

1 *Salix × sepulcralis* 'Erythroflexuosa'
2 *Cornus alba* 'Kesselringii'
3 *Helleborus niger*
4 *Eranthis hyemalis*
5 *Galanthus nivalis*
6 *Rubus cockburnianus* 'Golden Vale'
7 *Fragaria* 'Pink Panda'

BRIGHTENING UP A SEMI-SHADY SPOT IN EARLY SPRING

In this colourful planting, a witch hazel (hamamelis) provides the focal point. The witch hazels are among the aristocrats of shrubs yet could be more widely grown than they are. There are many selections to choose from, but those with yellow flowers are perhaps the most striking since their winter or early spring flowers light up the gloom more noticeably than those with darker orange or red ones. Contrary to general opinion, they do not have to have acid soil to succeed, but they do dislike thin, chalky soils. They grow well in sun or light shade, requiring a soil that is moist, yet well-drained and friable and to which ample humus in the form of well-rotted compost, leaf mould or composted bark is added.

For late winter and early spring, the yellow-flowered *H. mollis* 'Pallida' is one of the best. It has a spreading habit and fragrant, strap-like petals. The flowering period is determined by climate to some extent and in milder areas may be over before spring, in which case *H. ×. intermedia* 'Primavera' or *H. × i.* 'Westerstede', the latter among the latest, are worth looking for.

Any plants growing beneath the low-branching stems – here a selection of bulbs and perennials with winter and early spring interest – should make their show when the leaves are absent.

Snowdrops can surround the main stem, perhaps interspersed with *Chionodoxa luciliae* which has light blue, white-centred flowers, or the deeper blue flowers of *C. sardensis.* The nodding rose-pink flowers of *Helleborus orientalis* 'Winter Cheer' last for several weeks from late winter, depending upon the climate; there are many other choices among named or selected seedlings. Flowering at the same time is *Narcissus* 'February Silver', a dwarf cyclamineus daffodil with yellow trumpets and open, creamy white petals. Once the bulbs have finished flowering, they will not be seen until the following spring, but *Pulmonaria saccharata* 'Leopard' has leaves which are arguably the most spotted of all the lungworts and have summer-long attraction. In early spring its leaves take second place to the deep rosy-red flowers which continue for weeks. The *Dicentra* 'Snowflakes' will soon give a show of pendulous white lockets for many months. If space allows, this would be an ideal bed for a blue-leaved or variegated hosta for extra summer interest.

Snowdrops can be planted "in the green" as divisions after winter flowers have finished, or as with the chionodoxa bulbs in late summer. All the other plants can be planted from pots from spring to late autumn.

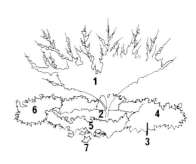

1 *Hamamelis mollis* 'Pallida'
2 *Chionodoxa lucilliae*
3 *Galanthus nivalis* (not in flower)
4 *Pulmonaria saccharata* 'Leopard'
5 *Narcissus* 'February Silver'
6 *Helleborus orientalis* 'Winter Cheer'
7 *Dicentra* 'Snowflakes'

DIRECTORY OF PLANTS

DIRECTORY OF PLANTS

This directory introduces hundreds of versatile plants that can add colour and interest to your garden in autumn, winter and spring as well as at other times of the year.

Most of the plants listed are hardy and adaptable to most soils, except where stated. A soil-testing kit will tell you whether your soil is acid or alkaline.

Unless you already have good, friable, fertile soil, you will probably need to dig thoroughly to a depth of 35-45cm/14-18in. Mix in organic material such as well-rotted compost or manure to help to retain moisture in light soils and aerate heavier types.

Before planting soak plants in their containers – for an hour or two if the compost is dry or a few minutes if it is moist. Make the hole deep enough so that the level of the soil in the container is just below the surface of the soil. Add some fertilizer – a slow-release type for conifers, shrubs or trees, but a quicker-acting, balanced one for perennials. Fill in with soil, firming gently on heavier soils but more firmly on lighter soils, and water in. Do not compact the soil too much. Mulch to retain moisture, protect new roots from frost and keep down weeds (page 67). Water regularly until established, for a tree at least a year.

TREES
Make the planting hole two or three times the width and depth of the rootball; on heavier soils break up the clay at the bottom. Provide a sturdy stake for anything over 90cm/3ft and use proper tree ties. Leave a circular ridge of soil just beyond the circumference of the rootball and fill with a good mulch.

SHRUBS
Mulch around newly planted shrubs, particularly shallow- or fibrous-rooted ones, and then annually or every two years. Apply a general, slow-release fertilizer in spring if shrubs lack colour or vigour. Protect susceptible new shrubs from wind or frosts with close-woven or shade netting. More details on pruning etc. are given in the Directory section.

CONIFERS
Most conifers can be planted slightly deeper than the level of the soil in the container or the rootball. If the roots of containerized plants are congested or curled, prune away some and tease out others. Staking may be necessary for large specimens (1.8-3m/6-10ft high) but for abundant foliage a tripod of three stakes may be preferable. Although containerized conifers may be planted with care at any time of year, the beginning of autumn and towards the end of spring are best. If planting in a lawn leave a circle of soil at least 60cm/2ft in diameter.

Larger specimens or those grown in open ground, particularly if they have abundant foliage, will benefit when moving from one or two protective measures: use an anti-desiccant foliage spray or surround with a close-meshed shading material or netting, supported by four stakes. Many conifers benefit from pruning and shaping, but this must not be so overdone as to lose the natural shape of the tree. Upright conifers may be damaged by heavy falls of snow, so knock it off as soon as it builds up.

PERENNIALS
Hardy perennials can be planted at almost any time unless soil conditions are poor and as long as they receive appropriate care – water in summer, drainage in winter. Tender plants must be planted in spring. Open-ground plants must be planted as soon after arrival as possible or temporarily in moist compost, sand or peat. If they arrive dry, soak them. Most early spring-flowering perennials are best divided and planted in late summer and early autumn, autumn-flowering ones are usually divided in early spring. Advice on protecting tender perennials in winter appears on page 34.

GRASSES
Few open-ground grasses take kindly to being planted in late autumn and winter but most hardy containerized types can be planted at any time as long as they do not go into waterlogged conditions in winter.

FERNS
Hardy ferns appreciate a friable soil and, according to variety or species, sun, shade, moisture or good drainage; some can tolerate quite dry positions.

HEATHS AND HEATHERS
Summer-flowering heathers need an acid soil, although *Erica vagans* (Cornish heath) tolerates neutral soil. Winter-flowering heathers are all lime-tolerant and are the most valuable for winter colour. All heathers benefit from a generous 4-6cm/1½-2in mulch of medium- or large-grade composted bark.

ALPINES
Many plants classed as alpines grow quite happily in any sunny spot with reasonable drainage. Many hardy alpines require well-drained soil which does not dry out in summer; consult specialist books for advice creating an alpine or scree bed.

BULBS
Seldom succeeding in heavy, wet soils, most bulbs prefer reasonably good drainage. Those flowering in winter and early spring must be planted in autumn, although if you can get them, both aconites and snowdrops are best planted after flowering in spring. Bulbs should go in places that are not likely to be disturbed.

HARDINESS ZONES
The plant hardiness zones given in this book are determined by the United States Department of Agriculture. They are based on the average annual minimum winter temperature for each zone. Climate variation is much less in the British Isles: Zone 7 covers the eastern Scottish Highlands; Zone 8 includes most of inland and eastern Britain and Ireland; and zone 9 includes the western coastal areas of Britain and Ireland. Each plant in the directories has been allocated a zone range within which it is likely to thrive. Within any one zone, however, several microclimates can occur, and other factors, such as site, aspect and soil, many also affect a plant's growth.

KEY TO SYMBOLS
☼ full sun
☀ semi-shade
✸ shade
☐ dry soil
◩ moist soil
■ well-drained soil
⊕ alkaline soil
⊖ acid soil
☆ most soils
★ fertile soil
★ humus-rich soil

Trees Directory

There is something magical about the thought of planting trees, and for today's smaller gardens there are many suitable ones, including many that can be pruned regularly to keep within bounds. Listed here are some which give good autumn colour, show off outstanding bark or stems or bear early spring flowers. Most, with the exception of the silver birches, are small or slow-growing.

H: Approximate height after 10 years
W: Approximate width after 10 years
F: Months in flower
Z: Relevant hardiness zone(s)

Foliage colour in autumn

Alnus glutinosa 'Aurea'

Betula nigra 'Heritage'

ACER Maple

Deciduous. For more detail see Shrubs Directory, page 92. ☼ ☀ ■ ☆
A. griseum. Paper-bark maple. Year-round attraction. Slowly flaking, brown bark revealing orange-brown beneath. Leaves split into three smaller leaflets, often colouring well in late autumn. Very slow-growing. H3-4m/10-13ft, W1.5-2m/5-6ft. Z5. ☆
A. hersii (syn. *A. grosseri hersii*). Snake-bark maple. Small, shapely tree for autumn colour. Smooth, grey-green, silver-streaked or marbled bark. Broadly ovate leaves. On mature specimens pendulous greenish flowers in spring and greenish yellow fruits in autumn. Of similar value are *A. davidii* and its cultivars 'George Forrest' and 'Ernest Wilson', *A. rufinerve* and *A. capillipes.* H4-5m/13-15ft, W2-4m/6-13ft. Z7. ☆
A. pensylvanicum 'Erythrocladum'. Beautiful selection. In winter bright coral-pink young stems striped silvery white. Golden-yellow leaves in autumn. Can be difficult; dislikes chalk soils and is slow on all others. H3-4m/10-13ft, W2.5m/8ft. Z4-7.
A. rubrum 'Red Sunset'. Slender, vigorous. Glowing, scarlet leaves in autumn. 'Schlesingeri', eye-catching with similar colours. Both H8-10m/26-33ft, W5m/16ft. Z3-9.

ALNUS Alder

Deciduous. ☼ ◪ ☆
A. incana 'Aurea'. Slow-growing, golden-leaved, attractive in winter with orange-red young wood, reddish catkins fading to yellow followed by yellow shoots and leaves, which soon fade to light green, in spring. H5-6m/16-20ft, W2-2.5m/6-8ft. Z3.
A. glutinosa 'Aurea'. Faster growing than *A. incana.* Long pendulous catkins, brighter yellow leaves, the colour maintained well into summer. H10m/33ft, W3-4m/10-13ft. Z3.

AMELANCHIER

Small deciduous trees or shrubs with spring flowers and autumn colour. Neutral to acid soil. ☼ ☀ ■ ◪
A. lamarckii. Suckering, multi-stemmed shrub or tree. Massed stems with erect panicles of pure white flowers in spring, edible, blackish-purple fruits in autumn. Leaves turn orange to red in autumn. H5-7m/16-23ft, W4-5m/13-16ft. F3-4. Z4.

BETULA Birch

Deciduous. Most of the birches eventually make medium or relatively large trees but are so attractive for both foliage and bark that they warrant inclusion in any garden large enough. Relatively surface-rooting, reducing the availability of moisture to nearby plants. Mostly slower-growing types are listed here, all slower on drier soils. ☼ ◪ ■
B. costata. Eventually large but slow for some years. Stout trunk and branches with flaking creamy white bark revealing brownish inner skin. Good golden-yellow autumn colour. H7-10m/23-33ft, W4-5m/13-16ft. Z4.
B. nigra. River birch. From North America, grows well in damper ground. Brown peeling bark with age, brownish stems but variable from seed. The selection 'Heritage' is striking with glossy, dark green leaves, peeling bark revealing white then pinkish brown stems. Golden autumn colour. H6-10m/20-30ft, W4-5m/13-16ft. Z4.
B. pendula. Common silver birch.

Betula utilis jacquemontii

Pleasing white bark and graceful branching habit with pendulous twiggy branchlets. Usually good autumn colour, if brief. Does well on drier soils. 6-10m/20-33ft, W5-6m/16-20ft. Z4.
B. utilis jacquemontii. Perhaps the most striking white-barked birch, relatively slow-growing. Peeling bark, glossy green leaves, attractive catkins. The form '**Jermyns**' is more vigorous but quite stunning. H6-8m/20-26ft, W4-5m/13-16ft. Z5.

COTONEASTER
Several deciduous or evergreen forms can eventually make small trees. Often classed under the *watereri* hybrids these are mostly semi-evergreen, carrying abundant red or orange fruits into winter. Single stems are trained upright and side shoots removed until a trunk develops. Deciduous ☼; evergreen ☼ ☀; all ■
C. × watereri '**John Waterer**'. Clusters of red fruits show well against deep green leaves. H5-6m/16-20ft, W4-5m/13-16ft. F6. Z7.

CRATAEGUS Hawthorn, thorn
Deciduous. ☼ ☆
C. crus-galli. Cockspur thorn. Attractive small North American tree. Thorny branches, show of white flowers in late spring, abundance of persistent crimson fruits in autumn. Shiny dark green leaves turn yellow and red in autumn. H6m/20ft, W4m/13ft. F4. Z3-7.
C. monogyna. Common hawthorn or May. Attractive hedgerow or ornamental tree, tough and thorny. Good foliage takes clipping well. Fragrant white flowers in late spring, the mature tree generally well endowed with crimson autumn fruits. Several selections with cultivar names. H6-8m/20-26ft, W6-8m/20-26ft. F4-5. Z4-7.

Betula pendula

C. prunifolia. One of the most garden-worthy of the thorns. Small, round-headed tree with rich glossy green leaves, white flowers. Good display of deep red fruits and matching crimson autumn leaves, both falling early. H6m/20ft, W6m/20ft. F4. Z4-7.

EUCALYPTUS Gum tree
Evergreen trees with aromatic foliage. Need shelter. ☼ ☆ ■
E. niphophila. Snow gum. One of the hardiest, most ornamental, and one of the few that can be classed as a small tree. Leathery, oval juvenile grey-green leaves become grey, narrow and lance-shaped as plant matures. Main stem usually develops

Eucalyptus niphophila

Liquidambar styraciflua 'Worplesdon'

a "lean", the smooth grey-green bark flaking to reveal creamy white, green and brown. Grown from seed, like all the gums, it is best planted as a young pot-grown plant so early roots quickly establish to support the rapid growth. The foliage is excellent for flower arranging and if cut back by hand or frost vigorous new shoots will emerge from the base. H10m/33ft, W5-6m/16-20ft. Z7-9.

LIQUIDAMBAR
L. styraciflua. Sweet gum tree. Eventually quite a large tree of upright habit. Often spectacular crimson autumn colours and corky bark. Seed-raised plants are unreliable for autumn colour, so look for selected cultivars, particularly for cooler climates. All prefer reasonably fertile soils which are not too dry and colour best in sunny position. Variable but expect H8m/26ft, W4m/13ft. ☼ ◪ ☆
'**Worplesdon**', reliable for good display of rich crimson autumn colour and is slow enough for a

smaller garden. '**Lane Roberts**', also good. Both H7-10m/23-30ft, W5-8m/16-26ft. Z7.

MALUS Crab apple
Some of the most ornamental of flowering and fruiting deciduous trees, many suitable for the small garden. Any soil that is not too dry or wet. ☼ ☆
M. '**Evereste**'. Good value small tree, large white flowers, red in bud, deep green foliage, profusion of orange-yellow fruits in autumn. H 5-7m/16-23ft, W4-5m/13-16ft. F3-4. Z5.
M. '**Golden Hornet**'. White flowers followed by spectacular show of rounded, bright yellow crab apples well into winter. Can get straggly with age. H6-8m/20-26ft, W5-6m/16-20ft. F3-4. Z5.
M. '**John Downie**'. Considered the best of fruiting crabs. White flowers and attractive, comparatively large yellow and red fruits of good flavour, the best for making jelly. H8m/26ft, W6-7m/20-23ft. Z5.
M. '**Red Jade**'. Weeping shrub or

Malus 'Evereste'

small tree, bright green leaves, pink and white flowers, abundance of crimson fruits lasting into winter. H4-5m/13-16ft, W5-6m/16-20ft. Z5.

M. sargentii. Shrub-like, Japanese species of great merit making a rounded bush profusely covered in white, golden-anthered blossom in spring and abundant cherry-like, bright red fruits in autumn. H3-4m/10-13ft, W3-5m/10-16ft. Z5.

Populus alba 'Richardii'

POPULUS Poplar

Very fast-growing, deciduous trees with extensive roots. ☼ ◩ ▪ ☀

P. alba 'Richardii'. Slower-growing form of the white poplar. Maple-like leaves with white undersides, bright golden-yellow upper sides – a brilliant combination, especially where wind can ruffle the foliage giving flashes of silver and gold, the colour enhanced in autumn. Grey-green winter stems, eventually suckering habit. Can be pruned as a shrub or small tree. H8m/26ft, W4m/13ft. Z5.

PRUNUS Cherry

Large family of deciduous or evergreen trees and shrubs, the latter described in the Shrubs Directory, page 104. Some wonderful spring-flowering trees, including the Japanese cherries. Those listed here give good autumn colour, winter bark or early spring blossom. Deciduous ☼; evergreen ☼ ☀; all ☆

P. incisa. See Shrubs Directory, page 104.
P. maackii. Manchurian cherry.

Prunus serrula

Medium-sized, deciduous. Small, white flowers in spring, cinnamon-brown bark which flakes with age. Usually grown from seed and therefore variable; look for '**Amber Beauty**', a small-headed selection with amber bark. Excellent winter interest. H10-12m/33-40ft, W3-4m/10-13ft. F3-4. Z6.

P. serrula. The polished mahogany trunk and stems with peeling bark are a beautiful sight through winter, although the white spring flowers are of little note and autumn leaf colour is disappointing. H5m/16ft, W3m/10ft. F4. Z5-9.

P. subhirtella 'Autumnalis'. Succession of small white flowers during mild periods from late autumn to early spring. Prolonged cold weather may inhibit flowers, giving more in spring. Eventually of some size with a broad, spreading habit and attractively pendulous branchlets. H5m/16ft. W5m/16ft. F11-4. Z4-8.

RHUS See Shrubs Directory, page 105.
SALIX See Shrubs Directory, page 107.

SORBUS Mountain ash

A great number of attractive, fruiting, deciduous trees many of which also have good autumn foliage colour. Smaller, shrubbier types are mentioned in the Shrubs Directory, page 108. ☼ ☀ ▪ ◩ ☀

S. aucuparia. Mountain ash or rowan. Relatively small trees, growing widely throughout Britain. The pinnate leaves turn tints of orange-red and yellow in autumn. White, early-summer flowers are quickly followed by often heavy bunches of orange or red fruits. Many selections exist with somewhat different habits and fruits from crimson and red to orange and yellow. H5m/16ft, W2-3m/6-10ft. F5. Z3-9.

S. hupehensis. Large, prettily divided, almost bluish green leaves which turn reddish in autumn. Pendulous clusters of pink-tinged, white fruits often lasting well into winter. Selections with pink fruits such as var. ***obtusa***, '**Rosea**' and '**Rufus**' are worth looking for. H5m/16ft, W3m/10ft. F5. Z3-8.

SHRUBS DIRECTORY

SHRUBS ARE EVERGREEN OR DECIDUOUS woody plants which do not die down to the ground in winter. Some shrubs remain dwarf, growing to only a few centimetres, while others can grow into small trees.

To provide interest and colour in autumn, winter and early spring there are innumerable shrubs to choose from. The problem in making this selection was not what to include, but what to leave out. Among the plants I have listed here are some first class but little known shrubs which will help to provide form, colour, flower, fruit, foliage and fragrance for all sizes of garden. Generally speaking, plants that are sited in sunny positions, as long as these are tolerated by the plant, give the best autumn colour.

The approximate size of each shrub after ten years is given at the end of its description. Remember that geographical situation, climate, soil conditions and pruning affect size, flowering times and sometimes even a plant's appearance. The hardiness zones allocated to each shrub are even more approximate, with local micro-climates, as well as protection provided by sunny walls, providing an exception to every rule.

H: Approximate height after 10 years
W: Approximate width after 10 years
F: Months in flower
Z: Relevant hardiness zone(s)

Abeliophyllum distichum

ABELIA
Bright-foliaged evergreen or deciduous shrubs, late flowers. Best grown in a warm, shelted position. Trim or prune as required in spring. ☼ ■ ☆
A. x grandiflora 'Francis Mason'. Yellow-variegated leaves, fragrant, blush-pink flowers. H1.2-1.5m/4-5ft, W1.2-1.5m/4-5ft. F7-10. Z7-9.

ABELIOPHYLLUM White forsythia
Deciduous. ☼ ■ ☆
A. distichum. Masses of small, almond-scented, blush-white flowers in early spring. Prune old wood after flowering, as for forsythia. Grow against sun-facing wall in cool climates. H90-150cm/3-5ft, W90-

150cm/3-5ft. F3; occ. F8-9. Z5-9.

ACER Maple
Deciduous or evergreen. Some slow-growing species can be considered shrubs, others can be kept shrubby by annual pruning. Many produce best colour on neutral to acid soil; most Japanese maples tolerate non-acid soils if thoroughly prepared with humus or leaf mould. ☼ ☀ ■ ☆
A. japonicum. Japanese maple. Many excellent selections with coloured foliage and good autumn colour: 'Atropurpureum', purple; 'Aureum', light yellow; 'Bloodgood', reddish purple. All H1.2-1.5m/4-5ft, W90-120cm/3-4ft. F4-5. Z6-8.
Dissectum Group. Cascading branches, fern-like leaves. 'Atropurpureum', 'Garnet' and 'Inaba Shidare', purples. 'Viridis', bright green leaves, yellow, orange or red in autumn. Average H1.2-1.5m/4-5ft, W1.5-2.1m/5-7ft. Z5-8. 'Osakazuki', small, green-leaved tree, brilliant crimson in autumn. H2.1-3m/7-10ft, W1.8-2.1m/6-7ft. F4-5. Z5-8. 'Senkaki' (syn. 'Sango Kaku'), golden autumn leaves, coral-red stems. H1.8-2.4m/6-8ft, W1.2-1.5m/4-5ft. F4-5. Z5-8. 'Shishigashira', slow-growing tree, greenish stems, golden-yellow leaves with red tints. Good

Acer palmatum 'Osakazuki' in autumn

Acer palmatum 'Garnet'

Berberis thunbergii 'Dart's Red Lady'

Berberis × media 'Red Jewel'

container plant. H90-150cm/3-5ft, W60-90cm/2-3ft. Z5-8.

ARBUTUS Strawberry tree
Evergreen shrubs or small trees. ☼ ■ ☆
A. x *andrachnoides.* Hybrid similar to *A. unedo,* striking, cinnamon-red, peeling bark on older trees. H2.1-2.4m/ 7-8ft, W1.8-2.1m/6-7ft. F10. Z8-9.
A. unedo. Dark green leaves, clusters of white or pink autumn flowers, occasionally edible, orange or red fruits. 'Rubra', reddish flowers. Tolerates alkaline and seaside conditions. H2.1-2.4m/7-8ft, W1.8-2.1m/6-7ft. F10. Z7-9. ☼ ❉ ⊖

Arbutus unedo 'Rubra'

ARONIA Chokeberry
Flowering, fruiting, deciduous. Control size by hard pruning in late winter. Neutral or acid soil. ☼ ❉ ■ ☆
A. arbutifolia 'Erecta'. Upright, narrow habit, red autumn leaves, red fruits, white flowers. H1.8- 2.1m/6-7ft, W2.1-3m/7-10ft. F4-5. Z5-9.
A. melanocarpa 'Brilliant'. Red leaves and black fruits in autumn. H1.2-1.5m/4-5ft, W2.1m/7ft. F4-5. Z4-9.

ARTEMISIA Wormwood
Some retain their silvery foliage into winter, depending on climate. ❉ ■
A. 'Powis Castle'. Silver-grey mound. H90-120cm/3-4ft, W90-120cm/3-4ft. Z5-8.

Artemisia 'Powis Castle'

AUCUBA Spotted laurel
Evergreen. ☼ ❉ ❋ ☆
A. japonica. Japanese aucuba. A male plant, bearing panicles of purple-petalled flowers in spring, is necessary for females to set the red fruit. Easily pruned. 'Crotonifolia' (female) and 'Mr Goldstrike' (male), gold-speckled, green leaves. 'Picturata' (female), broad leaves, central gold splash. 'Variegata' (female), yellow-dotted leaves. H2.1-3m/7-10ft, W2.1-3m/7-10ft. F4-5. Z7-11.

BERBERIS Barberry
Wide range of deciduous and evergreen shrubs, many with good autumn colour and fruits. Some thorny types good for hedging. Most withstand pruning. Hardiness varies. Most ☼ ❉ ☆
B. × *carminea.* Deciduous. Thorny, arching branches. Good autumn foliage, startlingly colourful fruits. H1.2-1.8m/4-6ft, W1.2-1.8m/4-6ft. F4-5. Z6-9.
B. darwinii. Dense, evergreen. Arching branches, spiny, dark leaves. Racemes of orange-yellow flowers in late spring and often another flush in late autumn, plum-coloured fruit. Prune, if required, after flowering. H1.5- 2.1m/5-7ft, W1.2-1.5m/4-5ft. F4-5; occ. F9-10. Z7-9.

B. × *media* 'Red Jewel'. Dense, semi-evergreen. Thorny stems, bronze-purple leaves with brilliant autumn colours. H90-120cm/3-4ft, W90-120cm/3-4ft. F4-5. Z6-8.
B. × *ottawensis* 'Superba'. Vigorous, deciduous. Deep purple leaves, yellow flowers, sparse fruits. Prune hard every few years. H1.5-1.8m/5-6ft, W1.2-1.5m/4-5ft. F5. Z5-9. ■
B. thunbergii. Deciduous. Yellow spring flowers, excellent autumn colour, bright red fruits. Lightly prune taller cultivars every few years, or prune to the ground in early spring to rejuvenate. Purple-leaved forms need sun to colour well. H90-240cm/3-8ft, W90-240cm/3-8ft. F3-5. Z5-8. 'Atropurpurea Nana', compact bush, purple summer leaves, red fruits in autumn. H45cm/18in, W45cm/18in. F4-5. Z5-8. 'Dart's Red Lady', bushy, black-purple leaves turning crimson in late autumn. H60-75cm/24-30in, W75-90cm/30-36in. F4-5. Z5-8. 'Golden Ring', gold-margined reddy purple leaves, good autumn colour, red fruits. H1.5-1.8m/5-6ft, W1.2-1.5m/4-5ft. F4-5. Z5-8.

BUDDLEIA Butterfly bush
Deciduous, semi-evergreen or evergreen. Interesting form in winter,

Buddleia 'Pink Delight'

Camellia × *williamsii* 'Donation'

particularly if seed heads are left on. Many flower into autumn, especially if pruned late. Prune annually in late winter or early spring to within 15-30cm/6-12in of ground. Wide variety of shapes and sizes. All F7-9. Z5-9. ☼ ■ ★

BUXUS Box, boxwood
Slow-growing, evergreen, many with coloured or variegated foliage. ☼ ✸ ✸ ■ ☆
B. sempervirens. Common box. Used for low hedging and topiary. '**Aurea Pendula**', broad; pendulous branches, leaves splashed creamy yellow. H90-120cm/3-4ft, W90cm/3ft. Z7-8. '**Elegantissima**', dwarf, dense, rounded; leaves margined creamy white. H45-60cm/18-24in, W30-45cm/12-18in. Z7-8. '**Latifolia Maculata**', rounded; large leaves splashed golden-yellow, bright yellow new shoots. H45-60cm/18-24in, W30-45cm/12-18in.

CALLICARPA
Deciduous. Startling, mostly lilac or purple, glossy fruit, abundant when three or more shrubs are planted together. Prune lightly annually for shape. Prefers a slightly alkaline soil. ☼ ✸ ■ ★
C. bodinieri '**Profusion**'. The best for

cooler climates, fruits regularly as an individual, abundant pale violet berries. H1.5-1.8m/5-6ft, W90-120cm/3-4ft. F6-8. Z6-9.

CAMELLIA
Evergreen. Glossy green leaves, exotic flowers in late winter and spring. Ideal for pots or under glass. Best protected by a north or west wall or high shade in northern climates, but will not flower well in deep shade. Prune lightly for shape after flowering. Neutral or acid soil. ◪ ■
C. japonica. Japanese or common camellia. H1.5-1.8m/5-6ft, W90-120cm/3-4ft, but eventually, according to cultivar, much larger. F2-3. Most Z8-9.
C. sasanqua. Scented flowers in autumn and winter, likely to get frosted in cooler climates, eventually larger and more spreading than *C. japonica*. F10-2. Z7-9.
C. × *williamsii.* Blooms from an early age. '**Donation**', double, rich pink flowers. Both H1.8-2.1m/6-7ft, W1.5m/5ft. F2-5. Z7-9.

CARYOPTERIS Bluebeard, blue spiraea
Aromatic, deciduous, mostly dwarf or low-growing shrubs. Late bright blue flowers. Prune each spring to 10-

15cm/4-6in from the ground. In cold climates, grow against a sun-facing wall. Plant in spring. ☼ ■
C. x *clandonensis* '**Arthur Simmonds**'. Hybrid. Grey-green leaves, profuse bright blue flowers. '**Heavenly Blue**', more compact, deep blue flowers. '**Worcester Gold**', greeny gold leaves, bright blue flowers. All H60-75cm/24-30in, W60-75cm/24-30in. F8-9. Z6-9.

CERATOSTIGMA Hardy plumbago
The two species mentioned behave like perennials in cool, temperate climates. Both late-flowering, bright blue, periwinkle-like flowers. ☼ ■
C. plumbaginoides. Dwarf, spreading. Leaves turn reddish in autumn, contrasting with blue flowers. H15-20cm/6-8in, W30cm/1ft. F7-9. Z5-8.
C. willmottianum. Twiggy, upright stems, bright deep blue flowers. Prune to ground in late spring. H60-75cm/24-30in, W60-75cm/24-30in. F8-10. Z5-9.

CHAENOMELES
Japonica, flowering quince
Mostly very hardy, often sharply, thorned, deciduous shrubs used as ground cover and on walls. Early, apple-blossom-type, crimson, pink, orange or white flowers often on bare

branches, often followed by bitter, apple-like fruits. Prune as required immediately after flowering. For wall shrubs, cut back all the previous season's growth to original shoot; late-summer pruning of fresh growth helps flower buds swell and exposes flowers. ☼ ✸ ✸ ☆
C. japonica. Japanese quince. Low-growing, spreading, dense, thorny stems, profuse bright scarlet, orange or red flowers before leaves on year-old wood. Yellow-green fruit. H60-90cm/2-3ft, W1.2-1.8m/4-6ft. F3-4. Z5-9.
C. speciosa. Common flowering quince. More upright than *C. japonica*, broad, spreading, densely congested, thorny branches. Scarlet flowers often in late autumn, especially if against a sunny wall, continue through winter, becoming more plentiful in spring, some even appearing in summer. H1.2-1.8m/4-6ft, W90-120cm/3-4ft. F11-4. Z5-9.
C. x *superba*. Hybrids of *C. japonica* and *C. speciosa*. Mounded or prostrate. All H1.2-1.5m/4-5ft, W1.5-1.8m/5-6ft. F12-4. Z5-9.

CHIMONANTHUS Wintersweet
Deciduous or evergreen, winter-flowering. ☼ ■ ★
C. praecox (syn. *C. fragrans*). Upright, twiggy bush transformed by sweetly fragrant, waxy, bell-like, purple-centred yellow flowers. Excellent for cutting. Can be trained on walls. Prune to tidy, after flowering. '**Grandiflorus**', less fragrant but larger, clear yellow flowers. '**Luteus**', clear yellow, waxy flowers. All H1.5-1.8m/5-6ft, W1.2-1.5m/4-5ft. F12-1. Z6-9.

CHOISYA Mexican orange blossom
Evergreen foliage, fragrant flowers. Give shelter, particularly for young plants. Good patio or wall plants. Prune lightly in early summer, cut back harder if foliage is severely damaged by frosts. ☼ ■ ★

C. 'Aztec Pearl'. Hybrid. Clusters of pink buds open to white flowers in late spring, lasting several weeks. Usually another show in late summer. H1.5-1.8m/5-6ft, W1.2-1.5m/4-5ft. F5-6; occ. F8. Z7-9.

C. ternata. Dense, slow-growing. Glossy leaves, white flower clusters in spring, sometimes autumn. H1.5-1.8m/5-6ft, W1.2-1.5m/4-5ft. F5-6; occ. F9. Z7-9. 'Sundance', compact, bright yellow, year-round foliage, flowers on older plants. Ideal for patios but protect from frost. H1.2-1.5m/4-5ft, W90-120cm/3-4ft. F5-6; occ. F9. Z7-9.

CLEMATIS
A few of these climbers have winter interest. Shade roots. ☼ ❋ ❋ ■ ☆
C. armandii. First of spring-flowering clematis. Dark green, ribbed leaves, masses of fragrant flowers. Sunny, sheltered wall or fence. 'Apple Blossom', flushed pink sepals. Prune only every few years to restrict growth. H5m/16ft, W5m/16ft. F4. Z7-9.

C. cirrhosa. Flowers through winter in mild areas. Pendent, bell-shaped, creamy yellow flowers. The form *balearica* has purple-spotted, yellow flowers, but is less hardy. 'Freckles', larger, crimson-purple splashed

Clematis tangutica

Cornus mas 'Aurea'

flowers. Provide shelter in cold areas. Perfect for conservatories. All H3m/10ft, W3m/10ft. F10-3. Z8-9.
C. orientalis. Vigorous. Finely dissected leaves and pendent, subtly fragrant, long-lasting, yellow flowers followed by fluffy seed heads. H2.1-3m/7-10ft, W2.1-3m/7-10ft. F8-9. Z6-9. 'Bill Mackenzie', larger-flowered, silvery seed heads. Both H5-6m/16-20ft, W5-6m/16-20ft. F8-9. Z6-9.
C. tangutica. Similar to *C. orientalis.* H5-6m/16-20ft, W5-6m/16-20ft. F7-9. Z6-9.

CORNUS Cornel, dogwood
Deciduous. Some of the most spectacular shrubs for winter stem colour, but many also provide autumn leaf colour, fruits and early flower. ☼ ❋ ■ ☆
C. alba. Siberian dogwood. Many good selections. Vigorous, spreading, with erect, flexible, dark red stems. Good autumn leaf colour, clusters of white flowers on two-year old wood, small, bluish white fruit. If grown for winter stems, site in sunny, open position and cut to the ground annually in late spring. Good beside water. 'Aurea', year-round appeal, bright yellow leaves particularly in autumn, deep red stems

'Kesselringii', black-purple stems, purplish leaves, crimson-purple in autumn. 'Sibirica', the brightest red stems, green leaves, shorter and less vigorous than the species. 'Sibirica Variegata' and 'Elegantissima', variegated white and green leaves, red-tinged in autumn, red stems. Average H1.5-1.8m/5-6ft, W1.5-1.8m/5-6ft. F5-6. Z3-9.
C. mas. Cornelian cherry. Naked branches burst into yellow flower from buds that gradually swell through autumn and winter. Good against a dark background. 'Aurea', suffused yellow leaves in spring, greening in summer. Both H2.4-3m/8-10ft, W2.4-3m/8-10ft. F2. Z4-8. 'Elegantissima' and 'Variegata', slower-growing but offer summer interest, too. H1.8-2.4m/6-8ft, W1.2-1.5m/4-5ft. F3. Z6-8. ❋
C. sanguinea 'Winter Flame' (syn. 'Winter Beauty'). Superb golden-yellow autumn leaf colour for several weeks, stems are fiery orange-yellow at base and pink and red at tips. Prune as for *C. alba* cultivars. H1.5-1.8m/5-6ft, W1.5-1.8m/5-6ft. F5-6. Z4-8.
C. stolonifera 'Flaviramea'. Similar to *C. alba* but more erect, green leaves and yellowish green stems. H2.4-3m/8-10ft, W1.8-2.4m/6-8ft. F6-7. Z3-8. 'Kelsey's Dwarf', low-growing, narrow, upright stems and bright green, finely ribbed leaves. Good autumn colour. H60-75cm/24-30in, W60-90cm/2-3ft. Z3-8. 'White Gold', variegated gold leaves which turn creamy white. H1.5m/5ft, W1.5m/5ft. F6-7. Z3-8.

CORYLOPSIS Fragrant winterhazel
Choice deciduous shrubs. Upright or spreading habit, delicate, pendent yellow flowers on bare stems in early spring. Shelter from cold winds and spring frosts, away from early morning sun. Prune only to thin congested branches, immediately after flowering. Will grow on alkaline

Cornus stolonifera 'Flaviramea'

loam with peat or leaf mould added. ☼ ■ ◩ ☆
C. pauciflora. Dwarf, bushy, spreading habit, scented primrose-yellow flowers. H1.2-1.5m/4-5ft, W1.2-1.5m/4-5ft. F3. Z6-8.
C. spicata. Spreading, irregularly branched, long spikes of pale yellow, cowslip-scented flowers. H1.2-1.8m/4-6ft, W1.5-1.8m/5-6ft. F3. Z6-8.

CORYLUS Hazel, filbert
Easily grown deciduous shrubs or small trees, some with long-lasting, coloured foliage, all with catkins for winter and early spring interest. ☼ ❋ ■ ☆ ☆
C. avellana 'Contorta'. Corkscrew hazel or 'Harry Lauder's walking stick'. Contorted stems show well in winter, particularly if smaller branches are removed. Generously draped with long yellow catkins in spring which develop through winter. Remove suckers from base each winter. H1.8-2.4m/6-8ft, W1.8-2.4m/6-8ft. F2-3. Z5-9.

COTINUS Smoke bush, Venetian sumach
Deciduous, providing foliage colour well into autumn. Prune in late spring just before new growth

Cotinus 'Grace'

appears. To keep plants compact, prune annually to within 15-60cm/6-24in of the ground, at expense of flowers; for rejuvenation thin out a few older stems. ☼ ❋ ■ □ ✭

C. coggygria. Venetian sumach. Bushy. Oval, light green leaves turning yellow or red in autumn. Older plants, especially in open situations, are smothered in fluffy, beige-pink panicles in late summer, fading to beige or grey. H2.4-3m/8-10ft, W2.4-3m/8-10ft. F8. Z5-9. **'Foliis Purpureis'**, **'Notcutt's Variety'** and **'Royal Purple'**, dark purple, oval leaves, colour best in full sun, going green in shade. All H2.4-3m/8-10ft, W2.4-3m/8-10ft. F8. Z5-9.

C. 'Grace'. Hybrid. Tall, open bush, distinct, soft red-purple leaves through which the sun glows. Imposing pinkish inflorescences. H3-3.6m/10-12ft, W2.4-3m/8-10ft. Z5-9.

COTONEASTER

Extensive genera of invaluable deciduous and evergreen shrubs, ranging from dwarf to tree-like proportions. Most have white flowers, often spectacular displays of various coloured fruit in late summer and autumn, which attract birds. Prune only to shape or control vigour, in early spring. Many so-called evergreens are deciduous in

cold regions. Deciduous ☼; evergreen ☼ ❋; all ✩

C. 'Coral Beauty'. Excellent ground cover, taller in shade, dark, dense evergreen leaves, white flowers, coral-red fruit. H30-60cm/1-2ft, W1.5-1.8m/5-6ft. F5. Z6-8.

C. frigidus 'Cornubia'. Vigorous, deciduous or semi-evergreen, eventually a small tree. Large, dark green leaves, profuse bright scarlet fruit weighing branches down in autumn and winter. H3-4.5m/10-15ft, W2.4-3m/8-10ft. F6-7. Z7-8.

C. divaricatus. Dense, multi-stemmed, deciduous, spreading bush. Small, dark, glossy, green leaves turn crimson-red in autumn. Deep red fruit. Good as hedging. H1.5-1.8m/5-6ft, W1.5-1.8m/5-6ft. F6-7. Z5-8.

C. 'Exburiensis'. Tall, wide-spreading, semi-evergreen shrub or small tree, arching branches, profuse, pendulous clusters of pale yellow fruit well into winter. Very similar is **C. 'Rothschildianus'**. H2.4-3m/8-10ft, W2.4-3m/8-10ft. F6-7. Z6-8.

C. franchetii. Graceful, semi-evergreen shrub, arching branches, glossy, sage-green leaves, ovoid, orange-scarlet fruit. The form *sternianus* is similar but has round fruit and green foliage, silvery grey

Cotoneaster franchetti

beneath. Good autumn colour. Both H1.8-2.4m/6-8ft, W1.8-2.4m/6-8ft. F6-7. Z7-9.

C. horizontalis. Low, spreading shrub, often wall-trained where its herringbone branching pattern is effective. Dark green leaves, red in autumn, and bright red fruits. **'Variegatus'**, slower-growing, creamy white leaf margins, bright in summer, brighter in autumn with reddish tinges, less plentiful red fruit. Both H60-75cm/24-30in, W1.2-1.5m/4-5ft. F6-7. Z5-8.

C. 'Hybridus Pendulus'. Free-fruiting deciduous shrub, large, glossy, green leaves, graceful, open habit. Mostly trained up or grafted onto a stem with long, pendulous branches. Laden with bright red fruit in autumn. Non-grafted. H45-60cm/18-24in, W1.5-1.8m/5-6ft. F6-7. Z6-8.

C. simonsii. Vigorous, erect semi-evergreen used for hedging. Glossy leaves, white flowers, large scarlet fruit well into winter. H1.8-2.4m/6-8ft, W1.5-1.8m/5-6ft. F6-7. Z6-9.

C. 'Streibs Findling'. Controllable creeping habit, small-leaved, red fruit in autumn. Try on a bank, over a rock or a wall. H10-15cm/4-6in, W90-120cm/3-4ft. F6-7. Z6-8.

DAPHNE

Slow-growing, deciduous and evergreen shrubs, most with sweetly fragrant flowers. Often easier than reputed, requiring little or no pruning. Acccording to species flower in clusters or around stem, some from late winter until autumn, most in spring and summer. Poisonous berries, from golden-yellow to red and black. Add well-rotted leaf mould or peat when planting. Most ☼ ■ ◪ ✭; some ❋

D. blagayana. Evergreen, open, spreading habit. Terminal clusters of highly scented, creamy white flowers. Not easy but worth the effort. Peaty soil. H30-45cm/12-18in, W45-

Daphne mezereum

60cm/18-24in. F3-5. Z7-9. ❋ ◪

D. mezereum. Striking, deciduous shrub, stiff, upright branches. Fragrant, rosy purple flowers on naked stems. **'Alba'**, white flowers, yellow fruits. **'Rubra'**, deep purple-red flowers. All H75-90cm/30-36in, W60-75cm/24-30in. F2-3. Z5-8.

D. odora. Winter daphne. Bushy evergreen. Large, dark green leaves, terminal clusters of scented, rosy pink flowers. Shelter from frosts and cold winds. **'Aureomarginata'**, hardier; pale-centred rosy purple flowers, leaves margined creamy yellow. Both H60-90cm/2-3ft, W60-90cm/2-3ft. F2-5. Z7-9.

ELAEAGNUS Oleaster

Evergreen foliage, excellent for cutting for winter decoration. Dislikes thin, chalky soil. Resistant to heat and drought. ☼ ■ ✭ ✩

E. x ebbingei. Evergreen hybrid. Fast-growing, wind-resistant, useful for background. Dark, glossy green leaves, silver underneath, small, fragrant autumn flowers, orange fruits in spring. Hybrid and cultivars listed can suffer defoliation in bad winters, but usually recover. Prune dead wood and also to encourage bushiness, cutting back by a third or a half in spring. Slow-growing, variegated sports include **'Gilt Edge'**, deep green leaves irregularly

Euonymus planipes

margined golden-yellow, sometimes slow to establish; and '**Limelight**', central splashes of greeny yellow and gold. Both excellent for winter colour. All H1.8-2.4m/6-8ft, W1.5-1.8m/5-6ft. F10-11. Z6-9.

E. pungens. Cultivars include some of the best winter colour evergreens. Fragrant, silvery white flowers, seldom fruiting in cool climates. Prune as required in spring. Cut away any green shoots from variegated types at once. H1.8-2.4m/6-8ft, W1.8-2.4m/6-8ft. F9-11. Z6-10. '**Dicksonii**' (syn. '**Aurea**'), slow, with mostly yellow leaves, the rest margined irregularly golden-yellow. H1.2-1.5m/4-5ft, W90-150cm/3-5ft. F9-11. Z7-10. '**Goldrim**', more reliable, dark green leaves banded with gold. '**Maculata**', dark green leaves splashed liberally with gold. '**Variegata**', similar to the species but with a thin, pale yellow leaf margin. All H1.8-2.4m/6-8ft, W1.8-2.4m/6-8ft. F9-11. Z7-10.

ELSHOLTZIA

Deciduous. ☼ ■

E. stauntonii. Interesting, mint-like, clump-forming sub-shrub. Erect stems, narrow, aromatic leaves and thin spikes of late, tiny, purplish flowers. Cut back to ground in late winter. H1m/39in, W60cm/2ft. F10-11. Z5-7.

EUONYMUS

Variable shrubs and small trees, evergreen grown for colourful foliage, deciduous types for fruits and autumn leaf colour. Several plants together required for cross-pollination. Good on chalk soil.
☼ ☀ ■ ☆

E. alatus. Deciduous, upright, later spreading habit. Dark green leaves, in favourable climates brilliant crimson in autumn. H1.8-2.4m/6-8ft, W1.5-1.8m/5-6ft. F5. Z4-9. '**Compactus**', smaller but colours equally brilliant, ideal low hedge. H1.2-1.5m/4-5ft, W1.5m/5ft. F5. Z4-9.

E. europaeus. Common spindle. Large shrub or small tree, unnoticed until autumn when bearing dangling red fruits surrounded by fleshy, yellow arils. '**Albus**', white-fruited, less robust. '**Atropurpureus**', purple leaves in spring. '**Red Cascade**', free-fruiting. Autumn foliage on above forms can be spectacular, varying from yellow to reddish purple. All H2.4-3m/8-10ft, W1.5-1.8m/5-6ft. Z4-8.

Fothergilla gardenii

E. fortunei. Winter-creeper euonymus. Low-growing parent to numerous hardy, adaptable forms, many with coloured foliage, most excellent for ground cover, some self-clinging climbers. Prune occasionally in early spring to tidy bushes. Tolerates shade. As ground cover: H30-45cm/12-18in, W1.8-2.4m/6-8ft. Z5-9. '**Emerald Gaiety**', ground cover, low hedge or bushy shrub; round leaves, broadly margined in creamy white, sometimes tinged pink in winter. H90-120cm/3-4ft, W90cm/3ft. Z5-9. '**Emerald 'n' Gold**', small, glossy, green leaves, edged gold, tinged pink and cream in winter especially in exposed sites. Climbs. Several slightly different sports. H45-60cm/18-24in, W60-90cm/2-3ft. Z5-9. '**Sunspot**', deep green-margined, cream to yellow leaves. H30-45cm/12-18in, W60-90cm/2-3ft. Z5-9.

E. planipes (syn. *E. sachalinensis*). Large, upright, eventually spreading deciduous shrub or small tree. Purple winter buds open to light green leaves, usually turning crimson in autumn; yellowish green flowers, rosy red fruits in autumn. H3m/10ft, W2.4-3m/8-10ft. F4-5. Z6-9.

FORSYTHIA

Trouble-free, deciduous shrubs. Yellow flowers on bare stems in early spring. Larger forms make fine background with bright green summer foliage. Many can be wall-trained. To tidy, prune back some or all flowering stems in late spring as last flowers fade, or on mature plants remove a few older stems from the base. Severe late winter frost can damage buds. ☼ ■ ☀

F. '**Golden Nugget**'. Compact, densely branched, large, bright yellow flowers. Excellent for a small garden. H1.5-1.8m/5-6ft, W90-120cm/3-4ft. F3-4. Z5-9.

F. x intermedia. '**Lynwood**' (syn. '**Lynwood Gold**'). A sport. Erect, branching habit. H1.8-2.4m/6-8ft, W1.2-1.5m/4-5ft. F3-4. Z5-9. '**Minigold**', compact, large, pale yellow flowers. H1.2-1.5m/4-5ft, W90-120cm/3-4ft. F3-4. Z5-9. '**Spectabilis**', profuse flowers hide the branches. Excellent for cutting. H1.8-2.4m/6-8ft, W1.2-1.5m/4-5ft. F3-4. Z5-9.

F. suspensa. This and its forms are graceful and informal, but difficult to control. The form *atrocaulis* has dark purple young stems. '**Nymans**', more erect, browny purple, arching branches, large, lemon-yellow flowers. All H1.5-1.8m/5-6ft, W1.8-2.4m/6-8ft. F3-4. Z5-8.

F. '**Weekend**'. Very free-flowering selection. H1.5-1.8m/5-6ft, W90-120/3-4ft. F3-4. Z5-9.

FOTHERGILLA

Slow-growing, deciduous shrubs. Fragrant flowers on bare branches, good autumn colour. Peaty soil.
☼ ☀ ◪ ■ ⊖

F. gardenii (syn. *F. alnifolia*). Dwarf, twiggy stems, small, fragrant, white bottlebrush flowers. Dull green oval summer leaves turn yellow, orange and fiery red in autumn. H45-60cm/18-24in, W45-60cm/18-24in. F5. Z5-9.

F. major (syn. *F. monticola*). Erect, picturesque shrub, can reach 3m/10ft. Congested branches, small, white, honey-scented, cylindrical flowers. Variable in habit, most have excellent autumn colour of yellow, orange and crimson, sometimes on the same leaf. H90-120cm/3-4ft, W75-90cm/30-36in. F5. Z5-9.

FUCHSIA

Many hardy varieties among this large group of shrubs provide flowers well into autumn, particularly in mild or coastal districts. Semi- if not evergreen in milder areas. In colder areas will be cut to ground, protect roots in winter. Plant in spring. All Z8-10. ☼ ◨ ■ ☆

GARRYA

Evergreen. Needs shelter. ☼ ■ ☆

G. elliptica. Silk-tassel bush. Fast-growing. Glossy, leathery leaves. Clusters of long, silvery, grey-green, pendulous catkins on established male plants, which on '**James Roof**', can reach 30-40cm/12-16in. Female catkins are less showy. Dislikes cold, desiccating winds, especially when young – leaves scorch easily. Best on a wall. Prune in late spring, removing unruly branches or to keep within

Garrya elliptica 'James Root'

bounds. Both H3-4m/10-13ft, W3m/10ft. F11-2. Z8-10.

GAULTHERIA

A few of this large genus of evergreens are worth growing, all low-growing. Effective en masse as ground cover. Pendulous, bell-shaped flowers followed by coloured fruit. Can be invasive. Peaty soil. ☼ ☀ ◨ ⊖

G. procumbens. Slowly spreading prostrate carpet. Leaves are reddish purple in winter. White, urn-shaped flowers and numerous, bright red fruit, from late summer often lasting through winter. H10-15cm/4-6in, W60-75cm/24-30in. F5-6. Z3-8.

HAMAMELIS Witch hazel

Large deciduous shrubs renowned for autumn colour and winter flowers. Upright or spreading, twisting branches, broadly oval, hazel-like leaves. Mostly fragrant flowers with narrow, wavy, frost-resistant, strap-like petals on naked stems from autumn until well into spring, depending on type. Stems can be cut for indoor decoration. Most soils except thin chalk, with added humus, leaf mould, composted bark or peat, and a similar mulch every two or three years. ☼ ☀ ◨ ■ ☆ ★ ⊖

H. x intermedia. Hybrid group including some of the most colourful and varied forms. '**Arnold Promise**', free-flowering, upright, later spreading, branches. Yellow autumn leaves. Fragrant, deep yellow flowers, red sepals. F2-3. '**Diane**', crimson-red flowers, orange-red autumn colour. F2-3. '**Feuerzauber**' (syn. '**Magic Fire**'), bronze-red flowers, the most brilliant autumn leaves of all. F1-2. '**Jelena**' (syn. '**Copper Beauty**'), large, coppery orange flowers, lasting sometimes for months, orange-yellow autumn leaves. F12-2. '**Orange Beauty**', profuse, orange-yellow flowers, lasting for several weeks. F2-3. '**Primavera**', pale canary-yellow flowers, yellow-orange autumn

Hamamelis × intermedia 'Primavera'

colour, upright habit, good for small gardens. F1-2. '**Westerstede**', slightly later, canary-yellow, large flowers. F2-3. All H2.4-3m/8-10ft, W2.4-3m/8-10ft. Z5-9.

H. mollis. Upright, later spreading, bush. Downy, grey-green leaves turn butter-yellow in autumn. Clusters of fragrant, deep yellow flowers with bronze-red sepals for several months. '**Pallida**', copious, large, deliciously scented, bright sulphur-yellow flowers with bronze-red sepals. Site both against dark backgrounds to highlight their winter beauty. Both H1.5-2.4m/5-8ft, W1.5m-1.8m/5-6ft. F12-1. Z5-9.

H. vernalis. Variable, but tolerates a higher alkalinity and wetter soils than other species. Usually a multi-stemmed, compact bush. Yellow autumn colour and yellow-through-red flowers, lasting for several weeks, pungent rather than fragrant. '**Sandra**', purple young leaves, green in summer and rich flame-orange in autumn. Small, yellow flowers not always freely produced. Both H1.8-2.4m/6-8ft, W1.5-1.8m/5-6ft. F2-3. Z4-9.

HEBE

Large group of evergreen shrubs. Many are valuable garden plants,

others are borderline hardy in cold northern temperate zones. If cut back by frost, hebes often shoot from the base in late spring or early summer. Prune in late spring to tidy, remove faded flowers; rejuvenate old, woody shrubs by cutting back to 15cm/6in above ground. Late-flowering or good evergreen foliage types are mentioned here. ☼ ☀ ■

H. cupressoides. Upright, multi-branched, grey-green, scale-like leaves. Terminal clusters of pale blue flowers only in warm seasons. '**Nana**', seems identical. H60-120cm/2-4ft, W60-120cm/2-4ft. F7. Z8-10.

H. '**Great Orme**'. Compact, lance-shaped leaves, tapering racemes of bright pink flowers. H90cm/3ft, W90cm/3ft. F6-9. Z8-10.

H. ochracea. Dwarf, spreading habit, cypress-like, whipcord foliage, old gold in summer, bronzing in winter. White flowers, fewer in cool climates. Often confused with *H. armstrongii*, which has olive-green foliage. H75cm/30in, W75cm/30in. F7-8. Z8-10. '**James Stirling**', tidy, flat-topped, bright green in summer, bronze in winter. White flowers, rarely in cool climates. H30cm/18in, W75cm/30in. F7-8. Z8-10.

H. '**Red Edge**'. Compact bush, glaucous leaves red-tipped in winter

Hedera colchica 'Sulphur Heart''

Hydrangea arborescens 'Annabelle''

and spring. Pale lilac flowers. H45cm/18in, W45cm/18in. F6-8. Z8-11.

HEDERA Ivy

Most are well-adapted to climb, some are excellent ground cover, especially large-leaved types, in dry shade, or can ramble over stumps; most are attractive in containers. ☀ ☀ ■ ☆ ⊕

H. canariensis 'Gloire de Marengo'. Used as a house plant, but is quite hardy in shelter of a wall and poor, dry soil. Variegation greener in shade. Its variegated leaves, grey, green and creamy white, are smaller than those of *H. colchica*. Excellent as a patio plant. H30cm/1ft, W2.4-3m/8-10ft. Z9-11.

H. colchica. This and variegated forms need help to climb a wall, but eventually grow up trees unaided; the species has leathery, dark green leaves. Variegated or coloured leaf forms are brighter in good light. 'Arborescens', shrubby mound of broad green leaves, free-flowering and fruiting at same time. H90-120cm/3-4ft, W1.2-1.5m/4-5ft. Z6-9. 'Dentata', lighter, larger green leaves. 'Dentata Variegata', broad, grey-green leaves, margined creamy yellow. 'Sulphur Heart' (syn. 'Paddy's Pride'), irregular

central splash. On older plants heads of rounded green flowers usually followed by black fruits. All H30cm/1ft, W1.8-3m/6-10ft. Z6-9. *H. helix*. Common ivy. Innumerable selections, with variously shaped, coloured, marbled or variegated leaves for ground cover, climbing and containers. If they find no support upper stems become shrubby. Greenish flowers on older, arborescent stems in autumn followed by black fruits, leaves becoming rhomboid. 'Arborescens', classed as shrub, mound of dark green leaves, yellow flowers, black fruits. H90-120cm/3-4ft, W90-120cm/3-4ft. F9-11. Z4-9.

HYDRANGEA

Dwarf to large deciduous shrubs with varying types of flowers and foliage. Many flower well into autumn and flower heads turn to striking autumn colours, continuing to look attractive in winter when dry. Some are excellent for containers. According to species ☼ ☀ or ☀; most ◪ ■ ☆ ⊖ or slightly ⊕

H. arborescens. 'Grandiflora', large, round heads of creamy white, sterile flowers, or florets fading to green. Broad bush, the upright stems often weighed down by flowers, attractive even in winter. H1.2-1.5m/4-5ft, W1.5-1.8m/5-6ft. F7-9. Z3-9. 'Annabelle', similar, but more compact, enormous, domed flower heads, up to 30cm/1ft across. H90-120cm/3-4ft, W1.2-1.5m/4-5ft. F7-9. Z3-9. Both cultivars easy in any soil, sun or shade and flower on the same year's growth, prune by half or to ground in early spring. ☼ ☀ ☆

H. macrophylla. Includes mopheads and lacecaps, both dense bushes with erect branches, often weighed down by flowers, needing humus-rich soil. Buds can be damaged by winter or spring frost. Prune in spring, removing only the previous year's dead flower heads and, on older

plants, a few woody stems from the base if congested. Good patio plants. In very acid soils some *macrophylla* and *serrata* types produce real blue, the same plant on neutral or alkaline soil can be pink or red. For blue flowers on neutral or alkaline soils, add aluminium sulphate. Lacecaps have small flowers surrounded by large, showy, flat ray. ☼ ☀

H. paniculata. Superseded by many selections, all erect, dense shrubs, with large, usually pyramidal, flower panicles, first light green, then white or cream, later often pink. Panicles grow on current season's wood, so escape spring frosts. To keep compact can be pruned in spring to just above where previous year's growth started – usually half the height of the shrub. 'Kyushu', glossy leaves, profuse, long panicles of creamy white flowers. 'Pink Diamond', large, creamy white heads, then pink, finally red-brown. 'Unique', with large, erect heads, rosy-pink in autumn. All, unpruned H2.4-3m/8-10ft, W2.4-3m/8-10ft. F7-10. Z4-8. ☼ ☀ ☀ ◪ ☆

H. quercifolia. Native to south-eastern U.S.A. Grows only half its natural height of 1.8m/6ft in climates with cool summers. Dark green 'oak' leaves turn bronze to purple in

autumn. Small, erect, long-lasting, greeny white panicles. 'Snowflake', double-flowered; requires warmth and shelter. Both H90-150cm/3-5ft, W1.2-1.5m/4-5ft. F6-8. Z5-9. 'Snow Queen', more vigorous, large, erect, white heads, later tinged pink. Needs a hot summer. Large leaves turn bronze in autumn. Prune back only if stems damaged in winter or if required as foliage shrub. H1.2-1.5m/4-5ft, W1.2-1.5m/4-5ft. F6-8. Z5-9.

HYPERICUM

Large genus containing herbaceous plants, semi-shrubby alpines, deciduous shrubs, evergreen in mild winters, all with yellow flowers. Most grow 60-150cm/2-5ft high and flower from midsummer onwards, some with colourful fruits in late summer and autumn. Prune for tidiness and flowering; cut back previous year's stems by a third, and every three to five years to the base, in early spring, to rejuvenate old plants. ☼ ☀ ■ ☆ ☆

H. androsaemum. Tutsan hypericum. Adaptable ground cover, dense, low-spreading bush, dark green leaves, small yellow flowers. Red-brown fruits turn black in autumn. 'Gladys

Brabazon', new shoots mottled cream and pink, yellow flowers, bright red berries. '**Gold Penny**', free-flowering and fruiting, maroon fruits. '**Hysan**', hardy, maroon fruits turning black lasting all winter, excellent for cutting. All H90cm/3ft, W90-120cm/3-4ft. F7-9. Z6-8.

ILEX Holly

Deciduous and evergreen species, miniatures as well as trees. Usually male and female flowers on separate plants, the females bearing fruit but usually requiring a male nearby for pollination. Most take well to pruning and are often improved by shaping early growth to increase density. Many are tolerant of pollution and maritime exposure, and make excellent hedges; prune in early spring or late summer. Often slow to establish. ☼ ❋ ■ ☆

I. x altaclerensis. Several selections. Mostly tall, pyramidal shrubs or trees, excellent for hedging. Large leaves, small, white flowers, large fruit. Some leaf drop in severe winters. '**Belgica Aurea**' (syn. 'Silver Sentinel'), lightly spined, green-grey leaves edged with creamy white to yellow, orange-red fruits. '**Golden King**', female,

spineless leaves edged yellow, abundant red fruit. '**Lawsoniana**', golden-centred, green-edged leaves, bright red fruit. '**Purple Shaft**', purple stems, free-fruiting. All H3-4.5m/10-15ft, W1.8-2.4m/6-8ft. F5-6. Z7-9.

I. aquifolium. Common holly. Numerous foliage and fruiting garden forms, all hardier than *I. × altaclerensis.* Mostly spiny leaves, small, white flowers, making large shrubs and eventually pyramidal trees. '**Amber**', bronze-yellow fruit. '**Argentea Marginata**', bushy and free-fruiting, broad leaves edged silvery-white. '**Fructu Luteo**' (syn. 'Bacciflava'), bright yellow fruit. '**Ferox**', slow, low-growing male, fiercely spiny leaves. Variegated forms include '**Ferox Argentea**', yellow and white leaf margins, and '**Ferox Aurea**', central gold splash. Growth rate of all 'Ferox' forms about a third of that given below. '**Flavescens**', female, needs sun to show its golden-yellow leaves best; young spring growth also very striking. '**Handsworth New Silver**', purple shoots, dark green leaves edged white, red fruit. '**J.C. Van Tol**', male, yellow-edged leaves, good for

hedging. '**Madame Briot**', purple young stems, prickly leaves broadly edged golden-yellow, orange-red fruit. '**Silver Milkmaid**', striking, female, dark green, spiny leaves splashed with creamy white. Average H3-4.5m/10-15ft, W1.8-2.4m/6-8ft. F5-6. Z7-9.

I. crenata. Small-leaved, useful as dwarf, clipped hedge or container plant. Most are compact, evergreen shrubs with rigid branches, dense, small, dark, glossy, spineless leaves, inconspicuous white flowers, and black fruit on females. Most below, F5-6, Z5-8.

'**Golden Gem**', low and spreading, golden-yellow leaves in sun; female, but seldom flowers or fruits. H45-60cm/18-24in, W60-75cm/24-30in. '**Mariesii**', female, free-fruiting, erect, box-like leaves, ideal for troughs or bonsai. H45-60cm/18-24in, W30-45cm/12-18in.

I. x meserveae. Hybrids between *I. aquifolium* and *I. rugosa*, hardier and more adaptable than *I. aquifolium*. The following varieties are dense and bushy in habit, fruiting is less than spectacular in cool climates. All F4-5, Z4-5. '**Blue Angel**', dark green leaves, red fruits. H1.2-1.5m/4-5ft, W1.2-1.5m/4-5ft. '**Blue Prince**', male, shining dark green leaves, abundant flowers. H1.5-1.8m/5-6ft, W1.2-1.5m/4-5ft. '**Blue Princess**', blue-green leaves, free-fruiting. H1.5-1.8m/5-6ft, W1.2-1.5m/4-5ft.

I. verticillata. Common winterberry. Deciduous, broad, upright or spreading shrub or small tree. Dark green leaves, yellow in autumn. Small clusters of creamy white flowers in spring. A male is necessary for female to produce bright, long-lasting fruit. Unsuitable for chalk. All H1.5-1.8m/5-6ft, W1.5-1.8m/5-6ft. F3-4. Z4-9. ☼ ❋ ◢ ⊖

JASMINUM Jasmine

Deciduous or evergreen wall plants and climbers. ☼ ■ ☆

J. nudiflorum. Sprawling, eventually mounded habit, congested branches wreathed in yellow flowers in winter. Prune regularly after flowering, or the centre becomes woody and unsightly. H90-120cm/3-4ft, W2.1-3m/7-10ft. F11-3. Z6-9. As wall shrub, H2.1-3m/7-10ft, W2.1-3m/7-10ft.

J. officinale. True or common white jasmine. Vigorous, mostly trained as a wall climber, can reach 10m/33ft in mild areas. Also grown as semi-evergreen shrub over a support and kept bushy by annual spring pruning. Deliciously fragrant, white flowers. '**Aureum**', gold-splashed leaves. H60-90cm/2-3ft, W1.8-2.4m/6-8ft. As wall shrub H1.8-2.4m/6-8ft, W1.8-2.4m/6-8ft. F7-9. Z8-11.

KERRIA

K. japonica. Deciduous. Upright, graceful, arching branches, light green, serrated leaves, yellow, saucer-shaped spring flowers. Use free-standing, massed or against a wall. The only species in this genus has produced several forms. Green-leaved forms are suckering. All have distinctive green stems, attractive in winter, but these become congested; prune older branches from the base immediately after flowering. '**Golden Guinea**', similar to the species but larger, single, golden-yellow flowers. Both H1.5-1.8m/5-6ft, W1.5-1.8m/5-6ft. F3-5. Z5-9. '**Pleniflora**', showy, taller form, more upright stems, double, yellow flowers, needs regular pruning. H1.8-2.4m/6-8ft, W1.8-2.4m/6-8ft. F3-5. Z5-9. ☼ ❋ ■ ☆ ☆

LAURUS Laurel

Evergreen. Needs shelter. ☼ ❋ ■ ☆
L. nobilis. Bay laurel or sweet bay. Dense, pyramidal evergreen shrub or small tree. Dark, glossy, wavy-edged leaves, aromatic when crushed, culinary. Often container-grown as wall or conservatory plant, clipped into standards or formal pyramids.

Ilex crenata 'Golden Gem'

Lonicera fragrantissima

Small, yellow flowers, black fruits on females if pollinated by a male. Half hardy in cooler temperate climates, thrives in milder ones. '**Aurea**', golden-leaved, attractive in winter and early spring. Prune from late spring on as required, established shrubs breaking well from old wood. Good for coastal planting. Both H1.8-2.4m/6-8ft, W1.2-1.5m/4-5ft. F4-5. Z8-11.

LEUCOTHOE

Mostly evergreen. Leathery leaves, racemes of tubular or bell-shaped, often fragrant, flowers. Peaty soil. ☼ ☀ ◪ ⊖

L. fontanesiana (syn. *L. catesbaei*). Suckering. Long, arching stems, glossy leaves, dangling, pitcher-shaped, fragrant, white flowers. Bright green or red foliage in spring, turns glossy green in summer and purple-brown in winter. Ideal ground cover on acid soil. '**Rainbow**', creamy yellow and pink new leaves. Occasionally prune old stems to the base in early spring to promote new shoots; reduce stem length to improve density. Both H1.2-1.5m/4-5ft, W1.5-1.8m/5-6ft. F4-5. Z5-8. '**Scarletta**', compact, bright, glossy, reddish leaves from early summer, turning bronze-red in

autumn and winter. H30-60cm/1-2ft, W60-75cm/24-30in. Z5-8.

LONICERA Honeysuckle

Some worthwhile, fragrant, winter-flowering shrubs. Prune after flowering only to keep in shape or to restrict size. Climbers prefer their roots in shade. ☼ ☀ ■ ☆

L. fragrantissima. Unremarkable in summer, this and similar forms, including *L.* × *purpusii*, provide winter interest. Depending on climate, its lemon-scented, creamy white flowers can last for many months. Usually deciduous, semi-evergreen in mild areas. Prune flowering stems by a third after

Magnolia stellata 'Royal Star'

flowering, if necessary; occasionally remove old stems from base of old shrubs. H1.8-2.4m/6-8ft, W2.4-3m/8-10ft. F12-4. Z5-9.

L. × *purpusii*. Hybrid between *L. fragrantissima* and *L. standishii*. Easy, hardy deciduous shrub. Both it and the cultivar '**Winter Beauty**' are free-flowering plants with upright, spreading habit and fragrant, creamy white flowers. Both H1.8-2.4m/6-8ft, W2.4-3m/8-10ft. F12-4. Z5-9.

MAGNOLIA

Wide range of hardy spring-flowering shrubs or trees. Flowers, some fragrant, vary from the small, star-

shaped *M. stellata*, to goblet-like *M.* × *soulangeana* or the open saucers of *M. sinensis*. Early-flowering types may be hit by spring frosts, especially in northern Europe. Site near a tree or wall, to protect from early-morning sun. Prune only to shape young plants or thin, congested branches. Light pruning is best after flowering; leave severe pruning until late summer, painting large cuts with suitable dressing. Magnolias are relatively trouble-free, if chosen to match the site and soil; adding masses of enriched humus may help as will an annual mulch of composted bark, acid leaf mould or well-rotted compost. ☼ ☀ ◪ ■ ☆

M. × *loebneri*. Hybrids between *M. kobus* and *M. stellata*, include beautiful free-flowering garden forms for all soils, including chalk. Flower young, each year becoming more floriferous, the multi-petalled, star-like, fragrant flowers appearing before the leaves. All eventually make large, broad shrubs or small trees. '**Leonard Messel**', magnificent purple-pink flowers. '**Merrill**' and '**Snowdrift**', white. All H2.4-3m/8-10ft, W2.4-3m/8-10ft. F3-4. Z5-8.

M. × *soulangeana*. Most of these cultivars make tall, eventually wide-spreading shrubs or small trees. Goblet-shaped flowers on bare

branches. The species has profuse, large, creamy white, globe-shaped flowers stained rose-purple outside, flowering sometimes interrupted by spring frost. '**Alba Superba**', fragrant, white flowers. '**Alexandrina**', narrow, upright form, flowers rose-purple outside, white inside. '**Lennei**', vigorous, large leaves, broad, goblet-shaped flowers, wine-purple outside, white inside. '**Lennei Alba**', white flowers. All between H3-4m/10-13ft, W2.4-4m/8-13ft. F3-5. Z5-9.

M. stellata. Star magnolia. Automatic choice for a small garden. Free-flowering, rarely over 4.5m/15ft high, but eventually wide-spreading, broad, round bush; pruning can control size. Cloud of starry, white, multi-petalled, fragrant blooms, vulnerable to spring frost. Several clones may exist of the pink-flowered '**Rosea**'. Other selections include '**Royal Star**', hardy, floriferous, late-flowering, large, white flowers, and '**Water Lily**', larger fragrant flowers, pink in bud, opening pinkish white. All H1.5-1.8m/5-6ft, W1.5-1.8m/5-6ft. F3-4. Z5-9.

MAHONIA

Hardier forms provide shape and substance in a winter garden, and flower and fragrance from autumn

Mahonia aquifolium 'Atropurpurea'

until spring. Erect clusters or graceful racemes of yellow flowers, glossy, generally prickly, evergreen leaves. Low-growing, dwarf to large shrubs or small trees, all preferring shelter from strong, cold, desiccating winds. Prune only to tidy, but straggly old plants, especially *M. aquifolium* and *M. pinnata*, can be cut to within 10cm/4in of the ground in spring to rejuvenate. Leaf drop may occur after severe frost, but if drop as a result of poor drainage, move plants. Any reasonable garden soil, where not too dry. ✿ ✸ ◪ ✬ ☆

M. aquifolium. Oregon grape. Clusters of blue-black fruits in summer and autumn. Glossy, green leaves tinged purple in winter, tight clusters of barely scented flowers. Specimen or ground-cover plant, good in shade. **'Apollo'**, rich yellow flowers. **'Atropurpurea'**, red-purple winter foliage, deep yellow flowers. Both H90-120cm/3-4ft, W1.2-1.5m/4-5ft. F3-5. Z5-8. **'Smaragd'**, tall, hardy, reliable, bright yellow flowers, deep green leaves, tinged purple in winter. H1.2-1.5m/4-5ft, W1.2-1.5m/4-5ft. F3-5. Z5-8.

M. japonica. Eventually large, erect shrub. Long leaves divided into glossy, spiny leaflets. Terminal racemes of soft yellow, highly scented flowers for many weeks. Purple fruits

in summer. This and the similar **'Bealii'**, shorter, more erect racemes, need shelter from cold winds. Both H1.8-2.4m/6-8ft, W1.8-2.4m/6-8ft. F11-4. Z7-9.

M. × media. Hybrids between *M. japonica* and *M. lomariifolia.* Deeply divided leaves, erect, later pendulous, racemes of dark yellow, lightly fragrant flowers. Less hardy than some, flowers can be damaged by early frost but light shade or the shelter of a wall helps. **'Charity'**, **'Winter Sun'**, **'Buckland'**, **'Lionel Fortescue'** and **'Underway'**, all good. All H2.4-3m/8-10ft, W1.5-1.8m/5-6ft. F10-2. Z8-9.

MYRICA
Deciduous shrubs with aromatic foliage, some growing in extremes of dry and wet. ⊖

M. gale. Bog myrtle or sweetgale. Aromatic, erect stems, small blue-grey leaves in summer, golden-brown catkins in spring on naked branches. Tolerant of very boggy conditions, succeeds in drier, acid soils, too. H90-120cm/3-4ft, W90-120cm/3-4ft. F4-5. Z1-8.

NANDINA
Evergreen. ✿ ◪ ■ ✬

N. domestica. Tall, multi-stemmed but unbranched. Divided, compound

leaves, red or purple in autumn and winter. Large, erect, white flower plumes in hot summers followed by red fruit, if climate allows. May be cut to the ground by severe winters but usually recover, if late. Tall and dwarf forms prefer moist soil, need warmth and shelter in cool climates. **'Moyers Red'** and **'Richmond'**, crimson autumn and winter foliage, bright red fruit. H1.5-2.4m/5-8ft, W90-120cm/3-4ft. F6-8. Z7-9. **'Firepower'**, dwarf, particularly colourful. **'Nana'**, dwarf, low, green, leafy, non-flowering hummocks, pink, red, orange and purple through autumn and winter. **'Nana Purpurea'**, shorter, purple-tinged summer foliage. These colour better in sun. All H30-45cm/12-18in, W30-45cm/12-18in. Z7-9.

OSMANTHUS
Evergreen trees and shrubs of varying hardiness. Usually small, white, fragrant flowers, although some grown for foliage. To shape or control large plants, prune just after flowering or as new growth begins, according to species. ✿ ✸ ■ ✬

O. × burkwoodii (syn. *Osmarea burkwoodii*). Robust hybrid between *Phillyrea decora* and *O. delavayi* often confused with latter, but has stiffer, stronger branches, larger, smoother-

Oxydendrum arboreum

edged leaves and clusters of small, white, fragrant, trumpet-shaped flowers on terminal shoots. H1.8-2.4m/6-8ft, W1.8-2.4m/6-8ft. F3-4. Z7-9.

O. delavayi. Dense, twiggy bush, eventually large in mild climates. Small, oval, glossy, toothed leaves, profuse, small, creamy white, scented, tubular flowers. Needs shelter. H2.4-3m/8-10ft, W2.4-3m/8-10ft. F3-4. Z8-10.

O. heterophyllus (syn. *O. ilicifolius*). Large, round, dense shrub or small tree in mild climates. Shining, holly-like leaves, some spined, but mature leaves smooth-edged and oval. Small clusters of fragrant, white flowers in hot climates, followed by blue berries. All selections can be tender, especially when young. H1.8-2.4m/6-8ft, W1.8-2.4m/6-8ft. F9-11. Z7-9. **'Aureomarginatus'**, leaves edged in yellow. **'Aureus'**, bright gold summer leaves, greeny yellow in winter. **'Gulftide'**, compact, heavily spined leaves, fragrant autumn flowers. **'Latifolius Variegatus'**, wide leaves edged silvery white. **'Purpureus'**, striking, purple young shoots and leaves in spring. **'Tricolor'** (syn. 'Goshiki'), dark green, white and pink leaves. **'Variegatus'**, creamy white margins. Average H1.2-1.8m/4-6ft, W1.2-1.8m/4-6ft. F9-11. Z8-9.

Nandina domestica 'Firepower'

Osmanthus × burkwoodii

Parthenocissus henryana

OXYDENDRUM

O. arboreum. Deciduous. May reach 15m/50ft in its native eastern U.S.A. but seldom more than a large shrub in climates with cool summers. Open, erect branches, long, narrow, graceful leaves, turning yellow or crimson in autumn, given an open situation. Long, pendulous racemes of white, fragrant flowers. H1.5-2.4m/5-8ft, W1.2-1.5m/4-5ft. F7-8. Z5-9. ☼ ✹ ◪ ⊖

PARTHENOCISSUS Ornamental vine

Deciduous climbers which attach themselves by tendrils. Leaves often colour well in autumn. Usually insignificant flowers may be followed by small, grape-like fruits, particularly in warm summers. May need controlling during the growing season as most are vigorous. ☼ ✹ ■

P. henryana. Small, deep green leaves veined with silver, occasionally flushed with pink and turning bright red in autumn. Blue-black fruit in autumn after hot summers. Leaves show most variegation in shade. Tying in and training necessary. H6-8m/20-26ft, W6-8m/20-26ft. F5-7. Z8.

P. tricuspidata (syn. *Vitis inconstans*). Boston ivy. Vigorous, self-clinging climber, glossy, dark green, variable, maple-like leaves, which turn bright fiery crimson in autumn. '**Veitchii**',

Pieris japonica 'Pink Delight'

smaller leaves, purplish green when young, crimson-purple in autumn. Both H5m/16ft, W5m/16ft. F5-7. Z4.

PEROVSKIA Russian sage

Indispensable deciduous sub-shrubs. Long, late display of shimmering blue flower spikes. Quite hardy, but young stems can die back in cold winters, new shoots appearing from the base. Prune to 15-30cm/6-12in from the ground in spring to promote new flowering growth. ☼ ■

P. atriplicifolia. Aromatic, downy, grey-green, serrated leaves, white stems and hazy panicles of lavender-blue flowers. '**Blue Spire**', more deeply cut leaves and larger flower heads. H90-120cm/3-4ft, W90-120cm/3-4ft. F8-10. Z6-8.

PHOTINIA

Large shrubs or trees, usually depending on climate. In cool summers, evergreens are shy to flower, but make excellent foliage plants. White, hawthorn-like flowers borne in clusters or panicles, followed by red fruits. Evergreens need shelter in cold regions. For compact, dense

growth and ample new colourful shoots, prune leading shoots back by 30-60cm/1-2ft in spring, as new growth commences; hedges or screens might need a summer trim. Deciduous types dislike lime but evergreens thrive in it, even on chalky soil. Warm soil. ☼ ✹ ◪ ■

P. davidiana (syn. *Stranvaesia davidiana*). Background shrub or small tree. Irregular, erect branches, glossy, lance-shaped, evergreen leaves, a few turning red in autumn and winter, small clusters of white flowers, usually followed by bright red fruit. It and some varieties are susceptible to fireblight, a serious fungal disease. H2.4-3m/8-10ft, W1.8-2.4m/6-8ft. F7. Z7-9. '**Palette**', variable, but relatively bushy, leaves irregularly splashed and variegated white, pink and green, new shoots flushed reddish pink. White flowers do not always develop into impressive red fruit. H1.5-1.8m/5-6ft, W1.2-1.5m/4-5ft. F6-7. Z7-9.

P. x *fraseri* '**Birmingham**'. Robust evergreen, dark, glossy green leaves, copper-red when young. Denser and hardier than the closely related, more

colourful '**Red Robin**', with an almost continuous show of brilliant red new growth all summer. Both make outstanding focal points. Both H2.4-3m/8-10ft, W1.8-2.4m/6-8ft. F6. Z8-9.

PIERIS

Evergreen, attractive in flower and foliage. Most make slow-growing, mounded bushes, with lance-shaped, glossy leaves. Racemes often develop in autumn, opening in spring, with mostly pendulous, fragrant, bell-shaped, white flowers. New growth can be vulnerable to spring frosts. Prune only to tidy up bushes or remove old flower heads as new growth begins. Mulch with leaf mould or composted bark every two or three years. Peaty soil. ☼ ✹ ◪ ■ ⊖

P. '**Flaming Silver**'. One of several selections with variegated foliage and new growth of scarlet or crimson in late spring. Leaves edged silvery white. H1.2m/4ft, W1.2-1.5m/4-5ft. F3-5. Z5-8.

P. '**Forest Flame**'. One of the best hybrids. Dense flower sprays; scarlet young growth turns pink and white, then green. H1.5m/5ft, W1.5m/5ft. F4-5. Z6-8.

P. japonica. Source of most new European and North American cultivars. Usually glossy leaves, pendulous flower racemes, with waxy, often fragrant, bell-like flowers, showy even in winter as flowering racemes develop. Most prefer an open, sheltered spot. All F3-5. Most Z6-8. '**Debutante**', dense trusses of white flowers. H75cm/30in, W75-90cm/30-36in. '**Flamingo**', carmine-rose and white flowers, coppery young growth. H1.2m/4ft, W1.2-1.5m/4-5ft. '**Little Heath**', dwarf, variegated form, compact, seldom flowers; small white, pink and copper leaves. H60cm/2ft, W60cm/2ft. '**Mountain Fire**', coppery-red new leaves, sparse, white flowers.

Polygala chamaebuxus 'Grandiflora'

H90cm/3ft, W90-120cm/3-4ft. **'Pink Delight'**, profuse, fragrant, rose-pink flowers on red stalks. H1.2m/4ft, W1.2m/4ft. **'Red Mill'**, glossy wine-red leaves, white flowers. H1.2m/4ft, W1.2m/4ft. **'Valley Valentine'**, deepest red flowers, free-flowering. H1.5m/5ft, W1.5m/5ft. **'Variegata'** covers a fast-growing form with white margins, also called **'White Rim'** (H90cm/3ft, W90cm/3ft), and a compact form, with creamy yellow variegations, which needs shelter. H45-60cm/18-24in, W45-60cm/18-24in.

PITTOSPORUM

Evergreen shrubs or small trees grown for foliage, useful for cutting. Few are hardy in cool temperate zones, but for mild and seaside areas there are good species and cultivars, the latter mostly belonging to *P. tenuifolium*. Leaves are rounded and undulating, pale or olive green with more recent variations purple, silver, gold or variegated. Purple or brown flowers, often small and fragrant, on mature plants in warmer climates. In cold, inland areas, grow against a sunny wall. Wet soil and cold, desiccating winds are fatal. If cut back by frost, most make new growth from old wood. Overwinter containerized plants in greenhouse or conservatory. Plant in late spring. All below F4-5, Z9-11. ☼ ☀ ■ ■

P. **'Garnettii'**. Hybrid. Grey-green leaves, edged white and tinged pink. H3m/10ft, W1.5m/5ft.

P. tenuifolium. Bushy tree, columnar when young. Glossy, pale, wavy-edged leaves black stems. Good for hedging. Innumerable cultivars. H3m/10ft, W1.5m/5ft.
'Purpureum', red-purple leaves.
'Silver Queen', white-edged leaves. Both H1.8-2.1m/6-7ft, W1.5-1.8m/5-6ft. **'Tom Thumb'**, dwarf, purple-leaved form. H1m/39in, W1m/39in.

POLYGALA

Evergreen. ☼ ☀ ■ ☼
P. chamaebuxus. Dwarf, creeping. Bright, pointed leaves, profuse, large, long-lasting creamy white and yellow flowers a few centimetres above the ground. Good with alpines or in a peat bed. Any moist soil but chalk. H10cm/4in, W30-45cm/12-18in. F3-4. Z4-7. **'Grandiflora'** (syn. *rhodoptera*), taller and more lax in growth, deep green leaves, red and yellow, pea-like flowers. H15cm/6in, W30-45cm/12-18in. F2-3. Z5-7.

P. vayredae. Charming, creeping shrub. Glossy, green leaves, bright purple and yellow flowers, dense mat for moist positions. H2.5-5cm/1-2in, W30-45cm/12-18in. F3-4. Z8-10.

POTENTILLA Cinquefoil, shrubby cinquefoil

P. fruticosa. Among the most adaptable of hardy shrubs, often very long flowering period. Good for autumn flowers, wide range of colours, some best in cooler weather. Prune established plants annually as new shoots appear. Cut back by a third each year to improve vigour and flowering. Coloured forms may retain deeper hues in shade. ☼ ■
The following are hybrids mostly listed at one time under *fruticosa*, which is the parent of many. All F4-10. Most Z3-8. **'Abbotswood'**, the best white, profuse-flowering, blue-green leaves. H1.2m/4ft, W1.5m/5ft. **'Elizabeth'**, bushy, grey-green leaves, golden-yellow flowers, long-flowering. H90cm/3ft, W1.2m/4ft. **'Goldfinger'**, bright green leaves, golden flowers. H90cm/3ft, W1.2m/4ft. **'Goldstar'**, erect, open habit, huge, yellow flowers. H90cm/3ft, W1.2m/4ft. **'Hopleys Orange'**, orange flowers. H75cm/30in, W1m/39in. **'Kobold'**, dense, dwarf, small, yellow flowers. H30-45cm/12-18in, W40-60cm/16-24in. **'Pretty Polly'**, dwarf, low-growing, light rose-pink flowers. H35-50cm/14-20in, W45-65cm/18-26in. **'Princess'**, long-flowering, pale-pink, then paler, fading to white in heat. H75cm/30in, W1m/39in. **'Red Ace'**, bright vermilion-flame at best, fading to yellow in heat. **'Red Robin'**, similar but deeper red. Both H60cm/2ft, W80cm/32in. **'Snowbird'**, semi-double white flowers, light green leaves. H60-75cm/24-30in, W60cm/2ft. **'Tilford Cream'**, low habit, rigid branches, white flowers, can look scruffy. H60cm/2ft, W60cm/2ft.

Prunus × incisa 'Kojo-no-mai'

PRUNUS

Large family of trees and shrubs. Spectacular in flower. Deciduous ☼; evergreens ☼ ☀; all ■ ☼
P. × cistena (syn. 'Crimson Dwarf'). Deciduous. White flowers, reddish purple foliage. As a hedge, prune after flowering, then regularly through summer. H1.5-1.8m/5-6ft, W1.2-1.5m/4-5ft. F3-4. Z2-8.

P. incisa. Fuji cherry. Deciduous, many shrubby forms, eventually making small trees. Small leaves, lovely autumn shades. Brief small, white flowers, pink in bud, cluster on leafless stems. Small, purple fruits. **'Kojo-no-mai'**, slow-growing, contorted branches, ideal for bonsai, profuse flowers, year-round interest. H1.2-1.5m/4-5ft, W90cm/3ft. F3. Z4-7. **'Shidare'**, weeping, good winter outline and good as specimen for lawn, masses of pink-flushed flowers. H1.2-1.5m/4-5ft, W3-4m/10-13ft. F3. Z4-7.

P. laurocerasus. Cherry laurels. Evergreen. Generally vigorous and accommodating, dark green, useful as background or ground cover. Spring bottlebrush flowers. Plenty of cultivars. Prune only to control growth immediately after flowering; then trim hedges at regular intervals until late summer. Rejuvenate old, bare-stemmed plants by cutting to the ground in mid spring. Any soil except chalk, not too dry. F4-5. Most Z6-8.

P. lusitanica. Evergreen, dense bush or small tree. Glossy leaves good for winter foliage, usually profuse, small, white, fragrant flower spikes. Background shrub, screening or hedging. Prune as for *P. laurocerasus*, if required. '**Variegata**', red young stalks, white-edged leaves, tinted rose-pink in winter in a sunny spot. H3m/10ft, W3m/10ft. F6. Z7-9.

P. mume. Japanese apricot. Deciduous, worth space, even in a small garden. Slender, erect or spreading branches. Winter blossom for several weeks. Prune just after flowering. '**Alba Plena**', white, semi-double. '**Alphandii**', semi-double, pink, '**Beni-shidare**', profuse carmine, fragrant, saucer-shaped flowers. '**Omoi-no-mama**', profuse, white. Give shelter. H3m/10ft, W3m/10ft. F2-4. F7-9.

PYRACANTHA Firethorn

Vigorous, evergreen or semi-evergreen, upright or spreading, thorny bushes with small, glossy leaves. Clusters of white flowers, followed by showy, round, 'fiery' yellow, red or orange fruit, attractive to birds. Can be used as specimens, hedge, screen or a wall shrub, even on shady walls. Most species have been superseded by hybrids. Prune after flowering, to remove extended, non-flowering shoots and repeat in early autumn on any subsequent new growths. Every five years, remove extended stems to within 10cm/4in of main branches for vigorous new growth, no flowering for a year, but a reborn plant! ☼ ✸ ■ ☆ ✫

P. coccinea '**Lalandei**'. Erect habit, red fruits freely borne. H3m/10ft, W2.4m/8ft. F6. Z5-9.

Hybrids. The following are of complex parentage. All F5-6. '**Mohave**', vigorous, upright, free-

Rhododendron 'Olive'

flowering and fruiting, red-orange fruits. H3m/10ft, W2.4m/8ft. Z6-9. '**Orange Glow**', reliable, erect, dense habit, orange fruits. H3m/10ft, W2.4m/8ft. Z6-9. '**Red Cushion**', low, dense, spreading ground cover, red fruits. H60-90cm/2-3ft, W1.8m/6ft. Z6-9. '**Soleil D'Or**' ('Golden Sun'), broad, upright habit, spreading, large clusters deep yellow fruits. H2.4m/8ft, W3m/10ft. Z7.

RHODODENDRON

Vast range. Some, mostly deciduous azaleas, give autumn colour, a few offer considerable winter interest in foliage and flower, and many flower in spring – how early depends upon local climate. If rhododendrons will grow successfully in your garden, their early, exotic flowers are a welcome boost. Frost can damage winter and spring flowers; site plants facing away from early morning sun, under the shade of tall trees and out of a frost pocket. Severe winters or frosts can damage swelling buds. All, except those classed as tender, can be planted throughout the year as long as soil conditions are suitable, early autumn better than late spring for those less hardy for your area. Neutral or acid soil. ☼ ✸ ◪ ■

R. **Bric-a-brac**. Hybrid, early white flowers, dark green leaves. H1.2m/4ft, W1.2-1.5/4-5ft. F2-3. Z7-8.

R. dauricum. Semi-evergreen, small leaves, early rosy purple flowers. H1.2m-1.8m/4-6ft, W90-120cm/3-4ft. F2-3. Z4-8.

R. '**Golden Oriole**'. Cheery sight in full flower, cinnamon-brown peeling bark, golden-yellow flowers. H1.2-1.5/4-5ft, W90-120cm/3-4ft. F2-3. Z8-9.

R. moupinense. Parent of many excellent hybrids, dwarf, narrow tubular fragrant flowers, light or rose-

Rhus glabra 'Laciniata'

pink or white often speckled with red. H60-90cm/2-3ft, W60-90cm/2-3ft. F3-4. Z7-8.

R. '**Nobleanum**'. Eventually large-growing hybrid, striking early flowers, trumpets of deep rose-pink open from bright red buds. Needs woodland or shelter. '**Album**', white flowers and '**Venustum**', pink, are generally put in this 'Nobleanum' group and have equally early flowers. 'Nobleanum' H1.5-1.8m/5-6ft, W1.5-1.8m/5-6ft. F1-2. Z6-9.

R. '**Olive**'. Ample trusses of pale mauve flowers. H1.2-1.5m/4-5ft, W90-1.2m/3-4ft. F2-3. Z6-9.

R. '**P.J. Mezitt**'. Hardy, free-flowering, small, dark green leaves, purplish in winter, striking, rosy purple flowers with darker spots. H90-120cm/3-4ft, W60-90cm/2-3ft. F3-4. Z4-9.

R. '**Silkcap**'. Compact shrub, white flushed pink flowers with prominent brown anthers. H60-90cm/2-3ft, W60-90cm/2-3ft. F2-3. Z7-9.

R. '**Tessa**'. Hybrid between *R.* 'Praecox' and *R. moupinense*. Purplish pink, spotted crimson, brighter than violet purple 'Praecox'. '**Tessa Roza**', more striking, rosy pink flowers. Both H90-120cm/3-4ft, W60-90cm/2-3ft. F2-3. Z7-9.

RHUS Sumach

Deciduous. A few species grown for their summer and autumn foliage, some have striking fruit. Can be invasive. Their sap can be an irritant: wear gloves and avoid touching cut stems with bare skin. ☼ ■

R. glabra. Smooth sumach. Erect, spreading, deciduous shrub, smooth, purplish stems and bright green, pinnate leaves turning glorious orange and red in autumn. '**Laciniata**', deeply dissected leaflets, brilliant autumn colour. Dense, erect panicles of greenish flowers followed, on female plants, by bright crimson seed heads in autumn, often remaining long after leaf fall.

H2.4-3m/8-10ft, W2.4-4m/8-13ft. F6-8. Z3-9.

R. typhina. Stag's-horn sumach. Striking, unruly shrub or small, flat-topped tree, erect, spreading stems, gaunt in winter. Large, pinnate leaves usually turn bright orange and scarlet in autumn. Modest, greeny male and female flowers on separate plants, the female flowers followed, if a male is present, by hairy, crimson seed heads. 'Dissecta' (syn. 'Laciniata'), deeply cut leaves, orange and yellow autumn colours, is more garden-worthy. Both H3-4.5m/10-15ft, W3m/10ft. F6-8. Z3-9.

RIBES Currant

Deciduous or evergreen, among the first shrubs to flower, just before or as the new leaves appear. Pendulous, graceful flower racemes, although the broadly lobed leaves often detract, as does the pungent aroma emitted by *R. sanguineum.* Prune back older stems, at the same time shortening unruly stems as required. Pruning can be formal, but I prefer their more irregular, natural shape. ☼ ☀ ■ ☀

R. laurifolium. Lax evergreen, glossy, dark green, leathery leaves, small, pendulous clusters of greenish white flowers. Prune after flowering to improve density. H90-120cm/3-4ft, W1.2-1.5m/4-5ft. F3-4. Z7-8.

Ribes sanguineum 'Red Pimpernel'

R. sanguineum. Flowering currant. Stiff, upright habit; pendulous flower clusters on naked stems quickly joined by emerging, downy, bright green leaves. Coloured forms are brightest in bud. Unless otherwise indicated, all below H1.8-2.4m/6-8ft, W1.5-1.8m/5-6ft. F4-5. Z5-7. 'Carneum', best pink, softly coloured blooms. 'King Edward VII', best red for small garden, compact with large racemes of deep crimson flowers. 'Porky's Pink', white flushed with pink. 'Pulborough Scarlet', vigorous (eventually up to 3m/10ft), rose-red, white-centred flowers. 'Red Pimpernel', long-flowering, dense racemes of rose-red flowers. 'Tydeman's White', pinkish buds, masses of silver-white flowers on long trusses. 'White Icicle', large, white flowers, flushed pink with age.

ROSA Rose

A great many roses of most groups – shrub, species, ground cover, climbing and rambling, bush roses (hybrid teas and floribundas) patio roses (dwarf cluster roses) – flower well into autumn and in milder districts into winter. Take care when making a selection – some roses are either too large for most gardens or sucker and become invasive. Those mentioned have colourful autumn foliage and fruits or striking stems, and can be used as shrubs to mix with other plants. Prune in late winter or early spring only to shape or control size. Old or untidy stems of ground cover types can be pruned to 15cm/6in above the ground every two or three years.

R. 'Canina'. 'Dog Rose'. Variable, fragrant white or pink flowers, shining red fruits. H3-4m/9-13ft, W3-4m/9-13ft. F6-8. Z5-9.

R. damascena. Damask rose. Non suckering, spiny stems. Fragrant pink or white flowers used traditionally for perfume. Red, egg-shaped fruits last into autumn. H1.8-2.1m/6-7ft, W1.5-1.8m/5-6ft. F6-7. Z5-9.

Rosa virginiana

R. eglanteria (syn. *R. rubiginosa*) 'Sweet Briar'. Vigorous, upright species, thorny stems, scented leaves, fragrant pink flowers in summer followed by a generous show of oval, scarlet fruits lasting until winter. H1.8-2.4m/6-8ft, W1.8-2.4m/6-8ft. F6-8. Z5-9.

R. glauca (syn. *R. rubrifolia*). Excellent summer foliage, bristly reddish purple stems, greyish purple leaves until well into autumn. Single, cerise pink flowers, white centres followed by rounded bright red fruits in late summer and autumn. H1.8-2.1m/6-7ft, W1.5-1.8m/5-6ft. F6-7. Z5-9.

R. nitida. Low-growing suckering shrub, good ground cover. Reddish prickly stems attractive in winter. Single, rosy red flowers, glossy green leaves turn purplish red then crimson in autumn, accompanied by bright scarlet hips. H45-60cm/2ft, W1.2-1.5m/4-5ft. F6-11. Z5-9.

R. 'Penelope'. A musk rose. Salmon pink buds open to fragrant, semi-double, blush-pink flowers which continue into winter in mild areas. Coral-pink hips with greyish bloom. H1-1.5m/3-5ft, W1.5m/5ft. F6-11. Z4-9.

R. rugosa. Suckering shrubs good for ground cover and hedging varying from 90-150cm/3-5ft in height. Double-flowered cultivars flower well into autumn. Abundant tomato-like hips, as foliage turns to gold. Look for dwarf selected forms or hybrids. 'Alba', single white, fragrant flowers, orange hips in autumn. H1.8-2.4m/6-8ft, W1.2-1.8m/4-6ft. F6-10. Z4-9. 'Blanche Double de Coubert', intensely fragrant semi-double, white flowers into autumn. H1.5m/5ft, W1.5-2.1m/5-7ft. F6-10. Z4-9. 'Frau Dagmar Hastrup', compact, bushy hybrid, single, pink flowers, crimson hips. H90-120cm/3-4ft, W1.2-1.8m/4-6ft. F6-10. Z4-9. The form *rubra*, fragrant wine-red flowers, orange-scarlet hips in autumn. H90-120cm/ 3-4ft, W1.5-2.1m/5-7ft. F6-10. Z4-9.

R. virginiana. Impressive shrub (see front cover), can become invasive. Glossy green leaves in summer, lightly fragrant pink flowers. Foliage turns bronze and purple in autumn, rounded red fruits. H1.5m/5ft, W1.5-2.4m/5-8ft. F6-10. Z4-8.

ROSMARINUS Rosemary

Aromatic evergreen, good dark green winter foliage and light blue spring flowers. Prune if necessary after flowering. ☼ ■

R. officinalis. 'McConnell's Blue', prostrate mound, useful for tumbling over a sunny wall. H45cm/18in, W1.2m/4ft. F4-6. Z7-9. '**Miss Jessopp's Upright**' (syn. 'Fastigiatus'), good hedging, erect but informal habit. H1.2-1.5m/4-5ft, W90-120cm/3-4ft. F4-6. Z7-9. '**Sissinghurst Blue**', erect habit, rich blue flowers. H90-120cm/3-4ft, W90-120cm/3-4ft. F5-6. Z7-8.

RUBUS Bramble

A few of this genus are useful for their winter stems, displaying a silver-white bloom, although most require space. Most have spines or thorns, some vicious. Prune winter stems back to ground in late spring. ☼ ❋
R. biflorus. Twisted, spreading branches, thick stems. White flowers on previous season's stems, followed by edible yellow fruits. H1.8-2.4m/6-8ft, W3-4m/10-13ft. F5-6. Z5-9.
R. cockburnianus. Spreading habit, thorny, erect stems. In winter, purple stems are overlaid with a brilliant white bloom. H2.4-3m/8-10ft, W2.1-3m/7-10ft. F6-7. Z5-9. '**Golden Vale**', year-round interest, golden yellow leaves, silver-white arching branches in winter. H90-120cm/3-4ft, W1.2-1.5m/4-5ft. F6-7. Z5-9. ❋
R. thibetanus '**Silver Fern**'. Suckering shrub, grey-green, finely cut leaves, arching bright white stems in winter. Prune annually in late spring, to maintain a height of 90-120cm/3-4ft. Purple flowers only on two-year-old wood. Unpruned H1.8-2.4m/6-8ft, W1.5-1.8m/5-6ft. F6-7. Z6-9.

RUSCUS

Unusual evergreens, attractive foliage and winter fruits. ❋ ☆
R. aculeatus. Butcher's broom. Slow-spreading clump of rigid, green, erect stems clothed in dark green cladodes, which resemble leaves. Tiny, white flowers in the centre of the cladodes, followed on females, if males are present, by bright red fruit, excellent

Salvia officinalis 'Berggarten'

for winter decoration. Rare, self-fertilizing, hermaphrodite forms in cultivation. H60-75cm/24-30in, W60-90cm/2-3ft. F3-4. Z7-8.

SALIX Willow

Some excellent forms for winter stems and spring flowers or catkins, male and female catkins on separate plants, usually the male is showier. Most grow and look well beside water. ☼ ☆
S. alba. Little summer appeal, but rewarding in winter. '**Britzensis**' (syn. 'Chermesina'), shining, orange-red stems. '**Vitellina**', bright yellow stems. Prune both hard each year when new leaves appear, to the ground for a multi-stemmed shrub, or allow them to make a trunk (will reach 10m/33ft unpruned). Prune back to the same point each spring; annual stems of 1.8-2.4m/6-8ft. W1.8-2.4m/6-8ft.
S. gracilistyla '**Melanostachys**' (syn. *S.* 'Kurome'). Striking shrub, shiny, deep purple stems, black catkins. Prune every other year when catkins have finished. H1.8-2.4m/6-8ft, W1.5-1.8m/5-6ft. F3. Z5-8.
S. irrorata. Blackish purple winter stems with a whitish bloom, small catkins before bright green leaves, blue-grey beneath. Prune annually in late spring for best stem colour. Height

then 1.2-1.8m/4-6ft. Unpruned H3m/10ft, W3-5m/10-16ft. F4. Z5-9.
S. x *sepulcralis* '**Erythroflexuosa**' (syn. *S. erythroflexuosa*). Hybrid, small tree with curiously twisted branches and leaves. In winter orange-yellow, contorted stems are striking. Pruned to ground each spring it forms a fascinating dwarfer shrub for winter colour. H10m/33ft, W5-6m/16-20ft. F4. Z6-9.

SALVIA Sage

S. officinalis. Common sage. Indispensable evergreen. Plants are best kept young, prune back if required in spring every two or three years. Various coloured-foliage forms, but shy to flower in cool climates. '**Berggarten**', hardy, felted grey leaves. '**Icterina**' (syn. 'Variegata'), leaves splashed and variegated with creamy yellow, golden-yellow and light green. '**Purpurascens**', purple younger shoots, older leaves turning soft grey-green. '**Tricolor**', most tender but colourful, grey-green leaves boldly marked white and pink, new shoots purple-tinged red. All ☼ or ❋ ■ H45-60cm/18-24in, W75-90cm/30-36in. F6-7. Z7-9. ☼ ■ ⚹

SANTOLINA Cotton lavender

Dwarf, evergreen shrubs, cypress-like,

grey or green foliage on soft, semi-woody stems, making low, spreading mounds. Profuse, yellow, button flowers. Prune annually or every other year in mid-spring to keep tidy. Prune all branches away to just above newly developing shoots. ☼ ■
S. chamaecyparissus (syn. *S. incana*). Bright silver-grey, woolly foliage in summer, dull grey in winter, yellow flowers which last for several weeks. H45-60cm/18-24in, W60-90cm/2-3ft. F7. Z6-9.
S. virens. Bright green foliage, deep yellow flowers. H45-60cm/18-24in, W45-60cm/18-24in. F7-8. Z7-9.

SARCOCOCCA Sweet box

Related to box, glossy, evergreen shrubs. Insignificant flowers providing heady winter and spring fragrance commend them for garden use and indoor decoration. Spread slowly as clumps or suckers. Trim back tall forms which get untidy immediately after flowering. Best in light shade. ☼ ❋ ❋ ▨ ⚹
S. confusa. Clump-forming, dense, erect branches, pointed, dark, glossy leaves, clusters of fragrant, creamy white flowers, often black, shiny fruit. H1.5-1.8m/5-6ft, W1.5-1.8m/5-6ft. F2-3. Z7-8.
S. hookeriana digyna. Untidy habit, spreading by suckers, lance-shaped leaves, useful for fragrance. Pinkish flowers followed by black berries. H1.2m/4ft, W1.2m/4ft. F12-3. Z6-8.
S. humilis. Low-growing, dense shrub, glossy leaves, small, creamy white, winter flowers fill a garden with lovely fragrance, excellent near a door. Grows well in deep shade. H30-45cm/12-18in, W45-60cm/18-24in. F1-2. Z6-8.

SKIMMIA

Slow-growing, dwarf to medium-sized shrubs, evergreen leaves, mostly fragrant spring flowers, bright red fruit from late summer through winter. Except for hermaphrodite, or

Skimmia reevesiana

'self-fertilizing, *S. reevesiana*, a male form is needed to fertilize fruiting females. Female flowers are usually less showy than those of males. Benefit from fertilizer and an annual mulch of well-rotted compost. Little or no pruning is needed. Tolerate some lime on heavy soils, and sun if moisture is available. ☼ ✳ ◩ ⭐ ⊖

S. × confusa 'Kew Green'. First-class, male form, mounded bush of glossy, bright green leaves, darker with age and in shade. Large, pyramidal, freely produced heads of sweetly fragrant, creamy white flowers with golden anthers rival any spring-flowering evergreen. H90-120cm/3-4ft, W90-120cm/3-4ft. F2-4. Z7-9.

S. japonica. Choose named selections. '**Bronze Knight**', male, similar to 'Rubella'. '**Fructo Albo**', dense clusters of white flowers, white fruit, but can be difficult. '**Nana Femina**', female, dark green leaves and large heads of bright red fruit. '**Nymans**', one of the best, free-fruiting female types, narrow leaves, open habit, bright red fruit. '**Rubella**', one of the best male forms, often seen as a pot plant. Dense bush of dark green leaves, reddish brown in winter, as are the leaf stalks and flower spikes. Bronze-red buds in winter open to

reveal pink-flushed petals and yellow anthers; very fragrant flowers. '**Rubinetta**', similar to 'Rubella' but more compact. All H60-90cm/2-3ft, W60-90cm/2-3ft. F3-5. Z7-8.

S. reevesiana. Hermaphrodite, often seen containerized and laden with bright red fruit in garden centres, but not always so free-fruiting in the garden. Low, spreading, open plant with panicles of fragrant, white flowers. Dislikes lime. H45-60cm/ 18-24in, W60-90cm/2-3ft. F4-5. Z7-8.

SORBUS **Rowan, mountain ash**
Some excellent shrubs in this large genus of mostly trees, for attractive foliage, often with good autumn colour, and late summer and autumn fruit, popular with birds. ☼ ✳ ◩ ■ ⭐

S. cashmiriana. Beautiful, slow-growing, open, shrubby habit. Graceful, deeply divided leaves. Panicles of pink buds open white and, on older plants, reliably produce clusters of large, succulent, white fruit in late summer. H2.4-3m/8-10ft, W1.8-2.4m/6-8ft. F5. Z5-7.

S. koehneana. Easy-going shrub or small tree, dark green leaves, crimson-purple in autumn. Clusters of pure white flowers, bunches of small, porcelain-white fruit in late summer, even on young plants. H1.8-2.4m/6-8ft, W1.8-2.4m/6-8ft. F5-6. Z6-7.

SPIRAEA
Useful and hardy ornamental shrubs some with good autumn colour, others early spring flowers. Dislikes thin chalky soil. ☼ ◩ ■ ☆

S. betulifolia aemeliana. Dwarf, twiggy shrub, reddish brown stems, oval, bright green leaves which darken, with excellent autumn colour, flat heads of white flowers. H60-75cm/24-30in, W60-75cm/24-30in. F6. Z5-8.

S. prunifolia '**Plena**'. Arching stems, serrated, oval leaves, brilliant orange-red in autumn, white, densely

Sorbus koehneana

petalled, double flowers. Prune after flowering by a third. H1.5-1.8m/ 5-6ft, W1.5m/5ft. F4-5. Z5-8.

S. thunbergii. Free-flowering, dense, twiggy bush, arching branches. Profuse, white flowers display along the stems before the leaves. On established plants, prune away older and weakest stems after flowering. '**Mt. Fuji**', leaves edged with white, pink shoots, longer interest. Both H90-120cm/3-4ft, W1.2m/4ft. F3-4. Z5-8.

STEPHANANDRA
Spiraea-like in habit, leaf and flower, some are useful for winter stems. ☼ ✳ ◩ ⭐

S. tanakae. Large, oval leaves, good autumn colour, dull, creamy yellow flowers on widely arching, pendulous branches. Rich brown stems are of great value in winter. Prune oldest wood to the base in late winter or early spring. H1.5-1.8m/5-6ft, W1.5-1.8m/5-6ft. F7. Z6-8.

STRANVAESIA See under *PHOTINIA*

SYMPHORICARPOS **Snowberry**
Large-scale, colonizing ground cover, often spectacular autumn fruits, should be used with care. Many are vigorous so growth may need to be

restricted. Remove spreading suckers, prune old stems to base and shorten others by half in winter. Tolerate dryish shade. ☼ ✳ ◩ ⭐

ULEX **Gorse**
Almost leafless shrubs appearing as evergreens. ☼ ■ ⊖

U. europaeus. Prickly common gorse. Some forms are ornamental and were it not so often seen in the wild the species would be considered garden-worthy. Profuse, golden-yellow, pea-shaped flowers, in mild weather some flower at Christmas, and often on and off almost all year. To restrict size, prune immediately after flowering on younger, softer wood with shears, but older, straggly plants can be cut to the ground in spring as growth begins. H1.2-1.5m/4-5ft, W1.5-1.8m/5-6ft. F3-6. Z8-9. '**Aureus**', greeny yellow stems, spines and leaves turn clear yellow in summer. H1.2-1.5m/4-5ft, W1.5-1.8m/5-6ft. F4-5. Z8-9. '**Plenus**', denser, double flowers, ideal with heathers. H60-90cm/2-3ft, W90-120cm/3-4ft. F4-6. Z8-9.

VACCINIUM
Evergreen and deciduous shrubs. Ornamentals are mostly grown for fruit and foliage, not the modest flowers. Deciduous types have good

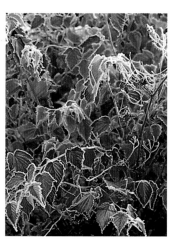

Stephanandra tanakae

autumn leaf-colour; the evergreens, often showy, mostly edible berries. Peaty soil. ☼ ☀ ◨ ■ ⊖

V. corymbosum. Blueberry. Ornamental. Upright, multi-stemmed, dark bluish green leaves, turning scarlet and bronze in autumn. Clusters of white-tinged pink, urn-shaped flowers before the leaves in spring, followed in summer by blue-black fruits covered in a blue bloom. The tasty fruits are much loved by birds. H1.5-1.8m/5-6ft, W1.2-1.5m/4-5ft. F4-5. Z4-8.

V. vitis-idaea. Cowberry. Dense, creeping shrub, dark, glossy green leaves, pinkish white, bell-shaped flowers, followed by abundant, shiny, red, edible fruit. H15-20cm/6-8in, W60-90cm/2-3ft. F6-8. Z4-7. '**Koralle**', pink, bell-shaped flowers, larger, if sparser, fruit than the species. Slightly more vigorous, making a carpet of small leaves; excellent ground cover in shade. H10-15cm/4-6in, W60-90cm/2-3ft. F6-8. Z4-7.

VIBURNUM

Among this varied group of deciduous and evergreen shrubs and small trees are many valuable for autumn colour, fruits and flowers, winter and early spring foliage and flower. Many have fragrance as an added bonus. Most grow in any soil, including chalk, some need moist soil; others, especially evergreens, may need shelter from cold, desiccating winds. ☼ ☀ ◨ ✿

V. × bodnantense. Erect, eventually large, bushes, fragrant flower clusters along the stems, even before the last leaves fall. Pink in bud, they open light pink, fading to white, and being frost-resistant, they last for many weeks. Perhaps the most striking is '**Charles Lamont**', deep rose-pink flowers. '**Dawn**', deeper pink in bud. '**Deben**', pink in bud, opening white flushed with pink. All H1.8-2.4m/6-8ft, W1.5-1.8m/5-6ft. F10-3. Z5-8.

V. davidii. Evergreen, low, spreading

Viburnum × *bodnantense* 'Dawn'

shrub, leathery, narrow, corrugated leaves, dull flowers, but bright metallic-blue fruit in autumn and winter, not always freely produced. Plant several to ensure cross-pollination – many nurserymen offer fruiting female plants with an identifiable male. Protect from severe frost and wind. H60-75cm/24-30in, W90-120cm/3-4ft. F6-7. Z8-9. ☼ ◨

V. farreri (syn. *V. fragrans*). Large, deciduous, erect shrub, bronze young leaves, fragrant flower clusters, pink in bud and opening white, continuing spasmodically through all but severe winters. '**Candidissimum**', light green leaves, white flowers. Both H1.5-1.8m/5-6ft, W1.2-1.5m/4-5ft. F11-3. Z5-8.

V. opulus. Guelder rose, European cranberry-bush viburnum. Deciduous, outstanding in late summer when hung with clusters of succulent, bright red fruit. Flat, white, lacecap flowers in early summer. Some have good autumn leaf colour, but fruit appears when leaves are green. '**Aureum**', bright yellow leaves which can scorch in full sun, but which stay yellow well through summer. Red fruit and reddish brown autumn tints. H1.5-1.8m/5-6ft, W1.2-1.5m/4-5ft. F6-7. Z3-8. '**Compactum**', dwarf,

free-flowering, red fruit persisting after leaves have dropped. H90-120cm/3-4ft, W90-120cm/3-4ft. F6-7. Z4-8. '**Notcutt's Variety**', large, red fruit, often purple autumn leaves. H2.4-3m/8-10ft, W1.8-2.4m/ 6-8ft. F6-7. Z4-8. '**Xanthocarpum**', bright green leaves, white flowers and golden-yellow fruits, becoming translucent with age. H2.4-3m/8-10ft, W1.8-2.4m/6-8ft. F6-7. Z4-8.

V. tinus. Valuable evergreens, winter form, dark, glossy leaves. Fragrant flower clusters can continue on and off for months, bright blue fruit are rare except in warm climates. For hedging or to retain density, prune immediately after flowering; to rejuvenate old, woody or open plants, prune to the ground in mid- to late spring when hard frosts are finished. Most plants sold are selected clones. Can be damaged in severe winters inland, especially when young. Exposed foliage is vulnerable to frost and freezing winds, although even if apparently killed, new shoots often break from the base in late spring. Flowers less in shade. H1.8-2.4m/6-8ft, W1.8-2.4m/6-8ft. F10-4. Z8-10. 8 '**Eve Price**', lower, more spreading, smaller leaves, rose-red flower buds, opening white, fragrant. '**Gwenllian**', compact habit, small leaves, pinkish

white flowers, deep pink in bud, free-fruiting. Both H1.2-1.5m/4-5ft, W1.2-1.5m/4-5ft. F11-4. Z7-8.

VITIS Vine

Ornamental grape vines are self-supporting, most are vigorous, ideal for covering walls, climbing up trees or training over pergolas, creating leafy shade. Most have maple-like leaves spectacular autumn colour, panicles of insignificant greenish white flowers followed by bunches of grapes, varying in ornamental and edible value. Prefers chalky soil. ☼ ☀ ■

V. coignetiae. Vigorous, probably the most spectacular ornamental vine for autumn leaf colour. Large green leaves in autumn turn from purple-bronze to bright crimson and scarlet, the best colour on poor, dry soil. Needs tying in before it becomes self-supporting, later requires considerable space, although it can be pruned. Purple-black grapes. H5-6m/16-20ft, W5-6m/16-20ft. F6-7. Z5-9.

V. vinifera '**Purpurea**'. Teinturier grape. Slow to establish, eventually makes a striking display of reddish purple leaves and, on older plants, deep purple, bloomy grapes, excellent autumn colour. Both H3-4m/10-13ft, W3-4m/10-13ft. F6-7. Z6-9.

Vitis coignetiae

CONIFERS DIRECTORY

CONIFERS COME IN ALL SHAPES *and sizes and may be slow or fast growing. They may be low, bushy and bun-shaped, narrow, upright, prostrate or semi-prostrate, wide-spreading, or any shape in between, and they are available in many shades of green, blue, gold or yellow as well as variegated colours. Some have soft, feathery foliage, others have sharp, prickly or needle-like foliage.*

Since the majority of conifers are evergreen, most give colour and form throughout the year. The selection that follows concentrates on those that are particularly attractive during the autumn, winter and early spring period. It is a personal selection that includes primarily dwarf and slow-growing types.

An indication of the approximate size, after ten years, appears after each description; inevitably, this is an estimate, since growing conditions, soils and climate can differ widely. The most important point to take into consideration when selecting conifers, however, is their rate of growth. For the best colour in both summer and winter, plant conifers in full sun.

H: Approximate height after 10 years
W: Approximate width after 10 years
G: Propagated by grafting
Z: Relevant hardiness zone(s)

Conifers contribute valuable colour and form in winter

Abies procera 'Glauca Prostrata'

ABIES **Silver fir**
The genus includes attractive, smaller cultivars. Cones usually stand above the foliage, and on some species, such as *A. procera* and *A. koreana*, can be most impressive. Generally prefer temperate zones, with cool winters. Most species are hardy; some dislike shallow, chalky soils and industrial atmospheres. ☼ ❋
A. lasiocarpa '**Compacta**'. Superb compact form of Arizona cork bark fir. Slowly makes a broadly pyramidal, dense, silvery blue bush with light brown winter buds. Foliage turns intense silver in midsummer. H60-90cm/2-3ft, W45cm/18in. G. Z6-7.
A. nordmanniana '**Golden Spreader**'. A form of Caucasian fir. Excellent winter colour. Slow and prostrate when young, eventually forming an irregular, compact bush with light gold summer leaves turning glowing, deep gold in winter. In hot climates, best in part shade. H45-60cm/18-24in, W45-60cm/18-24in. G. Z5-7.
A. procera '**Glauca Prostrata**'. Dwarf or prostrate form of noble fir. Bright, silver-blue foliage, deep crimson male flowers in spring. Very irregular, spreading bush unless pruned, ideal for the larger rockery or heather garden. Occasional upright shoots can be pruned, or left to make a small, controllable tree, occasionally

Calocedrus decurrens 'Aureovariegata'

with cylindrical cones. Unsuitable for chalk. H30-45cm/12-18in, W75-120cm/30-48in. G. Z6-7. ❋ ◪

CALOCEDRUS **Incense cedar**
C. decurrens '**Aureovariegata**'. Slow-growing, eventually forming a broadly conical tree. Deep green foliage, irregularly splashed golden-yellow. Pruning branch tips in early years promotes density. The species, with rich green foliage, is also attractive in winter. H2.1-3m/7-10ft, W90cm/3ft. G. Z6-8. ❋ ◪ ☆

CEDRUS **Cedar**
Genus of four species, most becoming large trees, pyramidal in mid-life, some flat-topped with age. Needle-like leaves spirally arranged in clusters along the branches. The upright cones often take two or three years to ripen. Deep soil. ☼ ❋ ◪ ■ ☆

C. deodara. 'Cream Puff', small pyramid, creamy white foliage, brighter in summer. Pruning will enhance density. H1.5-1.8m/5-6ft, W90cm/3ft. G. Z7-8. 'Golden Horizon', bright, golden-yellow needles in summer, golden-green in winter. Varies considerably in habit, perhaps according to grafting; in its best form low and prostrate, but can become semi-prostrate and sometimes throws up a leading shoot which, if not cut out, will develop into a large upright form. Approximate H45-60cm/18-24in, W1.5-1.8m/5-6ft. G. Z7-8. 'Karl Fuchs', distinctive pyramid, striking, blue-grey foliage. H3-5m/10-16ft, W1.5-2.1m/5-7ft. G. Z6-8. 'Nana Aurea', one of the best, although unexciting when young and perhaps prone to spring frost damage. Slowly develops into a dense, golden-yellow bush, keeps its colour throughout the year in a sunny position. If allowed to make a leading shoot, it forms a narrow, conical tree. For the smaller garden, prune the leading shoots to create a dome shape with pendulous branch tips. H (unpruned) 1.8-3m/6-10ft, W1.5m/5ft. G. Z7-8.

CHAMAECYPARIS False cypress

The selection below is but a fraction of the choice available for winter colour. ☀ ◩ ☆

C. lawsoniana. Most cultivars are hardy to Zone 6 but young golden- and cream-foliaged forms need shelter from cold winds and intense sunlight. 'Aurea Densa' and its sister plant, 'Minima Aurea' are two of the finest dwarf conifers. 'Aurea Densa' makes a very compact bush of stiff, golden-yellow foliage, eventually rounded in habit. Best in full sun. H30-45cm/12-18in, W30cm/1ft. Z7. 'Golden Pot', soft, feathery, upright branching foliage, slow-growing, year-round bright yellow colour. Excellent with contrasting foliage shrubs or heathers.

H90-120cm/3-4ft, W30-45cm/12-18in. Z7. 'Lane', a taller-growing Lawson, also known as 'Lanei', golden-yellow summer foliage, turning brighter, clearer yellow in winter. Eventually makes a broad pyramid, and can make an effective and colourful screen. H2.4-3m/8-10ft, W1.2m/4ft. Z6-7. 'Minima Aurea', rigid branches, dense sprays of bright golden-yellow leaves which appear brighter in winter. Eventually makes a dwarf pyramid; 'Aurea Densa' is more ovoid, but both are equally desirable. 'Moonshine', outstanding for bright yellow winter foliage, broad pyramid of soft, feathery foliage. Quite slow. H1.5-1.8m/5-6ft, W75-120cm/30-48in. Z6-7. 'Pygmaea Argentea', bright, year-round show, creamy white-splashed foliage. Needs sun but shelter from cold winds. H30-45cm/12-18in, W30-45cm/12-18in. Z7-8.

C. obtusa. 'Fernspray Gold', golden-leaved selection of fernspray cypress (*C. obtusa* 'Filicoides'), often straggly or open in habit unless trimmed from an early age. Fern-like foliage clothes the branches exposed to sunlight, giving bright, year-round colour. H1.5-1.8m/5-6ft, W90-120cm/3-4ft. Z6-8. 'Nana Lutea', dwarf, golden-yellow in summer and clear yellow in winter in an open position. Gradually forms a broad, irregularly pyramidal bush. H45-60cm/18-24in, W30-45cm/12-18in. Z5-8. 'Pygmaea', vigorous cultivar, belying its name. Bronze-green, glossy foliage, becoming deeper bronze in winter, grows in flat tiers, ending in thin, twisted, whipcord shoots. H30-45cm/12-18in, W60-75cm/24-30in. Z5-8.

C. pisifera. 'Filifera Aurea', first class for winter form and colour, eventually grows large but is extremely slow in early years. All 'Filifera' types have long, thin, thread-like foliage; on this plant it is

Cryptomeria japonica 'Elegans'

bright yellow all year round. It may be slow to produce upright shoots and pruning side shoots may help – hardly natural but most effective pruned as a narrow pyramid. H90-120cm/3-4ft, W90-120cm/3-4ft. Z5-8. 'Filifera Aureovariegata', sprawling and untidy when young but slowly forms a mounded bush of cascading, string-like, dark green foliage, irregularly splashed golden-yellow. H75-90cm/30-36in, W60-90cm/2-3ft. Z5-8. 'Squarrosa Lombarts', soft, heather-like foliage, grey-blue in summer, turning deep purple in winter, large bush in time. Dislikes extremely heavy or alkaline soils. H1.2-1.5m/4-5ft, W1.2-1.5m/4-5ft. Z5-8.

C. thyoides. Some attractive dwarf selections with juvenile foliage turning from greyish green in summer to shades of purple in winter. 'Heather Bun', 'Purple

Heather' and 'Rubicon', distinctive purple winter foliage, oval-shaped bushes, a little tender in exposed positions. H1.2-1.5m/4-5ft, W60-75cm/24-30in. Z7-8.

CRYPTOMERIA Japanese cedar

C. japonica. 'Elegans', finely cut, feathery foliage, soft to the touch. Eventually becomes broadly conical, varying according to climate and situation. Fresh-green summer foliage turns deep purple-bronze in late autumn and winter. Ideal for the winter garden, although not hardy in very cold climates. H1.8-3m/6-10ft, W1.2-1.5m/4-5ft. Z7-8. ☆ 'Sekkan-sugi', superlative, broad column of upright branches from which hangs looser, pendulous green inner foliage, which where exposed to the light is sulphur-yellow in winter and the most startling creamy white in summer. Shelter from strong sun and cold winds in early years. H1.5-1.8m/5-6ft, W90-120cm/3-4ft. Z6-9. 'Vilmoriniana', dwarf, very tight ball of dense, congested foliage, bright green in summer and bronze in winter, particularly in exposed situations. H30-45cm/12-18in, W30-45cm/12-18in. Z6-9.

× CUPRESSOCYPARIS

× *C. leylandii*. Leyland cypress. Fastest-growing conifer, popular for hedges (for which it is often unsuitable) and screening. Dark green foliage is useful in winter, but its windbreak qualities are greater than its ornamental value. Some attractive, garden-worthy selections with golden or variegated foliage. ☼ ■ ☆
'Golconda', one of the brightest golden conifers, excellent in winter. Open in habit when young, it fills in nicely with age. H5-6m/16-20ft, W1.5-2.1m/5-7ft. Z6-10. 'Gold Rider', similar. 'Silver Dust', vigorous, splashes of creamy white on dark green foliage. H5-6m/16-20ft, W2.4-3m/8-10ft. Z7-9.

CUPRESSUS Cypress

C. glabra. Hardy cypress, formerly considered a form of *C. arizonica*. ☼ ☆
'Conica', 'Glauca' and 'Pyramidalis', slow-growing, eventually large conical or pyramidal forms of striking blue-grey foliage, enhanced with large, round 'nuts' or cones. 'Blue Ice' and 'Silver Smoke', two new cultivars worth looking for. Ensure when planting that roots are not 'corkscrewed' within the pots. Often grafted. H3-5m/10-16ft, W1.2-1.5m/4-5ft. Z7-9.
'Sulphurea', striking column of densely packed, sulphur-yellow foliage, brighter in summer, as hardy as blue forms. Often grafted. H2.1-3m/7-10ft, W90-120cm/3-4ft. Z7-9.

JUNIPERUS Juniper

The junipers are among the most ornamental and adaptable conifers for garden use. Some have colourful winter foliage and an added bonus on mature specimens of attractive berries. Many are extremely hardy, surviving low and high temperatures, and thin and impoverished soils, including limy ones. ☼ □ ■ ☆
J. chinensis. 'Aurea', golden Chinese juniper, lovely but difficult to propagate and grow as a young plant. Prickly whitish yellow juvenile foliage and non-prickly golden-yellow adult foliage, eventually a narrow cone of deep golden-yellow, especially bright in winter. Hardy, but protect from cold winds and hot sun in early years. Often grafted. H1.2-1.5m/4-5ft, W60-75cm/24-30in. Z5-9. 'Japonica Variegata', often mistakenly sold as 'Kaizuka Variegata'. Semi-prostrate, almost vase-shaped, with juvenile foliage or, more commonly, an upright, irregular pyramid of mostly adult foliage, in each case splashed creamy white. H1.5-1.8m/5-6ft, W90-120cm/3-4ft. Z5-9. 'Kaizuka', upward, spreading bush with several leading stems, forming a plant of great character. Attractive clusters of blue-grey fruits on older plants. Excellent for specimen planting in a lawn or heather garden. To train it as a wall shrub or espalier, start early! H1.2-1.8m/4-6ft, W1.2-1.5m/4-5ft. Z4-9. 'Keteleeri', annual autumn and winter display of bluish grey berries, long-lasting when cut. Upright, grey-green, columnar form. H2.1-3m/7-10ft, W90cm/3ft. Z5-9.
J. communis 'Depressa Aurea'. Unusual semi-prostrate conifer, bronze-green in winter, changing to greeny yellow in spring, transformed in early summer when golden-yellow new shoots appear. The whole bush becomes butter-yellow, toning down

Juniperus chinensis 'Kaizuka'

later in summer. Full sun essential. At its best superb; excellent for ground cover. H30-45cm/12-18in, W1.2-1.5m/4-5ft. Z3-7. Many other *J. communis* forms have winter interest in foliage and habit – look for them in specialist books, nurseries and garden centres.
J. horizontalis. Creeping juniper. The many forms take some beating for year-round cover. However, most are duller in winter and few can be specifically recommended for autumn, winter or spring interest. Prune as necessary to keep a denser habit. Easy to grow on any well-drained soil. Semi-prostrate 'Plumosa Compacta' and 'Youngstown' change colour after first frosts from soft blue-grey to distinctive bronze-purple, effective next to a golden-foliaged heather, conifer or shrub. Both H30-45cm/12-18in, W75-90cm/30-36in. Z4-9.

Juniperus chinensis 'Aurea'

Juniperus communis 'Horstmann'

J. x *media*. Broad group includes first-class, mostly semi-prostrate cultivars of great ornamental value. 'Gold Coast', one of the best of many selections, keeping a good winter colour. Low-growing and wide-spreading habit with bright, mostly adult, golden-yellow foliage, less brilliant in winter. Takes pruning well. H60-90cm/2-3ft, W1.5-1.8m/5-6ft. Z4-9. 'Gold Sovereign', very compact cultivar, ideally suited to the smaller garden, with brilliant golden-yellow juvenile and adult foliage in summer, and in a sunny situation remaining bright in winter. Can be kept quite dwarf with annual pruning. H45-60cm/18-24in, W75-90cm/30-36in. Z5-9.

'Sulphur Spray', vigorous, semi-prostrate bush of striking, sulphur-yellow adult foliage, particularly in summer. Needs sun to produce the best colour. Regular pruning will keep it within bounds. H90-120cm/3-4ft, W1.2-1.5m/4-5ft. Z4-9.

J. scopulorum. Rocky Mountain juniper. Appealing upright, fastigiate forms. Perhaps most outstanding are 'Blue Moon', 'Gray Gleam' and 'Wichita Blue', all with silvery grey winter foliage, silver blue in summer and maintained well into autumn. All are of narrow, upright habit with tiny, scale-like leaves. Best in open positions in sun. Often grafted. Average H1.5-2.1m/5-7ft, W30-45cm/1-2ft. Z4-7.

J. squamata. 'Blue Star', quickly makes a compact bush, deep blue in winter, changing to a brilliant, silvery blue in summer. H30-45cm/12-18in, W45-60cm/18-24in. Z5-8.

J. virginiana. Most cultivars have thin, scale-like leaves, are generally very hardy and adaptable to a wide range of soil and climatic conditions. Among the many selections are some with columnar habits, whilst others are prostrate or semi-prostrate, their colour maintained well in winter. 'Grey Owl', one of the best junipers for ground cover where little else will grow. Thin, wide-spreading branches, smoky grey, scale-like leaves, blue-grey in winter. Its vigour and adaptability to sun, shade, flat ground, banks and heavy or light soils are remarkable! Lacy, overlapping foliage can be kept in check with regular trimming. H60-90cm/2-3ft, W1.8-2.4m/6-8ft. Z3-9. Similar but slower-growing is 'Blue Cloud', with curled and twisted branch tips. 'Helle', slowly forms a broad column of rich green foliage, maintained well in winter. Distinct but considered by some authorities to be the same as *J. chinensis* 'Spartan'. H1.5-1.8m/5-6ft, W45-60cm/18-24in. Z3-9.

LARIX Larch

L. decidua. European larch. One of the few deciduous conifers, along with *Ginkgo*, *Metasequoia* and *Taxodium*. In spring it bursts into clusters of bright green leaves, which darken through the summer before turning golden in late autumn. A beautiful tree, but rather large for average gardens, and not good on chalk soils. H8-10m/26-33ft, W3-5m/10-16ft. Z3-6. ☆

'Pendula', beautiful, if variable, with weeping branches. Often sold as a standard with shoots of 'Pendula' top-grafted onto the stem of a seedling of the species. Height is difficult to estimate, but growth can be vigorous, 30-45cm/12-18in a year. Pruning may be necessary. G. Z3-6.

L. kaempferi. Japanese larch. Grows to 30m/100ft or more. Broader, almost sea-green leaves and reddish winter twigs. Several forms have been selected from witches' brooms. H6-8m/20-26ft, W3-4m/10-13ft. Z5-7. 'Diana', peculiarly twisted and curly branches and long, light green leaves similarly curled. Estimated H90-120cm/3-4ft, W90-120cm/3-4ft. G. Z5-7. 'Nana', rare, in its best form it is truly dwarf, with shortened and congested branches and bright fresh-green leaves turning light gold in autumn. H30-45cm/12-18in, W45-60cm/18-24in. G. Z5-7.

Larix kaempferi 'Diana'

Picea glauca 'Coerulea'

METASEQUOIA Dawn redwood
M. glyptostroboides. Dawn redwood.
Rapid-growing, deciduous, conical
conifer. Delicate-looking, fresh-
green feathery foliage clothing erect
branching stems. In late autumn the
dying leaves turn pink, russet or
gold. Tolerates wide range of soils
and climates. H5-8m/16-26ft,
W1.2-1.5m/4-5ft. Z5-10. ☀ ◪ ◼ ☆

MICROBIOTA
M. decussata. Sole species of this
genus. Attractive ground cover of
gently overlapping lacy sprays of
foliage. Bright green in summer
changing to a deep rust-purple in
winter, a good contrast to golden
and variegated evergreens and
excellent with heaths and heathers. It
is adaptable to sun or shade. H15-
30cm/6-12in, W1.2-1.5m/4-5ft.
Z2-8. ☼ ❋ ☆

PICEA Spruce
There are attractive ornamental
species, but mainly the dwarf forms,
usually arising from selected
seedlings or witches' brooms, are
grown in the smaller, modern-day
garden. Although fairly adaptable to
a wide range of conditions, they are
less happy on very dry or thin chalky
soils and most dislike alkaline soils
P. abies. Norway spruce. '**Aurea
Magnifica**', brighter all year than
'Aurea' which is much less
ornamental, light yellow in summer
and much brighter in winter and
spring. Needs sun to colour well.
H2.1-3m/7-10ft, W1.5-2.4m/5-8ft.
G. Z3-7. '**Inversa**', totally prostrate,
but training the main stem to 2.1-
3m/7-10ft eventually produces a
weeping form of long, dark green
shoots cascading down. As a
specimen this creates a plant of
considerable year-round interest.
Annual growth rate 10-15cm/4-6in.
G. Z3-7. '**Will's Dwarf** ' (syn. 'Wills
Zwerg'), pyramid of short, rigid
branches, clothed in rich green
foliage, rather open at the top but
colour maintained throughout
winter. H1.2-1.5m/4-5ft, W60-
90cm/2-3ft. Z3-7.
P. glauca '**Coerulea**'. Slower-
growing in early years and more

Picea pungens 'Globosa'

compact than the species, making a
narrow pyramid with upward-angled
branches of short, soft, blue-grey
needles. Small green cones on quite
young trees on the branch tips,
maturing to light brown. Eventually
quite tall. H1.5-1.8m/5-6ft,
W90cm/3ft. G. Z3-7. ☀ ◪
P. omorika '**Nana**'. Attractive form
of Serbian spruce. Small for first ten
years, eventually forms a broad
pyramid 3-5m/10-16ft or more
high. Slow to develop leading
shoots, initially dome-shaped with
dark green upper leaves, bright

silver-blue beneath. H90-120cm/3-
4ft, W60-75cm/24-30in. Z5-8.
☀ ◪ ☆
P. orientalis '**Skylands**'. Beautiful
when well grown, one of the
brightest for colour. Prone to
sunscorch when young and slow to
make a leading shoot, hence its other
name, 'Aurea Compacta'; unless
trained when young it is almost
semi-prostrate. When established it
grows strongly, as much as 30cm/1ft
a year, into a narrow conical tree
with a rather open branching
system. The leaves are bright golden-

Picea pungens 'Prostrata'

yellow on the upper surface, but green underneath. Occasionally prune the more vigorous side shoots. H1.2-1.8m/4-6ft, W90-120cm/3-4ft. G. Z5-7. ☀ ◪

P. pungens. Colorado spruce. Some of the finest and most striking garden conifers for year-round colour. Nearly all cultivars are propagated by grafting, often using side shoots from upright trees, so young plants generally need their main shoot trained upwards on a cane for several years. Pruning vigorous side shoots in early spring helps maintain a better form and removes competition from the leading shoot. Species average: H2.1-3m/7-10ft, W1.2-1.5m/4-5ft. Z3-8. ☀ ■ ☆

'Globosa' (syn. 'Glauca Globosa'), closely set, congested branches slightly angled up from the centre, gradually forming a neat but irregular bush. Stiff, prickly needles are grey-blue in winter; in late spring soft, bright blue new leaves transform the colour for the whole summer. Unless grown from

cuttings (not easy) grafted plants may, within four or five years of planting, make one or more leading shoots. Prune away in early spring, unless you want an equally desirable compact pyramid. Mostly grafted. H45-60cm/ 18-24in, W45-60cm/18-24in. Z3-8.

'Hoopsii', soft, broad, bright silver-blue needles in summer, silver-grey in winter. Narrow pyramidal or broadly conical form, eventually large. Prune side shoots when young to improve habit. H1.8-2.4m/6-8ft, W90-120cm/3-4ft. G. Z3-8.

'Koster', difficult to train a leading shoot in early years, and even later the main terminal tends to bend or snake. Side shoots are irregular and need annual pruning to make a balanced specimen. Branches are angled sharply upwards from the

main stem. Good year-round silver-blue. Cones freely. H1.8-2.4m/6-8ft, W1.2-1.5m/4-5ft. G. Z3-8.

'Prostrata' (syn. 'Glauca Prostrata' and 'Procumbens'), covers any prostrate blue spruce but completely flat ones are rare, since most sooner or later try to make angled or vertical shoots. Cut these away to maintain a low-growing habit if required. These will make broad, spreading specimens, their bright silver-blue foliage showing brilliantly against golden heathers or conifers. Annual growth 15-30cm/6-12in. H30-45cm/12-18in, W1.5-1.8m/ 5-6ft. G. Z3-8. **'Thomsen'**, one of the best, narrow, with branches angled upwards and soft, thick needles, distinctive silver-grey in winter, bright silver-blue in summer. Difficult to propagate. H1.8-2.4m/ 6-8ft, W90-120cm/3-4ft. G. Z3-8.

P. sitchensis 'Papoose'. Eventually forms a dense, broadly conical bush whose blue-green leaves have showy silver undersides. H45-60cm/ 18-24in, W45-60cm/18-24in. G. Z4-8.

PINUS Pine

Extremely varied and valuable. All have needles growing in bunches of two to five. In spring many have cone-like male flowers which shed pollen, whilst female flowers produce cones. A great many offer colour, form and cones for winter interest, some turning from green to gold. Some cultivars root readily from cuttings but most must be grafted. ☀ □ ■ ☆

P. aristata 'Sherwood Compact'. Compact replica of its parent, erect branches forming a tight, conical, blue-green bush, the needles' scales much less and sometimes not at all noticeable. H45-60cm/18-24in, W20-30cm/8-12in. G. Z4-7.

P. cembra. Arolla pine. Excellent for garden and landscape. Formal column of upright branches, densely

Picea pungens 'Hoopsii'

Pinus mugo 'Winter Gold'

Pinus parviflora 'Glauca'

clothed young shoots in sets of five dark blue needles, with bright bluish white insides, covered with thick, orange-brown down. Most plants offered are from seed and may be variable. ◢ 'Glauca', attractive selection with dark blue needles, is grafted, as is the slower-growing 'Aurea', or 'Aureovariegata', which needs full sun, has paler foliage and gold-tipped needles, particularly in winter. *P. cembra* and 'Glauca': H1.5-1.8m/5-6ft, W75-90cm/30-36in. G. Z4-7.

P. koraiensis 'Silveray'. Correct name for plants listed as *P.k.* 'Glauca'. Very attractive selection of the rare, five-needled Korean pine. Hardy, adaptable, fairly slow when young. Rather open column of grey-green branches, clusters of blue-green needles, bright silver-grey underneath. Red male and female flowers often appear in spring, later on older plants. Quite large olive-green cones hug the stems, ripening brown. A distinctive pine for garden

and landscape. H1.5-1.8m/5-6ft, W60-75cm/24-30in. G. Z5-7.

P. leucodermis (syn. *P. heldreichii leucodermis*). Bosnian pine. Some first class seedlings and witches' brooms, which although a dark, rich green are invaluable in winter in association with gold, yellow and blue conifers. Distinctive for long, dark green, paired needles which in their first years press forward close to the branches. Bright blue cones ripen brown. Very useful on dry, poor and alkaline soils. Slow when young but eventually tall. H2.4-3m/8-10ft, W90-120cm/3-4ft. Z6-8. ☼ ◢ 'Compact Gem', compact and quite slow-growing when young, dense clusters of lustrous, deep green needles. My eighteen-year-old specimens are 3m/10ft tall and 1.8m/6ft across, so allow for its future development! H90-120cm/3-4ft, W60-90cm/2-3ft. G. Z6-8.

P. mugo. Numerous selections of the two-needled mugo pine, some very similar to each other. They take

kindly to pruning and many nurserymen prune them with shears just as they develop new shoots in early summer, still early enough for them to bush out and form buds for the following year. Most succeed in inhospitable conditions, including alkaline soils, as long as good drainage exists. Z3-7.

'Humpy', one of the most compact and attractive dwarf pines, forms a neat cushion with branches densely clothed in short, dark green needles. Prominent brown-purple winter buds. H30cm/1ft, W60cm/2ft. G. Z3-7. 'Ophir', nondescript in summer, but in winter its green needles gradually turn golden-yellow. An open, sunny position gives best colour. H60cm/2ft, W90cm/3ft. G. Z3-7. 'Winter Gold' differs from 'Ophir' in that its needles turn completely golden-yellow where light does not reach, while 'Ophir' needles remain green. Neither suffers sun- or frostburn. 'Zundert', similar but more compact. All H60-75cm/24-30in, W90cm/3ft. G. Z3-7.

P. parviflora 'Glauca'. One of many selections made from seedlings of the Japanese white pine, popular in Japan for their form and outline, particularly when pruned to allow light and air in. Widely used for bonsai. Bright blue-green needles, silvery beneath, borne in clusters at ends of branches and branchlets. Eventually attains 6-10m/20-33ft or more, although often sold as a dwarf. Prune if required to form a narrower outline, or for bonsai. Cones freely. H1.8-2.4m/6-8ft, W1.8-2.4m/6-8ft. G. Z5-8. ☼ ◢

P. strobus. Generally unsuitable for small garden use, but many cultivars have been selected and introduced from seedlings and witches' brooms. ☼ ◢ ■ 'Minima', dense, low, neat, round bush of thin, blue-green needles. Similar but even slower are 'Horsford' and 'Reinshaus'.

H30cm/1ft, W60-75cm/24-30in. G. Z4-9.

P. sylvestris. Scots pine. Two-needled, the only pine native to the British Isles. Old specimens reach 30m/100ft or more, so it is hardly suitable for the smaller garden. Slightly twisted needles, dark blue in winter, brighter in summer. Small rounded cones. A pine of picturesque outline as a mature specimen. Most soils and sites, including acid and alkaline ones. H3-5m/10-16ft, W2.1-3m/7-10ft. Z3-7. ■ ☆

'Aurea' covers several forms in cultivation, including a fairly rapid-growing one similar to the species, but with light grey-green leaves in summer changing to pale yellow in winter. Although grafted and starting a bit slower, estimated H3-4m/10-13ft, W2.1-3m/7-10ft. G. Z3-7. A much better and initially slower-growing form, sometimes referred to as 'Nisbets', has needles that turn a bright, deep golden-to-orange yellow in winter. Estimated

Taxodium distichum

Taxus baccatta 'Standishii'

H1.8-2.4m/6-8ft, W1.5-1.8m/5-6ft, developing more strongly each year. G. Z5. The so-called dwarf '**Gold Coin**' and '**Gold Medal**' have probably been grafted from small, secondary shoots or weak plants and, given time or rich, heavy soil, they soon want to become grown up, too! Unless continually pruned, with age they become much taller, with deep golden winter needles, exposure to sunlight producing the strongest colour. For a golden dwarf Scots pine, prune new growth with secateurs or shears each spring, just as the plant develops 5cm/2in or so of soft foliage. It will still bush out and make attractive winter buds by late summer, as though it had not been trimmed at all. Place against contrasting conifers and underplant with hardy cyclamen. Your plant could be kept for many years at, say, H60cm/2ft, W60-75cm/24-30in by this method. G. Z4-7.
'**Moseri**' (formerly *P. nigra* 'Pygmaea'), distinctive, long needles,

twisted and congested around the top of the branches, and buds surrounded by a sheaf of short green leaves. The needles are nondescript green but turn green-gold in winter, the colour in some winters more extreme than others. H75-90cm/30-36in, W60-75cm/24-30in. G. Z3-7.

PODOCARPUS
Some Australian species have produced forms of note for winter colour and fruit. The few dwarfs of note are similar to yews in appearance. Male and female plants must be in close proximity for the females to produce attractive, berry-like, brightly coloured, seed-holding receptacles, similar to *Taxus*. Like most yews they do well on chalky soils. ☀ ❋ ☆
P. alpinus. Slowly forms a prostrate bush of dark green needles, a few leading branches spreading beyond the mass of foliage. With age becomes a larger shrub. Provide shelter in early years from severe

frosts. Excellent as ground cover or in a rock garden. H20-30cm/8-12in, W60-90cm/2-3ft. Z8-11.
P. lawrencii. Similar to *P. alpinus*, but deeper blue-green needles, attractive against golds in winter.
P. nivalis. Recent breeding and selection by Graham Hutchins in England has resulted in a fascinating range of forms which turn bronze and purple in winter and which fruit readily. All are low-growing forms suitable for smaller gardens. Average H20-30cm/ 8-12in, W60-90cm/2-3ft. Z8-11.

TAXODIUM
Deciduous, for the larger garden. Thrive on moist, swampy soils, but dislike alkaline ones. ☀ ◿
T. distichum. Swamp cypress, bald cypress. Pyramidal habit, wide-spreading or ascending branches. Bare winter stems make picturesque outline, broken in spring by new, bright green shoots. Leaves turn a deep reddish brown in late autumn,

remaining for several weeks. Older trees have reddish brown bark. Beautiful at pond side. H4-6m/13-20ft, W1.5-2.4m/5-8ft. Z5-10.

TAXUS Yew
Useful conifers because of their adaptability. Many introductions have colourful foliage. Succeed in dry, dense shade. ☀ ❋ ☐ ☆
T. baccata. Common yew, known outside Britain as English yew. Variable from seed but leaves are glossy dark green, lighter green beneath; male and female flowers on separate plants but red-capsuled fruits borne only on females. Berries and foliage are poisonous, and one should be aware of possible dangers if children use the garden; avoid yew on boundaries accessible to livestock. Ideal for topiary and hedges, taking pruning, even hard pruning, well since shoots will develop from old wood. Growth rate per annum once established 15-30cm/6-12in. Z6-7.
'**Fastigiata Robusta**', outstanding accent plant, narrower than 'Fastigiata', dark green foliage untouched by severe frosts. Perfect where formality is required. H1.5-1.8m/5-6ft, W20-30cm/8-12in. Z6-7. '**Repens Aurea**', slow and low-growing when young, wide-spreading branches raised at tips. Orange-yellow shoots turn golden-yellow in spring, the foliage gracefully drooping along the outer branches. Colours best in sun. H45-60cm/18-24in, W1.2-1.5m/4-5ft. Z6-7. '**Semperaurea**', erect semi-spreading habit, intense orange-gold shoots in spring, and bright golden-yellow leaves the rest of the year. Excellent winter colour. Prune as necessary. H1.2-1.5m/4-5ft, W1.2-1.5m/4-5ft. Z6-7. '**Standishii**' (syn. 'Fastigiata Standishii'), best upright golden yew for the British climate. Slower and narrower than golden-leaved 'Fastigiata' types, also much brighter in summer and winter. In

Thuja orientalis 'Elegantissima'

open, sunny positions needle tips are deep old-gold. Often fruits. H1.2-1.5m/4-5ft, W30cm/1ft. Z6-7.

THUJA Arbor-vitae
Important ornamental conifers related to, and closely resembling, chamaecyparis. Most form conical trees with flattened foliage sprays, scale-like foliage, noticeably aromatic on certain species and cultivars. Most are hardy, although *T. orientalis* and some of its cultivars are much less so. ✿ ☀ ■ ☆

T. occidentalis. '**Holmstrup Yellow**', more open in habit than the narrowly pyramidal, dark green 'Holmstrup', forming a broad column of yellow-green summer foliage, bright yellow in winter, perhaps the brightest of any thuja. Can scorch when young in exposed positions. H1.5-1.8m/5-6ft, W90-120cm/3-4ft. Z4-8. '**Lutea Nana**', grows to 8m/26ft or more. Broad column of loose foliage sprays,

bright yellow in summer, deep golden-yellow in winter. H1.8-2.4m/6-8ft, W90-120cm/3-4ft. Z3-8. '**Marrison Sulphur**', slow-growing and broadly pyramidal with delicate, lacy, creamy-yellow foliage, even in winter. H1.5-1.8m/5-6ft, W90-120cm/3-4ft. Z3-8. '**Rheingold**', attractive bush of lacy, bright golden-yellow summer foliage, rich coppery bronze in winter. Excellent with heathers but colours best in an exposed spot. Prune as necessary, since with age it often gets too broad and untidy. Variable size but approximate H90-120cm/3-4ft, W90-120cm/3-4ft. Z3-8. '**Smaragd**', narrow column of bright, rich green foliage, loose, soft and, rare among the green-foliaged cultivars, maintaining its rich colour through winter. Excellent as a specimen or for suburban garden hedge, needing only occasional clipping. H1.8-2.4m/6-8ft, W60-75cm/24-30in. Z3-8. '**Sunkist**',

slower-growing and more densely pyramidal than 'Lutea Nana', soon forms a bush with several leading shoots, the flattened foliage sprays golden-yellow in summer, bronze-gold in winter. H1.2-1.5m/4-5ft, W90-120cm/3-4ft. Z3-8.

T. orientalis. Although considerably less hardy than the others, it provides attractive, colourful cultivars, most of which vary in hardiness. Z6-9. '**Collen's Gold**', narrow column of open foliage, bright golden-yellow in summer, well maintained in winter. H1.5-1.8m/5-6ft, W30-45cm/12-18in. Z6-9. '**Elegantissima**', stiff, upright habit, flat foliage sprays on curving branchlets. Deep golden-yellow leaves in summer, deep bronze in winter, particularly in an open sunny spot. Although slow when young, may reach 5m/16ft or more. H1.2-1.5m/4-5ft, W60-75cm/24-30in. Z6-9. A recent selection, '**Flame**', turns almost orange-red in winter in full sun. '**Purple King**', narrowly oval habit, green laminated foliage in summer, startling deep purple-brown in winter. Site against brighter foliage. H60-75cm/24-30in, W30-4cm/12-18in. Z6-9.

T. plicata. Fast-growing, tall, eventually broad-based pyramid, foliage flattened in fern-like sprays, from mid- to dark green, scale-like leaves glossy above and pale green beneath with silver markings. Excellent for hedges and screens, stands clipping well, and is one of the few conifers to produce new growth from its centre. The species has a most pleasant, fruity odour when the foliage is brushed or rubbed. Prefers areas of high rainfall. '**Atrovirens**', more formal, conical shape, erect branches clothed in deep, rich, glossy green foliage all year round. H4-5m/13-16ft, W90-120cm/3-4ft. Z6-8. '**Irish Gold**', one of the brightest conifers in winter, prone to sunscorch when

young. Pyramidal, creamy white foliage lightly flecked with green if grown in full sun. Shelter from cold, desiccating winds. '**Zebrina**', much denser and more yellow-green. H1.5-2.4m/5-8ft, W90-120cm/3-4ft. Z7-8. '**Rogersii**' (syn. 'Aurea Rogersii'), slowly forms a dense, round bush of congested foliage, dark green inside, deep golden-yellow to bronze at the tips. Cut away growths that break surface if they begin to grow too strongly. Good year-round colour, ideal for the rock garden. H30-45cm/12-18in, W30cm/1ft. Z6-8. '**Stoneham Gold**', one of the best plants in the winter garden. Slow-growing, often with several leading shoots to start with. Stems are reddish brown, especially in winter, foliage dark green inside, golden-yellow and green where exposed to sunlight, and orange-yellow, often bronze, at the tips. Excellent winter colour in exposed spots. Trim occasionally. H60-90cm/2-3ft, W45-60cm/18-24in. Z6-8.

TSUGA Hemlock
Not always easy to grow or establish. Need shelter from wind when young, even though the forms listed here are perfectly frost-hardy. ✿ ☀ ◪ ■ ⊖

T. canadensis. '**Everitt Golden**' (syn. 'Aurea Compacta'), very slowly forms an upright bush, eventually a small tree, upright, stiff branches, the small leaves golden-yellow all year round. Colours best in full sun but prone to damage from drying winds. H45-60cm/18-24in, W30cm/1ft. Z4-8. '**Gentsch White**', slow-growing, bushy, dark green foliage at its centre but the new season's brown stems bear startling white leaves still attractive in winter. Trim annually once well established. '**Dwarf Whitetip**' is similar. H60-90cm/2-3ft, W60-90cm/2-3ft. Z4-8.

PERENNIALS DIRECTORY

MOST HARDY PERENNIALS HAVE THE GOOD SENSE to disappear below ground in winter, hopefully to pop up and surprise us each spring. Luckily though, there are many that are evergreen, providing flower and foliage in winter and early spring. There are also many perennials that flower well into autumn. In large genera such as asters and dendranthemas (chrysanthemums) only a few of the vast range available can be mentioned here. Local and regional climates have a bearing on what can be grown successfully, what will flower and for how long in any area.

H: Approximate height
W: Approximate width
F: Months in flower
Z: Relevant hardiness zone(s)

Autumn flower and foliage

Aconitum carmichaelii 'Arendsii'

ACONITUM **Aconite, monkshood**
One or two species are excellent for late flowers, their blues welcome among autumn foliage colours. Tall types may need staking. Roots are poisonous, in the unlikely event of being eaten. Adaptable to heavy soil.
☼ ❋ ■ ☆
A. carmichaelii (syn. *A. fischeri*). Rich green summer foliage, light blue flower heads in autumn. H1.2m/4ft, W30cm/1ft. F9-10. Z3-8. '**Arendsii**', deeply divided leaves, erect stems topped in autumn with short spikes of deep amethyst-blue flowers. H1.8m/6ft, W30cm/1ft. F9-10. Z3-8. ◪

ADONIS
Indispensable for late winter flowers. Long-lived with fibrous roots, best lifted and divided for replanting when dormant, from mid-summer to late autumn. Provide shelter. ❋ ◪ ■
A. amurensis. Glistening, green-tinged, yellow flowers open from bronze-green shoots which become verdant, ferny foliage. H15cm/6in, W25cm/10in. F1-3. Z4-7. '**Plena**', large, double, green-centred yellow flowers. H15cm/6in, W25cm/10in. F3-5. Z4-7.
A. vernalis. Choice species. Erect little bushes, single, bright yellow, buttercup-like flowers. Green until late summer. H30cm/1ft, W30cm/1ft. F4-5. Z4-7.

Adonis amurensis

AGAPANTHUS **African lily**
Sterling plants for summer flowers, and even if only a few flower into autumn, their strap-like leaves turn golden and the seed heads remain attractive on slender stems. The newer, hardy kinds, mostly selections from the narrow-leaved Headbourne hybrids, are deservedly popular. Best covered with litter over winter in coldest areas. Move in spring, when new growth is about to begin. Most are Z8-10. Good, deep soil. ☼ ◪ ■

ANAPHALIS **Pearl everlasting**
A. triplinervis '**Summer Snow**'. Best form of the species with neat habit. Silvery, woolly leaves; flowers freely, close to pure white. H25cm/10in, W60cm/2ft. F7-9. Z7-10. ☼ ❋ ◪ ■

ANEMONE
There is some confusion in the naming of the very garden-worthy "Japanese anemones" which are all listed under *A.* x *hybrida*. Their beautiful, delicate flowers are enchanced by golden stamens.
☼ ❋ ■ ★
A. × *hybrida.* None needs staking, and they revel in limy soil. '**Alba**', strong growers, pure white flowers with contrasting yellow stamens. H75cm/30in, W45cm/18in. F8-10. Z5-8. '**Bressingham Glow**', rich deep pink, semi-double flowers. H60cm/2ft, W45cm/18in. F8-10.

Anenome × hybrida 'Lady Gilmour'

Z5-8. **'Hadspen Abundance'**, deep rose-pink, almost semi-double flowers, prominent golden-yellow stamens, very free-flowering. H60cm/2ft, W30cm/1ft. F8-10. Z5-9. **'Lady Gilmour'**, large, ivy-type basal leaves, large, semi-double, clear pink flowers. H60cm/2ft, W45cm/18in. F7-10. Z5-8. There are many others.

ARTEMESIA
Good foliage plants until winter. ☼ ■
A. canescens. Delicate, silvery, almost hoary or filigree leaves. Compact, somewhat shrubby, a good foil to other plants. H30cm/1ft, W30cm/1ft. Z5-9.
A. stelleriana. Quite large, deeply cut, felted, silver leaves on ground-hugging stems. Good ground cover. **'Mori'** (syn. 'Boughton Silver'), more compact. H30cm/1ft, W60cm/2ft. Z4-8.

ASARUM Wild ginger
Evergreen, ground-covering plants forming mounds of rounded leaves but with insignificant flowers. ✴ ◪ ■ ★
A. europaeum. Neat, clump-forming, highly glossy, kidney-shaped leaves, brownish flowers. H20cm/8in, W30cm/1ft. F5-6. Z4-7.

Aster amellus 'King George'

ASTER
Among this enormous family are some excellent late-flowering types for all sizes of garden. Most are easy to grow; many are valuable for cutting. ☼ ✳ ■ ★
A. amellus. First-rate, trouble-free plants. Single rayed, yellow-centred flowers seldom needing support. Long-lived, no faults or diseases, slow-growing, long-flowering. For autumn planting, pot-grown plants are best. All F8-10, Z5-8. **'King George'**, violet-blue. H60cm/2ft, W45cm/18in. **'Nocturne'**, rich lilac-lavender. H75cm/30in, W45cm/18in. **'Pink Zenith'**, the most prolific pink variety. H75cm/30in, W45cm/18in. **'Violet Queen'**, masses of deep violet-blue flowers. H60cm/2ft, W45cm/18in.
A. cordifolius. Heart-shaped leaves, wiry stems and graceful sprays of silvery blue flowers. **'Blue Heaven'**, deep blue. 120cm/4ft, W45cm/18in. **'Photograph'**, light blue. H1.3m/51in, W45cm/18in. **'Silver Spray'**, some need staking. H1.6m/63in, W45cm/18in. All F9-10.

Z3-8.
A. ericoides. Shapely bushes, tiny leaves and profuse, tiny flowers. Trouble-free, largely self-supporting, need dividing only after several years. **'Blue Star'**, light blue. **'Brimstone'**, soft creamy yellow. **'Pink cloud'**, delicate lilac pink. **'White Heather'**, white. All H70-90cm/28-36in, W30cm/1ft. F7-9. Z3-8.
A. x frikartii **'Wunder von Stäfa'** (syn. 'Wonder of Stäfa'). Taller, more branching and leafier than the type. Clear lavender-blue flowers. H1m/39in, W40cm/16in. F7-9. Z5-8. **'Mönch'**, similar, less branching, very long-flowering.
A. lateriflorus **'Horizontalis'**. Slender, twiggy, upright stems, horizontal sprays of small white or bluish flowers with pink stamens. Foliage turns purple-bronze in early autumn. H1.5m/5ft, W38cm/15in. F9-11. Z4-8.
A. novae-angliae. New England asters. Stout clumps from fibrous roots giving startling colour in late summer and autumn. Sturdy stems carry loose heads of single, yellow-

centred, ray-petalled flowers. Most soils, not too wet. All F9-10, Z4-8. **'Alma Pötschke'**, striking, warm salmon-rose. H1.5m/5ft, W60cm/2ft. **'Autumn Snow'** (syn. 'Herbstschnee'), large white flowers in bushy heads. H1.5m/5ft, W50cm/20in. **'Purple Dome'**, dwarfest to date, intense glowing purple. H60cm/2ft, W45cm/18in. **'Rosa Sieger'** and **'Harrington's Pink'**, similar, clear, clean pink. H1.5m/5ft, W60cm/2ft.
A. novi-belgii. Michaelmas daisy. Many varieties well worth including for their autumn colour. Some are prone to mildew and wilt; avoid tall kinds. Lift and divide in spring every two to three years. All Z4-8. **'Ada Ballard'**, large mauve-blue flowers. H90cm/3ft, W45cm/18in. F8-10. **'Carnival'**, intense, semi-double, cherry-red, erect-growing. H60cm/2ft, W45cm/18in. F9-10. **'Coombe Rosemary'**, fully double violet-purple flowers. 3-5cm/1¼ - 2in across. H90cm/3ft, W45cm/18in. F9-10. **'White Ladies'**, strong-growing, white flowers, dark foliage. H1.2m/4ft, W45cm/18in. F9-10.

Dwarf hybrids, sometimes listed under *A. dumosus*, are less prone to diseases, grow vigorously and do not need support. **'Audrey'**, mauve-blue single, one of the best. H30cm/1ft, W45cm/18in. F9-10. **'Jenny'**, double red. H30cm/1ft, W45cm/18in. F9-10. **'Little Pink Beauty'**, the best semi-double pink. H40cm/16in, W45cm/18in. F9-10. **'Snow Cushion'**, low-growing, compact, with white flowers. H30cm/1ft, W45cm/18in. F9-10.
A. pringlei **'Monte Cassino'**. Very late-flowering cut-flower variety, a mass of white. H1.2m/4ft, W60cm/2ft. F9-11. Z4-8.
A. spectabilis. Dwarf, mat-forming. Dark, leathery foliage, wiry stems and late sprays of blue, yellow-centred flowers for several weeks. Disease-

resistant. H30cm/1ft, W25cm/10in. F8-10. Z4-9.

A. thomsonii 'Nanus'. Shapely, bushy habit, greyish foliage, rayed, light blue, starry flowers for weeks on end. Best left undisturbed. H40cm/16in, W25cm/10in. F7-10. Z4-9.

BERGENIA

Useful and attractive for both foliage and flowers, although both can be damaged by late spring frost. Mainly evergreen, shiny leaves vary in size up to 25cm/10in across. Surface-expanding from shallow-rooting rhizomes. Many listed here notable for leaves which turn purple, bronze and red in late autumn. ☼ ✳ ■

B. purpurascens. Narrow leaves turning almost beetroot-red in winter, brownish red underneath. Good ground cover among shrubs. Deep pink flowers. H30cm/1ft, W30cm/1ft. F3-5. Z3-8.

Hybrids. 'Abendglut' (syn. 'Evening Glow'), slow-spreading, almost prostrate purplish leaves, purple-red stumpy spikes. H25cm/10in, W30cm/1ft. F3-5. Z3-8. 'Baby Doll', close-set spikes of sugar-pink flowers. H20cm/8in, W30cm/1ft. F3-5. Z4-8. 'Bressingham Ruby', outstanding intense, deep red flowers and almost beetroot-red leaves in winter, which seem to withstand both winter frosts and summer heat. H35cm/14in, W30cm/1ft. F3-5. Z3-8. 'Bressingham White', white flowers, handsome, rounded leaves. H30cm/1ft, W30cm/1ft. F3-5. Z4-8.

Bergenia 'Bressingham Ruby'

'Eric Smith', glossy, rounded leaves turn bonze-purple in winter, reddish beneath. Red flowers. H45cm/18in, W30cm/1ft. F3-5. Z4-8. 'Wintermärchen', small, pointed, somewhat upright leaves turn bronze-purple, carmine beneath, in winter. Rose-red flowers. H30cm/1ft, W30cm/1ft. F3-5. Z4-8.

CHRYSANTHEMUM

C. nipponicum see *Nipponanthemum nipponicum*

C. rubellum see *Dendranthema rubella*

C. uliginosum see *Leucanthemella serotina*

C. yezoense see *Dendranthema yezoense*

CIMICIFUGA Bugbane

Beautiful, trouble-free plants, some late-flowering. Slender, graceful stems, bottlebrush spikes of often scented, small white or cream flowers in late summer or autumn. Leaves often turn yellow in autumn. Support not necessary. Appreciates a good deep soil that is not too limy. ☼ ✳ ◪

C. ramosa. Large, divided leaves and lofty, tapering, branching spikes, creamy white, late in the season.

Cimicifuga simplex 'Elstead'

H2.1m/7ft, W60cm/2ft. F8-9. Z4-8. 'Atropurpurea', purplish leaves and stems, white flowers. H2.1m/7ft, W60cm/2ft. F8-9. Z4-8. 'Brunette', black-purple foliage. H1.8m/6ft, W60cm/2ft. F8-10. Z4-8.

C. simplex 'White Pearl'. The latest to flower, with full, arching spikes of pure white to brighten the autumn scene. Deservedly popular. 'Elstead', similar, but with purplish buds. H1.2m/4ft, W60cm/2ft. F9-10. Z4-8.

COMMELINA

C. coelestis. Tuberous, tender plant that can be treated as *Cosmos atrosanguineus* with which it associates well. Spreading habit. Azure blue flowers in autumn. H60cm/2ft, W60-90cm/2-3ft. F6-10. Z8-9. ☼ ■ ✶

COREOPSIS Tickseed

Yellow daisies, with yellow or orange central discs, some flowering into autumn. ☼ ■ ✶

C. verticillata. Shapely bushes of finely divided leaves. Studded with small, bright yellow flowers for many weeks. H40cm/16in, W45cm/18in. F7-9. Z4-9. 'Golden Gain', larger flowers, more clump-forming habit.

H60cm/2ft, W38cm/15in. F7-9. Z4-9. 'Grandiflora', larger, deeper yellow flowers. H50cm/20in, W45cm/18in. F7-9. Z4-9. 'Moonbeam', light lemon-yellow flowers, scented foliage, multi-branched growth. H40cm/16in, W30cm/1ft. F7-9. Z3-9. 'Zagreb', clear yellow flowers, dwarf bushy growth. H35cm/14in, W30cm/1ft. F7-10. Z3-9.

COSMOS

C. atrosanguineus (syn. *Bidens atrosanguinea*). Long succession of chocolate-scented, rich deep crimson, single, dahlia-like flowers above bushy, dark green, divided foliage. Tuberous root. Survives outdoors only if covered to prevent frost penetration; roots may be lifted and stored as for dahlias. H80cm/32in, W38cm/15in. F7-10. Z8-9. ☼ ◪ ■

CROCOSMIA

Some of these South African plants create vivid splashes of colour in late summer and into autumn. Parentage is very mixed; montbretia types, indicated with (M), are less hardy and more tender. Best planted in spring and either protected by leaves or dug up for winter. ☼ ◪ ■

C. 'Citronella' (M). Masses of small, soft yellow flowers. H60cm/2ft, W15cm/6in. F7-8. Z6-9.

C. 'Emily MacKenzie' (M). Large-flowered late variety, deep orange petals and mahogany-crimson throat. H50cm/20in, W15cm/6in. F8-10. Z6-9.

C. 'Jenny Bloom'. Soft butter-yellow flowers, strong-growing and prolific. H80cm/32in, W15cm/6in. F7-10. Z5-9.

C. 'Star of the East' (M). Large, warm orange, turning apricot-yellow. H90cm/3ft, W30cm/1ft. F7-9. Z5-9.

DENDRANTHEMA

To many gardeners these will always be chrysanthemums, but the name

Epimedium pinnatum colchicum

Eupatorium purpureum 'Glutball'

change is being followed by all nomenclature authorities. For cheery autumn colour, there is little to beat the "crysanths" or "mums", and now breeders are producing an amazing range of both hardy and pot-plant varieties. Only a few of the hardy species and hybrids that flower reliably late in the year can be mentioned. Some shade where not too dry is acceptable. ☀ ■ ★

D. rubella (syn. *Chrysanthemum rubellum*). Some excellent garden-worthy cultivars which look natural among other perennials and grasses. All are single ray-petalled, with yellow eyes. Replant every year or two to avoid congestion. '**Apricot**', glowing orange-yellow. H75cm/30in, W45cm/18. F9-10. '**Clara Curtis**', clear pink. '**Duchess of Edinburgh**', bright bronzy crimson. '**Mary Stoker**', yellow. All H60-90cm/2-3ft, W60cm/2ft. F8-9. Z5-9.
Hybrids. Much confusion as to parentage exists, but singles, doubles and pom pom flowers are available in all colours, heights, shapes and sizes. Taller, larger-flowered hybrids have a tendency to flop and need staking. Here are a few well-tried varieties. All Z7-9. '**Anastasia**', compact, double, rose-pink, button flowers.

H75cm/30in, W45cm/18in. F10-11. '**Brennpunkt**', brilliant cherry-red. H75cm/30in, W45cm/18. F10-11. '**Mandarin**', bushy, double, orange-yellow. 60cm/2ft, W30cm/1ft. F9-10. '**Mei Kyo**', double, rose-pink. H5cm/18in, W30cm/1ft. F10-11. '**Peter Sare**', fully petalled, single, clear pink. H60cm/2ft, W30cm/1ft. F9-10. '**Pink Procession**', masses of single, bright pink flowers. H90-120cm/3-4in, W45cm/18. F9-10. '**Sunbeam**', bushy, double pom pom, golden yellow. 60cm/2ft, W30cm/1ft. F9-11.

ECHINACEA Purple coneflower
Reliable, daisy-like perennials. Radiating crimson-magenta petals, often with lighter tips and dark centres. Good, light soil. ☀ ■ ★
E. purpurea '**Magnus**'. Outstanding for flower size, almost 10cm/4in across. Warm purplish rose. H90cm/3ft, W38cm/15in. F7-10. '**Robert Bloom**', a selection from the more variable Bressingham hybrids. Sturdy stems, rounded, dark brown cones and flattened, deep rose-pink petals. H90cm/3ft, W38cm/15in. F7-10. '**White Lustre**'. Yellow-centred, ivory-white flowers. H90cm/3ft, W45cm/18in. F7-10.

EPIMEDIUM Barrenwort
Ground cover, some forms are virtually evergreen, whilst others have veined and rose-tinted leaves. Trim back semi-evergreen foliage in winter to display spring flowers. Only evergreens are listed as most flowers appear in late spring. ☀ ☀ ◪ ■ ★
E. x *perralchicum*. Evergreen hybrid. Quite large, yellow flowers. H30cm/1ft, W30cm/1ft. F3-5. Z5-9. '**Fröhnleiten**', neater, yellow flowers and marbled foliage. Evergreen. H25cm/10in, W25cm/10in. F4-5. Z5-9.
E. perralderianum. Strong-growing evergreen. Glossy leaves, bright green and bronzy red when young, copper-bronze in winter, and yellow flowers. H35cm/14in, W35cm/14in. F3-5. Z5-9.
E. pinnatum colchicum. Semi-evergreen foliage is brightly coloured in autumn and winter. Profuse, large yellow flowers. H25cm/10in, W25cm/10in. F3-5. Z5-9.

EUPATORIUM
Small, fluffy flower heads. Easy in most conditions. ☀ ☀ ◪ ■
E. fraseri (syn. *E. ageratoides*). Dense, bushy clumps of light green leaves and effective heads of puffy white

flowers. H1.2m/4ft, W60cm/2ft. F8-10. Z4-9.
E. purpureum. American Joe Pye weed. Stately, late-flowering background plant. Stiff stems with whorls of pointed leaves carry wide, flat, rose-purple flower heads. '**Atropurpureum**', deep purple heads. '**Album**', white flowers. H1.8-2.1m/6-7ft, W90cm/3ft. F8-10. Z3-9. Some new selections of dwarfer habit are worth noting, particularly '**Glutball**' with large heads of intense purple-red. H150cm/5ft, W60cm/2ft. F8-10. Z3-9.

EUPHORBIA Spurge
Among the spurges are some evergreen species with attractive winter foliage and early spring flowers. Most of these: ☀ ☀ ◪ ■
E. amygdaloides '**Rubra**'. Purple-leaved form of the wood spurge. Free-seeding evergreen foliage plant, with contrasting greenish yellow spring flowers. H30cm/1ft, W30cm/1ft. F4-5. Z7-9.
E. characias. Still confused with *E. wulfenii*. The former has brown centres to the greenish yellow flowers; the latter has yellow-centred flowers, carried in broader spikes and with broader leaves. Both have evergreen,

glaucous foliage and bushy growth habits; if stems die back to the base after flowering, prune away. H1.2m/4ft, W90cm/3ft. F3-5. Z7-10.

E. dulcis 'Chameleon'. Early spring growth. Clumps of purple leaves, followed by greenish yellow flowers. Foliage throughout year with good autumn colour. H45cm/18in, W30cm/1ft. F5-6. Z7-9.

E. myrsinites. Blue-grey, fleshy leaves closely set along trailing stems which carry heads of sulphur-yellow flowers. H15cm/6in, W30cm/1ft. F5-7. Z5-8.

E. robbiae. Evergreen ground cover. Rounded leaves forming attractive basal rosettes, and flattish heads of almost green flowers. Roots spread quite rapidly but are easily curbed. H50cm/20in, W50cm/20in. F3-5. Z8-9.

E. wulfenii. Yellow-green flowers, no brown centres, carried in broader spikes than *E. characias*. Sturdy habit, with glaucous leaves. Several named cultivars. Some dwarfer with nodding heads in early spring like 'Humpty Dumpty', compact blue-grey stems. H75cm/30in, W75cm/30in. F3-5. Z7-10. Some tall with enormous heads like 'Lambrook Gold' and 'Spring Splendour'. H1.5m/5ft, W90cm/3ft. F3-5. Z7-10.

Euphorbia wulfenii 'Humpty Dumpty'

GAURA

G. lindheimeri. Willowy, branching stems carry a long succession of small, pinkish white flowers. H1.2m/4ft, W90cm/3ft. F7-10. Z6-9. ☼ ■

GENTIANA Gentian

Some valuable perennials for late summer and autumn colour.
☼ ❁ ◪ ■ ★

G. asclepiadea. Willow gentian. Wiry stems, willow-like leaves, terminating in many pairs of deep blue trumpets. Colour varies a little; the form 'Alba' is white. H60-70cm/24-28in, W60cm/2ft. F8-10. Z6-9. ❁

GERANIUM Crane's bill

Deservedly popular perennials. Most flower in summer but some make quite a show in autumn. See also Alpines Directory, page 137. Most ☼ ☆

G. 'Ann Folkard'. Wide-spreading, with magenta-purple, saucer-shaped flowers. Yellow-tinged leaves early in the year. Excellent if allowed to scramble among other plants. H30cm/1ft, W30cm/1ft. F6-9. Z5-8.

G. macrorrhizum. Semi-evergreen sweet briar-scented leaves, colouring well in autumn, somewhat woody stems and short sprays of magenta flowers, 4cm/1½in across. The form

Geranium 'Russell Pritchard'

Helianthus salicifolius

album is white, 'Ingwersen's Variety', is soft pink, and 'Variegatum' has variegated leaves. 'Bevan's Variety', deep rose-pink flowers. Good, quick-spreading, weed-proof ground cover for sun or shade. All H25cm/10in, W60cm/2ft. F6-7. Z4-8.

G. procurrens. With self-rooting runners forms rapid ground cover of light green leaves and pale magenta flowers. H15cm/6in, W60cm/2ft. F6-10. Z5-8.

G. × *riversleaianum*. Long-flowering on wide-spreading stems, greyish leaves. 'Mavis Simpson', masses of light pink flowers. H30cm/1ft, W60-90cm/2-3ft. F 6-10. Z7-8. 'Russell Prichard', vivid magenta-rose, slightly greener foliage. Good for frontal or sloping positions with full sun. H15cm/6in, W45cm/18in. F6-10. Z6-8.

G. wallichianum 'Buxton's Variety'. Wonderful for a frontal position. Dense, deep green summer growth studded for weeks with lavender-blue, saucer-shaped flowers, white at the centre. H30cm/1ft, W90cm/3ft. F6-10. Z4-8. ☼ ■

HACQUETIA

H. epipactis. Uncommon, spring-flowering plant. Tight umbels of tiny,

sulphur-yellow flowers set in leafy bracts, followed by a mound of tufted, deeply lobed, dark green leaves. A rare form with variegated leaves is attractive. Humus-rich soil. H15cm/6in, W23cm/9in. F3-5. Z5-7. ❁ ◪ ★

HELIANTHUS Perennial sunflower

Many species and varieties, all with golden-yellow flowers, mostly in late summer and early autumn. ☼ ■

H. salicifolius (syn. *H. orygalis*). Distinctive for its long, willow-like stem, foliage and sprays of yellow flowers. Tall and for the larger garden. H2.1m/7ft, W60cm/2ft. F9-10. Z6-9.

HELLEBORUS Christmas rose, Lenten rose

One of the most important groups for winter and early spring colour. Cup- or bowl-shaped flowers with prominent stamens and thick petals. Subtle range of colours and colour combinations. Ideally a north-facing position without excessive competition from tree roots. Light mulch of humus to retain moisture. Hellebores resent disturbance, so young plants are most successful, flourishing for years if left alone.

Helleborus foetidus

Divided plants of *H. niger* are apt to sulk, producing only occasional flowers and little foliage thereafter, but it seldom varies from seed. A healthy plant remains evergreen at least until early winter. Most *orientalis* types make new sets of leaves after flowering, providing a shady canopy for the seeds to ripen slowly. Recent developments have produced some excellent, sought-after strains. ☼ ✳ ◪ ■ ☆

H. argutifolius (formerly *H. corsicus*). Evergreen, rather lax in habit, grey-green, attractively veined, divided leaves and large clusters of pale apple-green flowers. H60cm/2ft, W90cm/3ft. F3-5. Z7-9.

H. foetidus. Deep green, upright growth, fingered, dark evergreen leaves and greenish flowers with maroon-edged petals in spring. Not a long-lived plant but naturalizes by self-seeding freely. 'Wester Flisk', reddish stems, even more attractive. H60cm/2ft, W60cm/2ft. F2-4. Z6-9.

H. niger. Christmas rose. Nodding white flowers, often tinged greeny pink, and dark green, leathery leaves, usually flowers after Christmas until early spring. Resents being moved or divided. All H25-30cm/10-12in, W45cm/18in. F1-3. Z4-8.

H. x nigercors. Cross between *H. argutifolius* and *H. niger.* Handsome,

dark leaves, rather loose stems carrying sprays of open, creamy flowers. H30cm/1ft, W45cm/18in. F2-4. Z6-9.

H. orientalis. Lenten rose. Scarcely obtainable now in the true species, but hybrid strains are excellent, including white, greenish yellow, pink, maroon and blue-black shades, with many flowers delicately spotted crimson or pink. Some forms almost come true from seed, but there are named selections which must be grown from division. All are virtually evergreen, with new leaves following the flowers, and they make good ground cover. Cut away any tatty leaves before flowers start. H30-60cm/1-2ft, W30-60cm/1-2ft. F2-4. Z4-9.

HEUCHERA

Those with coloured foliage are useful for autumn, winter and early spring. Selection and breeding is beginning to show results with some – purple, cream, bronze and marbled leaves. When replanting, discard old woody sections; fibrous roots encourage free flowering.

☼ ✳ ◪ ■ ☆

H. micrantha. 'Palace Purple', excellent garden-worthy form with large, glossy, richly coloured, almost beetroot-red leaves, but is variable from seed. 'Bressingham Bronze', a reliable selection with large bronze-surfaced crinkled leaves, whitish flowers. H70cm/28in, W30cm/1ft. F6-8. Z4-8.

HOSTA Plantain lily

Many hostas remain interesting in late summer, if left alone by slugs! Dying leaves are often attractive, turning to gold and beige before collapsing. All Z3-9 ✳ ◪ ■ ★

IRIS

A few are certainly worthy plants for autumn, winter and early spring interest, although the majority are

Iris foetidissima 'Variegata'

Iris stylosa

summer flowering. Requirements depend on type.

I. foetidissima. Gladwyn or gladdon iris. Insignificant, buff-yellow flowers followed in autumn by decorative scarlet or orange seed pods, valued in dried-flower arranging. Grows almost anywhere, including dry shade under trees. H60-70cm/24-28in, W45cm/18in. Z5-9. 'Variegata', evergreen, creamy white variegated form, shows up brightly in winter, although seldom flowers. H50cm/20in, W45cm/18in. Z5-9.

I. pallida. Two variegated forms have year-round interest because their sword-like leaves remain attractive until frosts and start growing again in early spring. Rich, slightly alkaline soil. 'Argentea' (formerly *I. p.* 'Variegata'), white and grey striped leaves, and 'Variegata' (formerly *I. p.* 'Aurea Variegata'), golden-yellow stripes. Both have clear blue flowers. Both H60-75cm/24-30in, W30cm/1ft. F6-7. Z4-8.

I. stylosa (syn. *I. unguicularis*). Mainly winter-flowering iris, good for sunny, sheltered spot. Flowers occasionally in early autumn but freely through to mid-spring. Fragrant light blue flowers, deeper in 'Mary Barnard'. H30cm/1ft, W30cm/1ft. F1-3. Z8-9.

KNIPHOFIA Red hot poker

Indispensable for their architectural value, but some need plenty of space. Vary from 35cm/14in to 1.8m/6ft in height, flower from late spring to mid-autumn according to type. Plant in spring; pot-grown plants can be planted in autumn if protected in their first winter. Moist soil in summer.

☼ ■ ☆

K. 'Bressingham Comet'. Bright orange, red-tipped spikes, grassy leaves. H60cm/2ft, W45cm/18in. F8-10. Z6-9.

Kniphofia rooperi

K. caulescens. Large, yucca-like glaucous-leaved rosettes; stumpy, yellow-tipped red flower spikes. H70cm/28in, W60cm/2ft. F9-10. Z6-9.

K. 'Cobra'. Upstanding, long-flowering. Tight leaves, deep bronze in bud, changing through copper to creamy white. H90cm/3ft, W60cm/2ft. F8-10. Z6-9.

K. 'Little Maid'. Charming, narrow leaves, profuse, ivory-white spikes. H60cm/2ft, W45cm/18in. F7-9. Z5-9.

K. rooperi (syn. *K.* 'C.M. Prichard'). One of the latest to flower. Deep orange spikes rise from broad foliage. H1.5m/5ft, W60cm/2ft. F9-10. Z6-9.

LAMIUM Deadnettle
This genus includes useful ground cover, a few of greater garden value, some with evergreen leaves. ☀ ◩ ■
L. galeobdolon 'Florentinum' (syn. 'Variegatum'). Semi-evergreen, surface-rooting, rapid spreader good for wild garden. Silvery green leaves on straggly stems, brief, patchy show of yellow flowers in spring. H25-30cm/10-12in, W30cm/1ft. F5-6. Z4-8.
L. maculatum. Shallow-rooting ground cover, easy to curb if

necessary. Silver-pink speckled leaves, purplish pink flowers. 'Beacon Silver', excellent for leaf colour, silvered, semi-evergreen leaves, H15cm/6in deep pink flowers in early summer. 'White Nancy', similar foliage, pure white flowers. H15-30cm/6-12in, W60cm/2ft. F4-7. Z4-8.

LIRIOPE
Slow-spreading evergreen perennials. Broadly grassy, mostly deep green, leaves, erect spikes of bead-like lilac flowers from midsummer to mid-autumn. Some make good ground cover even in shade, but flower more freely in the open. Drought-resistant. ☀ ☀ ■

Lamium maculatum 'White Nancy'

L. muscari (syn. *L. macrophylla*). Most reliable selection for cooler temperate zones. Tussocks of deep green, blade-like leaves, fading slightly in winter. Bright display of short spikes set with grape hyacinth-like flowers of lilac-purple from late summer to late autumn. H30cm/1ft, W30cm/1ft. F8-10. Z6-10.

OMPHALODES Navelwort
Dwarf perennials for shade and ground cover. ☀ ☀ ◩ ■
O. cappadocica. Mounds of green leaves, pretty sprays of forget-me-not-type, bright blue flowers; several selections are similar. H13cm/5in, W30cm/1ft. F3-5. Z6-9.
O. verna. Blue-eyed Mary. Spreading mats, bright blue flowers, good under trees. 'Alba', white. H10cm/4in, W60cm/2ft. F3-4. Z6-9.

ORIGANUM Marjoram
Several worth growing as ornamentals, each very different. ☀ ■ ⊕
O. 'Herrenhausen'. Mauve-pink hybrid, rather lax habit. H60cm/2ft, W30cm/1ft. F7-10. Z5-8.
O. laevigatum. Dense, twiggy sprays of tiny, deep purple-violet flowers from late summer, small, rounded, glaucous leaves. 'Hopleys', brighter, deep blue flowers. H40cm/16in, W30cm/1ft. F8-10. Z5-9.
O. vulgare. Culinary marjoram. Insignificant flowers. Good ground cover. 'Aureum', more or less evergreen, golden-leaved form. H15cm/6in, W30cm/1ft. Z4-8.

PENSTEMON
Some hybrids have good, late display and are a deservedly popular group of semi-hardy perennials, which need protection in cold regions. Leafy spikes, continuous show of tubular flowers in many colours. Best planted in late spring or early summer; autumn-purchased plants need protection under glass.
All F6-10 unless noted otherwise.

All Z9-10. ☀ ◩ ■ ⋆
Hybrids include the following. 'Firebird', bright red. H40cm/16in, W45cm/18in. 'Garnet', wine-red. H50cm/20in, W45cm/18in. 'King George', salmon-red, white throat. H60cm/2ft, W45cm/18in. 'Hewell's Pink', light pink. H45cm/18in, W30cm/12in. 'Hidcote Pink', pink and red. H60cm/2ft, W45cm/18in. 'Rubicunda', large, warm red, white centre. H60cm/2ft, W45cm/18in. 'Sour Grapes', large, pale purple flowers, strong-growing. H70cm/28in, W45cm/18in. F6-9. 'Snowstorm', distinctive white flowers. H70cm/28in, W45cm/18in. F6-9.

Physalis franchetii

PHYSALIS Cape gooseberry, Chinese lantern
P. franchetii. Rapid, invasive spreader needing to be planted with care. Insignificant white flowers followed by bright orange inverted cones, or 'lanterns', in autumn, within each is a gooseberry-sized, orange berry. Excellent for drying and effective in patio container. H60-80cm/24-32in, W90cm/3ft. F8-10. Z5-8. ☀ ☀ ■

PHYSOSTEGIA Obedient plant
Useful, late-flowering. Squarish

stems, tubular flowers. Spreading but easy to curb. Frequent lifting, dividing and replanting advisable. ☼ ◩ ■ ☆

P. virginiana (syn. *P. speciosa*). '**Rose Bouquet**', rosy lilac. H80cm/32in, W60cm/2ft. F7-10. '**Summer Snow**', white. H70cm/28in, W60cm/2ft. F7-10. '**Variegata**', quite tall, lilac-pink spikes, variegated leaves. H50cm/20in, W45cm/18in. F8-10. '**Vivid**', much dwarfer and later, deep pink. H50cm/20in, W45cm/18in. F8-10.

POLYGONUM (syn. PERSICARIA) Knotweed

Some members of this family have a bad name, overshadowing the fact that there are many good garden plants, many with a very long flowering period. ☼ ✳ ◩ ■

P. affine. Good ground cover with shallow roots. Narrow, leathery leaves, bottlebrush flowers. H15-23cm/6-9in, W38cm/15in. F6-7. Z3-9. '**Darjeeling Red**', deep pink. H20cm/8in, W45-60cm/18-24in. F6-10. Z3-9. '**Dimity**', fuller, long-lasting pink, more reliable, good

autumn colour. H15cm/6in, W45cm/18in. F6-10. Z3-9. F6-7. Z3-9.

P. amplexicaule. Abundant, bushy growth, long succession of thin terminal spikes before dying back to a sturdy but not invasive root. H1.2m/4ft, W75cm/30in. F6-9. Z5-9. '**Arun Gem**' (syn. '**Pendula**'), distinct bright pink tassels dangling above a leafy, compact base. H30cm/1ft, W75cm/30in. F6-10. Z5-9. '**Atrosanguineum**', deep crimson. H1m/39in, W60cm/2ft. F6-9. Z5-9. '**Firetail**', outstanding bright red. H1.2m/4ft, W1.2m/4ft. F6-10. Z5-9. '**Taurus**', deepest crimson, larger, longest-lasting. H75cm/30in, W1.2m/4ft. F6-11. Z5-9.

P. campanulatum. Dense, leafy growth, light pink flower heads for weeks until the frost, from shallow, spreading roots. Good for dampish place. '**Rosenrot**', deep rose-pink. '**Southcombe White**', white. All H90cm/3ft, W90cm/3ft. F7-11. Z5-9.

P. milletii. Clumps of narrow leaves, intensely crimson-red pokers on and

Pulmonaria officinalis 'Sissinghurst White'

off all summer. Choice plant. Good, deep soil. H30cm/1ft, W30cm/1ft. Mainly F6-10. Z5-9.

POTENTILLA Cinquefoil

P. x tonguei. Flowers freely into autumn. Low clump of bronze-green leaves, prostrate rays of crimson-centred, apricot flowers for months. H10cm/4in, W45cm/18in. F6-10. Z5-7. ☼ ■

PRIMULA

Only a few of this enormous family can be selected for early spring flowering. Requirements depend on type.

P. denticulata. Drumstick primula. Dense, round heads of flowers on single stalks in spring. Colours range from white to mauve, lilac, lavender-blues and deep pink. Deep-rooting and long-lived. Propagate named selections by root cuttings. '**Alba**', many white forms. '**Rubin**', many with red drumstick flowers. '**Bressingham Beauty**', free-flowering powder-blue. H30-45cm/12-18in, W25cm/10in. F4-5. Z6-8. ☼ ✳ ◩ ■

P. rosea. Short sprays of bright pink flowers in early spring. Leaves open as these lengthen. '**Delight**', best cultivar. H25cm/10in, W25cm/10in. F3-5. Z6-8. ☼ ✳ ◩

P. vulgaris. Primrose. Cheerful yellow spring flowers. Divide regularly. Heavy soil. ☼ ◩ ■

Singles: '**Garryarde Guinevere**', purple-red; '**Wanda**' and '**Wisley Red**', bright red; '**Schneekissen**', briliant white; the form *sibthorpii* is pink. Doubles: '**Alan Robb**', apricot; '**Dawn Ansell**', white; '**Easter Bonnet**', prolific, large, lilac-blue flowers; '**Miss Indigo**', compact, purple-blue, edged white; '**Sue Jervis**', shell-pink. '**Sunshine Susie**', golden-yellow. All H10-15cm/4-6in, W15-25cm/6-10in. F3-5. Z5-8.

PULMONARIA Lungwort

First class early spring display. Ground-covering foliage, prettily spotted on many, lasts until the first hard frost. Good infill between deciduous shrubs. ☼ ✳ ◩ ■ ☆

P. angustifolia. Almost the first to flower in early spring. Narrow leaves follow the flowers. The form *azurea* is the earliest, intensely blue. '**Munstead Blue**', a shade deeper. All H15cm/6in, W30cm/1ft. F3-4. Z3-8.

P. longifolia. Conspicuously spotted leaves 15cm/6in long, blue flowers on terminal sprays; white in the form *alba*. '**Bertram Anderson**', deep violet-blue flowers. '**Roy Davidson**', lighter blue flowers. All H25cm/10in,

Polygonum amplexicaule 'Atrosanguineum'

W45cm/18in. F4-5. Z5-8.

P. officinalis 'Sissinghurst White', white sprays, white-spotted leaves. H25cm/10in, W60cm/2ft, F3-5, Z4-8.

P. rubra. Early flowering, coral-red blooms, evergreen leaves softer than most. 'Bowles' Red' is usually listed, but 'Redstart' is superior. H30cm/1ft, W60cm/2ft. F3-4. Z5-8.

P. saccharata. Bethlehem sage. Widest range of choice. Overlapping evergreen leaves. All Z4-8. 'Argentea', almost entirely silvered leaves. 'Highdown' (syn. 'Lewis Palmer'), outstanding for deep blue flowers, vigour and attractive foliage. 'Leopard', spotted summer leaves, deep rose-pink spring flowers. 'Pink Dawn', spotted silver all summer. All H25cm/10in, W60cm/2ft, F3-5, except 'Highdown', H30cm/1ft.

RUDBECKIA Cone flower, black-eyed Susan

Daisy-like flowers with central cone and rayed petals. ☼ ☀ ◪ ■ ☆

R. deamii. Wide clumps of grey leaves, masses of yellow flowers. H80cm/32in, W38cm/15in. F7-9. Z4-9.

R. 'Goldsturm'. One of the finest plants ever raised. Rayed, deep yellow, black-centred flowers for weeks. Dark green leaves on slow-spreading plants. H70cm/28in, W30cm/1ft. F6-10. Z4-9.

R. laciniata 'Goldquelle'. Leafy, deep green bushy growth covered in fully double, chrome-yellow flowers, 8cm/3in across. H1m/39in, W60cm/2ft. F7-10. Z3-9.

SALVIA

Some good garden plants in this vast genus, many of which flower non-stop until frosts. Some tender salvias are worth the extra care required to keep them over winter: the dwarf red *S. blepharophylla*, the silver-leaved, blue-flowered *S. farinacea*, the carmine-red *S. involucrata* 'Bethellii' and the taller red *S. neurepia* give a bright display. Most are best lifted, divided and replanted every three or four years. ☼ ■ ☆

S. ambigens (syn. *S. guaranitica* 'Blue Enigma'). Shapely bushes, small, deep green leaves, short spikes of royal blue flowers. Protect by covering with leaf mould, bark or

Saxifraga fortunei 'Rubrifolia'

litter in cold districts. H1.1m/43in, W45cm/18in. F7-10. Z5-8.

S. uliginosa. Tall, distinctive, late species. Delicate sprays of long-lasting, sky-blue flowers above deep green foliage. Warm, sheltered spot; needs supporting. H1.5m/5ft, W45cm/18in. F9-11. Z8-9.

SAXIFRAGA

Other saxifrages are described in Alpines Directory, page 138.

S. fortunei. Shallow-rooting rosettes of round, glistening leaves, red beneath, in spring and, in mid-autumn, airy sprays of starry white flowers. Light soil; give shelter, a light spring mulch and, in cold areas, some winter cover. H30-45cm/12-18in, W30cm/1ft. F10-11. Z4-7. 'Rubrifolia', reddish foliage. H25cm/10in, W20cm/8in. F10-11. Z6-7. 'Wada's Variety', almost beetroot-red leaves. H25cm/ 10in, W20cm/8in. F10-11. Z6-7. All ☀ ◪ ☆

SCABIOSA Scabious, pincushion flower

Many species and cultivars continue to flower well into autumn, particularly if dead flower heads are removed. Plant in spring. ☼ ■ ☆

S. 'Butterfly Blue'. Deep blue flowers all summer. Similar, but with pink

flowers is *S.* 'Pink Mist'. H30cm/1ft, W25cm/10in. F5-10. Z5-8.

S. caucasica. Valued for cutting. 'Blansiegel' ('Blue Seal'), vigorous light blue. 'Bressingham White' and 'Miss Willmott', good whites, the latter more ivory. 'Clive Greaves', prolific mid-blue. All H60-80cm/24-32in, W45-60cm/18-24in. F6-9. Z4-9.

S. graminifolia. Excellent for frontal groups. Dense mats of narrow, silver-grey leaves, long show of light blue flowers. H30cm/1ft, W30cm/1ft. F6-10. Z7-9. 'Pink Cushion', light pink, less robust. Light soil for both. H25cm/10in, W25cm/10in. F6-9. Z7-9.

SCHIZOSTYLIS Kaffir lily

Valuable for late flowering. Mats of spreading foliage, rush-like leaves, bright gladioli-like flowers. Cover with leaves or bark in cold districts, to protect in winter. ☼ ☀ ◪ ☆

S. coccinea. All Z6-9. The form *alba* has clean white flowers on slender stems. H60cm/2ft, W25cm/10in. F9-11. 'Major', fine crimson-red. H60cm/2ft, W25cm/10in. F9-11. 'Fenland Daybreak', bright green foliage, satin pink blooms. H60cm/2ft, W25cm/10in. F8-11. 'Mrs Hegarty', pale pink. H50cm/20in, W25cm/10in. F9-11. 'November Cheer', clear pink. H50cm/20in, W25cm/10in. F9-11. 'Snow Maiden', white. H50cm/20in, W25cm/10in. F10-11. 'Sunrise', almost salmon. H60cm/2ft, W25cm/10in. F9-11.

SEDUM Stonecrop

Some of these succulent-like perennials are indispensable for late summer and autumn colour, attracting bees and butterflies. Their flat heads remain interesting throughout winter. ☼ ■ ☆

S. 'Autumn Joy' (syn. 'Herbstfreude'). One of the best of all perennial plants. Spring growth of

Salvia uliginosa

glaucous, fleshy stems and leaves remaining attractive all summer. Glistening pink flower heads widen to 25cm/10in across, turning a deep bronze, then coppery red. Divide and replant regularly. H50cm/20in, W50cm/20in. F8-10. Z3-10.
S. spectabile. Fleshy glaucous foliage all summer before wide heads of bright pink flowers appear. **'Brilliant'**, wide, bright pink heads; **'Iceberg'**, pale foliage, creamy white flowers; **'Indian Chief'**, smaller heads, deeper rose-pink; **'September Glow'**, broad, glowing pink heads. All H30-40cm/12-16in, W30-40cm/12-16in. F8-10. Z4-9.

SERRATULA
Late fluffy flowers on stiff, branching stems, and deeply divided deep green leaves. ☀ ■ ✭
S. macrocephala. Shapely, bushy growth, profuse, small violet flowers. H30cm/1ft, W25cm/10in. F7-9. Z5-8.
S. seoanei (syn. *S. shawii*). Similar to above, more delicate leaves. H25cm/10in, W25cm/10in. F8-10. Z5-8.

SOLIDAGO Goldenrod
Wide range of easily grown perennials, some lasting into autumn and giving a splash of golden yellow. Ideal with blue asters. All Z4-9. ☀ ☀ ■

TRADESCANTIA
Easy growing with long-flowering season into autumn, although apt to be untidy by then. Bright, three-petalled flowers amid copious narrow foliage. Cultivars listed are hybrids of *T. virginiana* and other species.
☀ ☀ ✭
'Caerulea Plena', double light blue flowers. **'Carmine Glow'**, crimson flowers, neat habit. **'Iris Prichard'**, white flowers stained azure-blue. **'Isis'**, warm Oxford blue. **'Osprey'**, white, lilac-centred flowers. **'Pauline'**, light lilac-pink flowers. **'Purple**

Sedum spectabile 'Brilliant'

Dome', rich velvety purple flowers. All approx. H50cm/20in, W50cm/20in. F6-9. Z5-9.

TRICYRTIS Toad lily
Late show of distinctive flowers, most of which are spotted and bell-shaped.
☀ ☀ ◨
T. formosana. Clumpy plant, erect leafy stems carrying open heads of mauve, yellow-throated flowers with a hint of brown. H75cm/30in, W45cm/18in. F8-10. Z5-9. ☀
T. hirta. Near white, heavily spotted lilac flowers along stems; hairy leaves. The form **alba**, is less vigorous, pleasing white. Both H90cm/3ft, W60cm/2ft. F8-10. Z4-9.
T. macropoda. Purple-spotted, greenish yellow flowers, broad leaves. H1m/39in, W60cm/2ft. F9-10. Z5-9.
T. stolonifera. Vigorous spread, a little paler than *T. formosana.* H90cm/3ft, W60cm/2ft. F8-10. Z5-9.

VERBENA
Although long-flowering and useful, few verbenas are hardy. ☀ ■
V. bonariensis. Hardy plant making late contribution of form and colour. Little heads of lavender-blue, fragrant flowers above slender, sparsely leaved, branching stems. Pretty as a group. Not very long-lived, but self-seeds

freely. H1.5m/5ft, W60cm/2ft. F6-9. Z7-10.

VINCA Periwinkle
Evergreen ground cover, useful for foliage, and in *V. minor* for early flower. Some are invasive and wide-spreading. ☀ ☀ ☆
V. major. Greater periwinkle. Larger, rounded leaves and taller than *V. minor.* Blue flowers are sparse, but the bright foliage throughout winter in the cream-variegated **'Variegata'** (syn. 'Elegantissima') makes up for this. Both H30cm/1ft, W90cm/3ft. F4-5. Z7-9.
V. minor. Lesser periwinkle, trailing myrtle. Flowers more freely than *V. major.* Small dark green leaves. Many colours. **'Argenteovariegata'**, creamy white-edged leaves, blue flowers. **'Atropurpurea'**, reddish purple. **'Aureovariegata'**, golden-edged leaves, white flowers. **'Azurea Flore Pleno'**, double blue. **'Bowles' Variety'** (syn. 'La Grave'), the best, least rampant single, free-flowering blue. **'Gertrude Jekyll'**, free-flowering white, better than *alba.* **'Mutliplex'**, double reddish purple. All H15cm/6in, W60-90cm/2-3ft. F3-7. Z4-9.

YUCCA
Often listed as shrubs, these evergreen

plants, with their sword-like foliage, have considerable character and appeal through the winter. They are generally hardy and long-lived. ☀ ■
Y. filamentosa. Adam's needle. The most reliable species. Almost stemless, has evergreen, greyish foliage with hair-like fibres along the edges. Few variations, all with basically ivory-white, bell-shaped flowers most years. H1.5m/5ft, W1.5m/5ft. F7-8. Z5-10. **'Bright Edge'**, dark green, narrow leaves edged yellow. **'Golden Sword'**, light yellow-centred leaves with green edges. **'Variegata'**, covers perhaps more than one selection with green-centred, white- or yellowish-edged leaves, sometimes tinged pink. Variegated forms are less free to flower. Foliage reaching 60-90cm/2-3ft, W60-90cm/2-3ft. F7-8. Z5-9.

ZAUSCHNERIA
Showy, late-flowering, semi-shrubby perennials, fuchsia-like flowers. ☀ ■
Z. californica 'Glasnevin'. Grey-green leaves, intensely red flowers. H35cm/14in, W35cm/14in. F8-10. Z8-10.
Z. canescens. Twiggy summer growth, small grey leaves, brilliant, trumpet-shaped, orange-scarlet flowers. H35cm/14in, W35cm/14in. F8-10. Z8-10.

Yucca filamentosa

FERNS DIRECTORY

HARDY FERNS ARE SELDOM CONSIDERED as plants which have autumn and winter interest, but both the deciduous ferns, whose foliage often turns golden in autumn, and the evergreen ferns provide colour and form throughout winter. The latter, like the ornamental grasses, can be quite magical in their appearance as mist and frost play on their foliage. Hardy ferns are relatively easy to grow in the garden, some requiring some shade where not too dry, others being quite happy in sun. Only a few can be selected for inclusion in this book

H: Approximate height after 2 years
W: Approximate width after 2 years
F: Months in flower
Z: Relevant hardiness zone(s)

ADIANTUM Maidenhair fern
A. pedatum. American or northern maidenhair. Branching fronds made up of many toothed lobes on slender black stems. H45cm/18in, W30cm/1ft. Z3-8. ☀ ◢ ★

ASPLENIUM
Hardy, easily grown evergreens (formerly *Phyllitis* and *Scolopendrium*) growing well on lime soils. ☀ ◢
A. scolopendrium. Hart's tongue. British native. Long, leathery leaves. Given shade it is easy to grow, even in crevices or on walls. H up to 35cm/14in, W40cm/16in. Z4-8. 'Cristatum', curiously dissected crests on the light green fronds. H35cm/14in, W40cm/16in. Z4-8. 'Undulatum', narrow fronds with attractive wavy edges. H30-40cm/12-16in, W30-45cm/12-18in. Z4-8.

BLECHNUM Hard fern
B. spicant. Common hard fern, or deer fern. Produces two types of pinnate frond: arching, spreading, sterile ones and erect, spore-bearing, deciduous ones; both deep glossy green and highly ornamental. A clump-forming species for humus-rich soil but once established will succeed in less. H30-60cm/1-2ft, W45cm/18in. Z3-8. ★
B. tabulare. Shade lover, reliably

hardy only in mild districts or sheltered gardens. Forms a spreading mass of deep green leathery fronds. H30-100cm/1-3ft, W30-60cm/1-2ft. Z7-9. ☀ ◢

Blechnum tabulare

CYRTONIUM
C. falcatum. Holly fern. Attractive clump of erect, glossy deep green fronds. H60cm/2ft, W45cm/18in. Z7-9. ☀ ◢

DRYOPTERIS Buckler fern
In milder climates or winters many remain evergreen until spring or severe frosts. ☀ ◢
D. borreri (syn. *D. affinis* and *D. pseudomas*). 'Crispa' is a select form with arching, deep green, crisped fronds. The form *cristata* 'The King', a selection of the golden-scaled male fern, has evenly crested, arching fronds from a symmetrical

Dryopteris borreri 'Pinderi'

central crown. Tolerates dry soil. 'Pinderi' has narrow, deeply pinnate fronds of dark green, an attractive form. All H80-90cm/32-36in, W80-90cm/32-36in. Z4-8.
D. erythrosora. Japanese shield fern. Unusual pink- or bronze-tinged young fronds that mature to light green. Evergreen according to weather. H60cm/2ft, W30cm/1ft. Z5-9. ☀ ★

MATTEUCCIA Ostrich fern, shuttlecock fern
M. struthiopteris. Spectacular, with large, shapely fronds forming shuttlecock-like rosettes from stout stocks and spreading runners which are likely to colonize in rich, moist soil. The fertile fronds are dark brown in winter. H1m/39in, W60-90cm/2-3ft. Z2-8. ☀ ◢

POLYPODIUM Common polypody
P. cambricum. Mass of evergreen fronds in mounded clumps. Adaptable to fairly dry soil. H25cm/10in. W45-60cm/18-24in. Z5-8. ☀ ◢ ■
P. vulgare 'Pulcherrimum'. Good for ground cover and for rock gardens or wall crevices. The evergreen fronds are fresh green, tinted in autumn. Tolerant of dry soil but less vigorous in alkaline soil. H25cm/10in, W40cm/16in. Z5-8. ☀ ◢ ■

POLYSTICHUM Shield fern, holly fern
Evergreen ferns with large, broad fronds, many variations in their intricate form. Most are adaptable even where soil is poor, dry or limy, if given a good start. ☀ ☀ ◢ ■
P. aculeatum. Hard shield fern. Bold, deep, lacy, feathery fronds. H60-75cm/24-30in, W60cm/2ft. Z4-8.
P. polyblepharum. Year-round, elegant greenery with broad, shining fronds from hairy central crowns. Hardy and reliable. H50cm/20in, W30cm/1ft. Z5-8.
P. setiferum. Soft shield fern. Produces bulbils, or potential babies, along its midrib, adding to its charm. The several forms differ in the pattern of the broad, deeply cleft fronds, arching from a stout central crown. H up to 90cm/3ft, W90-120cm/3-4ft. Z5-8. 'Divisilobum', finely divided fronds, tolerates fairly dry conditions. H50cm/20in, W50cm/20in. Z5-8. 'Herrenhausen', dense clumps of spreading fronds of finely feathered, mid-green foliage. H45cm/18in, W75cm/2.5ft. Z5-8. 'Plumosum', soft, semi-prostrate, densely clothed, evergreen fronds. H30cm/1ft, W50cm/20in. Z5-8.

Polystichum setiferum 'Herrenhausen'

GRASSES DIRECTORY

ONE OF THE GREATEST ATTRIBUTES *of ornamental grasses, an increasingly appreciated group of plants, is their interest and beauty during autumn, winter and early spring. They can be planted with many different groups of plants, but they associate particularly well with perennials, conifers, heathers and shrubs, softening harsh or bright colours and adding their own in summer, with more subtle whites, browns and beiges in winter. Most of the grasses listed here are hardy and none of them is invasive. Container-grown plants can be planted at any time of year in free-draining soil, but most field-grown plants, which are sent out bare rooted, may not establish so it is best to purchase and plant these in spring. Although generally they tolerate a range of conditions, they mostly prefer well-drained soil.*

H: Approximate height
W: Approximate width
F: Months in flower
Z: Relevant hardiness zone(s)

Bouteloua gracilis seen here in winter

ACORUS
A. gramineus 'Ogon'. Not strictly a grass but looks like one with rush-like foliage. Narrow, gold and green leaves arching in fan-like sprays are almost brighter in winter than summer. 'Variegatus', less showy with white and green striped leaves. Both H20cm/8in, W30cm/1ft. Z4-10. ☼ ✳ ◩

ANDROPOGON
A. scoparius. Upright, shapely, slow-growing evergreen, with narrow blades of a bluish coppery hue particularly in autumn. Light soil. H60cm/2ft, W60cm/2ft. Z5-8. ☼

BOUTELOUA Mosquito grass
B. gracilis (syn. *B. oligostachya*). Short sprays of curious, brownish flower spikes, at right angles to the stems, resembling hovering mosquitoes, above a tufty, semi-evergreen, deep green base. Attractive in winter frost. H25cm/10in, W20cm/8in. F6-8. Z5-9. ☼ ◩ ★

BRIZA Common quaking grass
B. media. Small clump with panicles of tiny, greenish purple, locket-like flowers which nod in a breeze. The flowers are popular for drying. Best where not too dry. H60cm/2ft, W30cm/1ft. F6-8. Z5-9. ☼ ■ ★

CALAMAGROSTIS
C. x acutiflora. 'Karl Foerster'. Attractive hybrid with erect habit, rich green foliage followed by plum-brown spikes which remain until spring. H1.5m/5ft, W60cm/2ft. F7-8. Z5-9.

CAREX Sedge
Low-growing, mostly clump-forming plants with much year-round interest. ✳ ◩ ★
C. buchananii. Leatherleaf sedge. Evergreen, erect tufts of unusual, coppery brown, thin, needly blades,

reddish towards the base. H60cm/2ft, W20cm/8in. Z6-9.
C. comans. More mounded, wide-spreading habit. The thin, dense growth has a decidedly light brownish hue, held all year round. Flowers are not conspicuous. There are various forms of the species. 'Bronze', deep bronze-green foliage. Very similar in form but classed as a hybrid is 'Frosted Curls' which looks, even in summer, as though its narrow foliage is frosted with creamy white. All H45cm/18in, W60cm/2ft F6-8. Z6-9.
C. morrowii (syn. *C. oshimensis*). 'Evergold' is one of the brightest year-round plants, forming large clumps with narrow, shiny, dark green leaves, striped golden-yellow. H25cm/10in, W60cm/2ft. Z7-9.
C. testacea. Another hummock type, similar to *C. comans* but with wide-spreading leaves, yellow-green in summer, bronze-green in winter. H45cm/18in, W90cm/3ft. F6-8. Z6-9.

CHIONOCHLOA
C. rubra. Finely spaced, arching leaves rounded and graceful in habit, olive-green in summer, bronzed in winter. H60cm/2ft, W60cm/2ft. F7-8. Z7-9.

CORTADERIA Pampas grass
Spectacular flowering grasses, unsuitable for the smaller garden. Evergreen in mild climates, but die back to ground in cold ones. Plumes excellent for drying. ☼ ◩ ✪
C. selloana. Several variations, from 1.5m/5ft to 3m/10ft high, making large clumps and silvery white plumes in autumn which, particularly in 'Pumila' and others in sheltered situations, last until spring. 'Gold Band', narrow, golden-green striped leaves and silvery plumes. H1.8m/6ft, W1.2m/4ft. F9-10. Z8-10. 'Silver Comet', leaves margined white and a good display of flowers,

Deschampsia caespitosa 'Golden Dew'

Festuca glauca 'Blue Glow'

Cortaderia selloana 'Pumila'

but needs a warm, sheltered spot. H1.5m/5ft, W90cm/3ft. F9-10. Z8-10. **'Sunningdale Silver'**, strong-stemmed, finely plumed, free-flowering. H2.5-3m/8-10ft, W1.8m/6ft. F9-11. Z7-10.

DESCHAMPSIA Tufted hair grass
D. caespitosa. Large tufts of narrow, deep green leaves and sheaves of very graceful spikes, valuable for autumn and winter interest. Self-seeds freely. ☼ ❋ ◪ **'Bronze Veil'** (syn. 'Bronzeschleier'), effective bronze plumes. **'Gold Veil'** (syn. 'Goldschleier'), strong, clumpy

evergreen with plumes of green stems and flowers which turn a warm golden-yellow. H90cm/3ft, W90cm/3ft. F6-8. Z4-9. **'Golden Dew'** (syn. 'Goldtau'), similar growth with fountains of green stems and flowers which mature to a rich golden-brown. Good, compact form. H70cm/28in, W50cm/20in. F6-9. Z4-9.

FESTUCA Fescue
F. glauca. Blue fescue. Neat, bluish evergreen tufts, useful as edging, ground cover or frontal groups. Several selections worth looking for: **'Blue Glow'** (syn. 'Blauglut'), striking silver-blue leaves and a good show of flowers; **'Elijah Blue'**, compact, silver-blue. Colour good into winter. Best divided every two or three years. Average H25cm/10in, W25cm/10 in. F6-7. Z4-8. ☼

HAKONECHLOA
H. macra **'Alboaurea'.** One of the best dwarf grasses. Although not evergreen has winter interest in beige pendulous foliage. Spring brings a lovely show of green- and yellow-striped leaves, gradually ageing to reddish brown and effective until late autumn. Plants spread slowly,

appreciating good soil. Excellent in a container as a patio plant. H25cm/10in, W38cm/15in. F8-9. Z7-9. ☼

LUZULA Woodrush
L. sylvatica. Greater woodrush. Bright green leaves, slow-spreading, tufted habit, and open heads of greenish flowers. Good ground cover for dry shade. **'Marginata'** (syn. 'Aureomarginata'), white leaf margins. Attractive in winter. Both H30cm/1ft, W30cm/1ft. F5-6. Z5-9.

MISCANTHUS Silver grass
Some first class selections with great autumn and winter appeal through flower and foliage. Heights range between 60cm/2ft and 3m/10ft, nearly all are clump-forming, making annual growth of bladed leaves, some green-silver or variegated. Although none is evergreen, the foliage remains attractive over winter. Cut back foliage in spring. They flower best in hot summers. Some good selections, mainly raised by Ernst Pagels in northern Germany, flower regularly in cooler, northerly climates. A number are quite dwarf. ☼ □ ☀
M. sinensis. Chinese silver grass.

Miscanthus sinensis 'Cascade'

Ample green- and silver-striped foliage but seldom planted. H1.8m/6ft, W90cm/3ft. F7-9. Z5-10. Its many erect-growing and non-invasive cultivars are more garden-worthy. All Z5-10. **'Cascade'** (syn. 'Kaskade'), pendulous, silvery white flowers. H1.2m/4ft, W60cm/12ft. F8-10, **'Flamingo'**, deep crimson flowers fading white. H1.2m/4ft, W60cm/2ft. F8-10. **'Gracillimus'**, elegant, narrow leaves, a shapely habit, seldom flowers in autumn. H1.5/5ft, W45cm/18in. F7-9. **'Kleine Fontane'**, tall, free-flowering with pendulous, silver

heads. H1.5/5ft, W90cm/3ft. F7-10. '**Malepartus**', vigorous, broad, silver-striped leaves, crimson flowers fading pink then beige. H1.8m/6ft, W90cm/3ft. F8-10. '**Morning Light**', outstanding variegated Japanese selection, compact, densely foliaged, silver and white. Needs heat to flower. H1.2m/4ft, W60cm/2ft. F9-10. '**Purpureus**', reddish leaves, profuse but small flowers. H1.2m/4ft, W60cm/2ft. F8-9. '**Silver Feather**', sprays of white flowers arching above luxuriant green foliage. Majestic where space allows. H2.4m/8ft, W90cm/3ft, F8-10. '**Variegatus**', stately and brightly variegated with vertical white stripes. H1.5m/5ft, W90cm/3ft. '**Zebrinus**', or zebra grass, lateral bands of gold across green leaves. H1.5m/5ft, W90cm/3ft.
M. yakushimensis. Dwarf, late-flowering with erect, beige plumes. H90cm/3ft, W60cm/2ft. F9-10.

MOLINIA Moor grass

M. altissima.(syn. *M. litoralis*). Strong-growing, free-flowering, good autumn colour as stems fade. The terminal flower sprays are greenish purple, turning brown in autumn. Some good selections: '**Fontane**', pendulous heads; '**Transparent**', slender stems, wispy flower heads; '**Windspiel**', smaller heads, all turning golden brown autumn colours. All 1.5-1.8m/5-6ft, W45cm/18in. F8-10. Z5-9.
M. caerulea. Purple moor grass. British native for damp, acid soils. '**Moorhexe**', a good green-leaved selection with purplish flower heads, brown in autumn. H40cm/16in, W40cm/16in. F8-9. Z5-9. '**Variegata**', stout clumps of soft, deciduous, creamy yellow-green leaves and long-lasting, small, purplish buff flowers. Prefers a light, deep soil and sun. H60cm/2ft, W60cm/2ft. F7-10. Z5-9.

Molinia altissima 'Transparent'

Stipa gigantea

PANICUM Switch grass

P. virgatum '**Rubrum**'. Clump-forming, narrow, erect reddish autumn foliage, panicles of airy reddish brown seed heads. H1.2m/4ft, W60cm/2ft. F8-9. Z5-9. ☼ □ ★

PENNISETUM

Large, deciduous tussocks, but not all produce their bottlebrush flowers freely. Long, arching and narrow grey-green leaves. ☼ □ ☆
P. alopecuroides (syn. *P. compressum*). Shy to flower in cool temperate zones but '**Hameln**' and '**Woodside**' are much freer, and their flowers attractive well into winter. All H90cm/3ft, W60cm/2ft. F8-10. Z5-10.
P. orientale. Hairy leaves, tufty growth. Its bottlebrush, silvery pink flowers are long-lasting and reliable fading to grey. H45cm/18in, W30cm/1ft. F7-9. Z6-9.

STIPA Feather grass, needle grass

S. arundinacea. Compact clump of narrow-leaved, arching, bronze-green stems, diffuse, brownish flowers. Foliage tinged red, bronze, yellow and orange in winter. H45cm/18in, W60cm/2ft. F7-9. Z7-9. ☼ ◩ ☆
S. calamagrostis. Clump-forming species which flowers freely with dense, buff-white plumes which arch gracefully. H1.2m/4ft, W60cm/2ft. F7-9. Z5-10.
S. gigantea. Imposing specimen clumps. Narrow green leaves above which tall stems remain erect, carrying oat-like flowers for months which are still attractive in winter. H1.8-2.1m/6-7ft, W60-75cm/24-30in. F6-10. Z5-10.
S. tenuifolia. A beautiful ornamental grass forming a dense, grassy, deep green clump which is topped in mid-summer by fluffy plumes which turn from beige to white. H60cm/2ft, W45cm/18in. F6-9. Z7-10.

HEATHS AND HEATHERS DIRECTORY

ALTHOUGH THEY ARE CLASSED AS EVERGREEN SHRUBS, heaths and heathers stand alone as a group which, where they can be grown successfully, can have a tremendously colourful impact the year round but especially in winter. Even for those who do not have acid soil and therefore are not be able to grow the summer-flowering types, there are many lime tolerant winter-flowering ones to choose from.

Heathers have a wide selection of flower colour as well as a vast range of foliage colour – shades of green, bronze, gold, yellow, orange, crimson, grey and silver – which often changes with the seasons and, given sunny situations, lights up the winter garden. They can be used as frontal groups to shrub beds or borders, as edging for paths or as a heather garden. Smaller-growing cultivars are ideal with alpines or dwarf shrubs in rock gardens. They can be used in window boxes, containers and raised beds. Heathers and slow-growing conifers complement one another particularly well, the various forms, textures and colours of the latter providing dramatic contrast. Heathers work well with ornamental grasses, too.

Well over 500 cultivars are currently in cultivation and wider selections can be found from specialists. Those described here are some of the most outstanding in my experience. As a guide to planting densities, the approximate widths of heathers after only 3-4 years are given, this being the period within which plants will have matted together. All require well-drained, humus-rich soil.

H: Approximate height after 8-10 years
W: Approximate width after 3-4 years
F: Months in flower
Z: Relevant hardiness zone(s)

Massed heathers make a striking display in early spring

Calluna vulgaris 'Anne Marie'

CALLUNA **Common heather, ling**
C. vulgaris. Hundreds of cultivars of this heathland plant offer an amazing range of colours, shapes and sizes. Prune all except the dwarfest and very prostrate types in early to mid-spring, before growth really begins. All flowers are single unless otherwise stated. All Z5-7. ☀ ⊖
'**Allegro**', profusion of deep red flowers, dark green foliage. H45-60cm/18-24in, W45cm/18in. F8-10.
'**Anne Marie**', bushy habit, dark green foliage. Flowers open bright pink, gradually deepening to brilliant carmine-rose. H23-30cm/9-12in, W45cm/18in. F8-11. '**Beoley Gold**', one of the best yellow-foliaged cultivars, bushy year-round foliage, contrasting white flowers. H30-45cm/12-18in, W45cm/18in. F8-9. '**Boskoop**', superb, dense, feathery foliage, golden-orange in summer, bronze-red in winter. Light mauve-purple flowers. H30-45cm/12-18in, W45cm/18in. F8-9.
'**Dark Beauty**', compact, bushy

Calluna vulgaris 'Boskoop'

plant, dark green foliage, bright crimson flowers over long period in autumn. H30cm/12in, W30-45cm/12-18in. F8-10. **'Golden Carpet'**, low, prostrate mat of golden-yellow foliage, tinged bronze and red in winter. Mauve flowers often sparse. H10cm/4in, W40cm/16in. F8-9. **'Golden Feather'**, first-class foliage form, bright gold, feathery summer foliage, turning reddish orange in winter. Occasional mauve flowers. H30-45cm/12-18in, W45cm/18in. F8-10. **'H.E. Beale'**, vigorous, with strong, erect spikes of soft, double, silver-pink flowers lasting for weeks. H30-45cm/12-18in, W50cm/20in. F9-11. **'Peter Sparkes'**, similar to 'H.E. Beale', but with double, much deeper, pink flowers on sturdy, erect spikes. H45-60cm/18-24in, W45cm/18in. F9-10. **'Robert Chapman'**, changes from gold to yellow, orange to bronze and red. Lower winter temperatures enhance the colour intensity. Purple flowers. H30-45cm/12-18in, W45cm/18in. F8-9. **'Sir John Charrington'**, arguably the best foliage cultivar, compact and bushy, golden-yellow foliage, orange with bright red and crimson tips in winter. Excellent in bloom, with short spikes of crimson flowers. H30-45cm/12-18in, W40cm/16in. F8-9.

DABOECIA Irish bell heather
Summer-flowering. ⊖

D. cantabrica. Long flowering period, glossy green leaves and bell-shaped flowers. Resent drought almost as much as severe frost, but where they can be grown offer a contrast to other heathers. Stronger-growing cultivars can get straggly with age and should be pruned each year, either lightly once the flowers have finished in late autumn, then more severely in spring, or, preferably, leave it all until spring. All Z7. ☼ ☀ ◢

Calluna vulgaris and *Erica × darleyensis* 'Ghost Hills'

Erica carnea 'Pink Spangles'

'Atropurpurea', one of the hardiest and most reliable. Bronze-green leaves, rich purple flowers. H60cm/2ft, W50cm/20in. F6-10. **'Snowdrift'**, bright green foliage, masses of white bell flowers. H45cm/18in, W45cm/18in. F6-10. *D.* x *scotica* **'William Buchanan'**. One of several dwarf hybrids between *D. azorica* and *D. cantabrica.* Glossy green leaves, masses of crimson flowers. One of the hardiest cultivars. H30cm/1ft, W30cm/1ft. F5-10. Z7.

ERICA Heath
E. carnea (syn. *E. herbacea*). Winter heaths are among the most valuable garden plants. Most cultivars are low-growing with a bushy or spreading habit, and flower from late autumn to late spring, some lasting several months. Very few need pruning, except to prevent spreading into other plants or to tidy them occasionally. All Z5-7. All ⊖; some ⊕ **'Ann Sparkes'**, superb foliage sport of 'Vivellii', slowly makes a compact bush of deep orange-yellow foliage, tipped bronze-red. Deep carmine-red flowers. H15cm/6in, W25cm/10in. F2-4. **'Eileen Porter'**, reputedly less hardy than some, but has endured temperatures of -20°C/-4°F in my garden. Out-performs all others in length of flowering. Rich carmine flowers, producing a bicoloured effect. H15-20cm/6-8in, W25cm/10in. F10-5. **'Foxhollow'**, low-growing, spreading habit. One of the finest foliage heathers, brilliant golden-yellow foliage in late spring and summer, deep gold in winter, often flecked with red. In low-lying areas, new growth can be caught by late spring frost. Pale pink flowers, rarely borne. H15-25cm/6-10in, W45cm/18in. F2-4. **'King George'**, compact, bushy habit, dark green leaves, bright pink flowers, rose-red with age. Always reliable, one of the best. H20-25cm/8-10in,

W30cm/1ft. F12-3. '**Myretoun Ruby**', magnificent, smothering display of deep ruby-red flowers. Dark green foliage. H30cm/1ft, W35cm/14in. F3-4. '**Pink Spangles**', first-class spreader, large, bicoloured, pink and cream flowers, deepening to rose-pink. H20-30cm/8-12in, W35cm/14in. F1-3. '**Springwood White**', excellent ground cover, spreading, bright apple-green foliage. Roots as it goes, may need curbing. Smothered in pure white blooms. H20-30cm/8-12in, W60cm/2ft. F2-4. '**Vivellii**' (syn. 'Urville'), attractive for foliage and flower. Dark, bronze-green foliage, ideal against gold, silver or blue evergreen plants. Deep carmine-red flowers. H10cm/4in, W35cm/14in. F2-3. '**Westwood Yellow**', similar to 'Foxhollow' but more compact, flowers more freely. H15cm/6in, W40cm/16in. F2-4.
E. cinerea. Bell heather. Grows on cliffs by the sea, on moorlands and mountains, surviving with less moisture than most species. Long flowering period, as with some of the cultivars. Late flowers, attractive in winter even when flowering has finished and some with colourful foliage. Prune in spring, just as new growth begins. All Z7. ☼
'**Eden Valley**', bushy and compact, soft lavender and white bicoloured flowers. H15-20cm/6-8in, W25cm/10in. F7-10. '**Purple Beauty**', easy and reliable, with bushy, spreading habit, dark green foliage, large, bright purple flowers, one of my favourites. H30cm/1ft, W40cm/16in. F6-10. '**Rock Pool**', low, spreading form, deep golden-yellow foliage in summer, rich copper-bronze, often with red tints, in winter. Occasional purple-red flowers. Excellent contrast to blue spruce. H15cm/6in, W25cm/10in. F7-9. '**Windlebrooke**' similar to 'Rock Pool' but brighter yellow foliage in summer, orange-yellow in

Erica arborea 'Albert's Gold' with *Erica carnea* 'Pink Spangles'

winter. Purple flowers. H25-30cm/10-12in, W30cm/1ft. F7-9.
E. x darleyensis. First-class cultivars from an original cross between *E. carnea* and *E. erigena*. Excellent ground cover in broad drifts or on banks. Prune only to tidy up any unkempt growth, if necessary. All Z7-8. Tolerate ⊕
'**Arthur Johnson**', reputedly a hybrid between *E. erigena* 'Glauca' and *E. carnea*, taller than others, making a looser plant with long, narrow stems, dark green foliage and pink flowers. Superb garden plant, useful for cutting. H60-75cm/24-30in, W60cm/2ft. F11-4. '**Darley Dale**', robust, spreading dark green bush, profuse pale mauve-pink flowers, untroubled except by severe frosts. Somewhat similar are '**George Rendall**' (F12-3), '**Furzey**' (F1-4) and '**Ghost Hills**' (F11-4). All H30-45cm/12-18in, W50cm/20in. '**Jack H. Brummage**', bright golden-yellow foliage in summer in full sun, orange-gold in winter. Bright pink flowers. H30-45cm/12-18in, W40cm/16in. F1-4. **Kramer's Red**, deep green leaves, long-flowering truly red flowers. H25-30cm/18-12in. F10-4. '**Silberschmelze**' (syn. 'Molten Silver'), formerly appeared

under various names such as 'Silver Beads', 'Silver Bells' and 'Silver Mist'. Similar to 'Darley Dale' but has silvery white, sweetly scented flowers over long period. H30-45cm/12-18in, W50cm/20in. F12-4.
E. erigena. Irish heath. Useful garden plants, although less hardy than some winter-flowering species. Long flowering period, honey-scented. The species varies in height from 60cm/2ft to 2.4m/8ft, although most modern cultivars are compact and bushy. All Z8. Tolerate ⊕
'**Golden Lady**', a sport of 'W.T. Rackliff'. Dense bush, year-round bright yellow, colours well in light shade. Sparse white flowers. Shoots can revert to green. Prone to sunscorch in exposed situations. H45-60cm/18-24in, W35cm/14in. F4-5. '**Irish Dusk**', compact and bushy, erect branches of dark to mid-green foliage and deep salmon-pink flowers. Older plants can get open and woody. H45-60cm/18-24in, W40cm/16in. F12-5.
'**W.T. Rackliff**', dense, rounded rich green bush, white flowers. H60-75cm/24-30in, W40cm/16in. F3-5.

E. vagans. Cornish heath. Old flower heads remain attractive through winter and although frost damage can occur plants usually sprout from the base in spring. Prune in spring just as new growth begins. All Z7-8. ☼ ☀ Tolerates some ⊕
'**Cream**' and '**Cornish Cream**', creamy white flowers, the latter with longer spikes. H45cm/18in, W50cm/20in. F8-10. '**Lyonesse**', light green leaves, reliable annual show of white flowers with golden anthers. The faded, buff heads are equally attractive. H45cm/18in, W45cm/18in. F8-10. '**Mrs D.F. Maxwell**', perhaps the most outstanding of all the cultivars, neat, mounded habit, sprays of deep cerise-pink flowers. H45-60cm/18-24in, W40cm/16in. F8-10. '**Valerie Proudley**', slow-growing, compact, bright yellow bush. Good in light shade; can scorch in exposed positions. Flowers white but seldom occur. H15-20cm/6-8in, W35cm/14in. F8-9.

TREE HEATHS
Provide the height lacking in most other heathers, and have a flowering period that knits together the late winter- and spring-flowering types with the earliest summer ones. In exposed spots and colder regions can suffer damaged or broken foliage. In sheltered positions make magnificent, free-flowering plants, useful for cutting. Some are sweetly scented. All ☼ ☀; most ⊕ ⊖
E. arborea. '**Albert's Gold**', remarkably hardy, upright branches, bright golden-yellow foliage, tolerant of cold winds and frost. White flowers a bonus. Ultimate H1.5-1.8m/5-6ft, W60-75cm/24-30in. F3-5. Z8. '**Estrella Gold**', slow-growing, less bright bush, greeny yellow foliage, white flowers. H90-120cm/3-4ft, W60-75cm/24-30in. F3-5. Z8.

ALPINES DIRECTORY

USUALLY REFERRED TO AS ALPINES OR SOMETIMES AS ROCK PLANTS, this group of plants is a diverse one that can be confusing to beginner and expert alike. Many of the plants offered by garden centres in this category are not necessarily native to mountainous regions, but are usually of dwarf or compact stature and really can be classed as dwarf perennials. In their natural habitat, most either die back in autumn or spend the winter covered by snow, and flower from early spring onwards. The majority, therefore, are somewhat limited in appeal during the period covered by this book.

In addition to those that do flower early enough to be included here, I have included those that have some interesting foliage during the quiet season, such as houseleeks, sempervivums, dianthus, raoulias and thymes. All of these have an invaluable contribution to make to alpine or scree gardens when interplanted with dwarf shrubs and dwarf conifers. They all have another season of interest as well. Most alpines prefer reasonable drainage and all those mentioned can be safely planted in autumn unless otherwise indicated.

H: Approximate height after 2 years
W: Approximate width after 2 years
F: Months in flower
Z: Relevant hardiness zone(s)

A group of alpines, perennials and dwarf shrubs add colour in spring

ACAENA New Zealand burr
Creeping, semi-evergreen plants with finely cut leaves, small flowers and rounded burr-like seed heads. Best as ground cover or between paving as can be invasive. Several forms. ☼ ☀ ■
A. 'Blue Haze'. Good foliage, bluish grey leaves, brown burrs. H10cm/4in, W60cm/2ft. F7-8. Z6-8.
A. microphylla. One of the best. Coppery bronze mats, reddish flowers and burrs. H2.5cm/1in, W60cm/2ft. F7-9. Z5-8.

Ajuga reptans 'Braunherz'

AJUGA Bugle
Creeping, semi-evergreen, flowering plants, colourful ground cover between taller plants. ☼ ☀ ◪ ☆
A. reptans. Common bugle. Green leaves. Best foliage selections are **'Braunherz'**, glossy purple-bronze leaves, blue flowers, and **'Burgundy Glow'**, wine-red, bronze and cream leaves, pale blue flowers. H15cm/6in, W30-45cm/12-18in. F5-6. Z3-9.

ALYSSUM Gold dust
A. saxatile (correctly *Aurinia saxitalis*). Early spring-flowering alpines, ideal for banks, walls and frontal groups. **'Citrinum'**, grey-green leaves, lemon-yellow flowers; **'Dudley Neville'**, compact, silvery leaves, primrose-yellow flowers. **'Dudley Neville Variegated'**, creamy edges to leaves. All H25cm/10in, W45cm/18in. F4-6. Z3-7. ☼ ■

ARABIS Rock cress
Showy, spring-flowering, taller forms, good for banks or over walls. ☼ ■
A. caucasica. White flowers well above grey-green leaves. **'Plena'**, double white flowers. **'Corfe Castle'**, deep magenta. **'Variegata'**, single white flowers, creamy-edged white foliage. H20cm/8in, W45cm/18in. F3-5. Z4-7.
A. ferdinandi-coburgii. Mat-forming rosettes, white flowers. Best are **'All Gold'**, gold and green leaves, and **'Variegata'**, creamy variegations. H10cm/4in, W20cm/8in. F4-6. Z5-7.

ARMERIA Thrift
Evergreen, grassy-leaved hummocks, flowers in late spring. ☼ ■
A. caespitosa (syn. *A. juniperifolia*). First alpine thrift to bloom, pink. **'Alba'**, white. **'Bevan's Variety'**, bright pink. H10cm/4in, W15-20cm/6-8in. F4-7. Z4-8.

Aubrieta 'Bressingham Pink'

AUBRIETA

Wonderfully coloured flowers in spring for frontal groups, slopes or over walls, but of no value for rest of the year. Clip back after flowering. Seed-raised varieties are less effective than good named cultivars. 'Alix Brett', double, carmine-purple. 'Bob Saunders', double, reddish purple. 'Bressingham Pink', single, bright pink. 'Dr. Mules', single, violet-purple. 'Red Carpet', best single red. 'Silver Edge', leaves narrowly margined with cream, blue flowers. Average H10-15cm/4-6in, W30-45cm/12-18in. F4-6. Z5-8. ☼ ■

AZORELLA

A. trifurcata (syn. *Bolax glebaria*). Dense mats of glossy evergreen rosettes with small, yellow flowers. H5cm/2in, W25cm/10in. F6-7. Z6-7. ☼ □

DIANTHUS Rock pinks

Includes perennial and alpine types. Although few of the alpines flower in the autumn to spring period, many provide attractive mats or hummocks of silver or grey foliage for the scree garden. Many suitable for troughs. Slightly alkaline soil for most. Average H5-15cm/2-6in, W10-30cm/4-8in. F5-7. Z4-8. ☼ ■

DRABA

Cushions of green foliage, bright yellow flowers in early spring. Good for alpine house. Gritty soil. All Z4-6. ☼ ■
D. aizoides. Easy to grow from seed. H5cm/2in, W20cm/8in. F3-5.
D. bruinifolia. Miniature hummocks. H8cm/3in, W20cm/8in. F3-5.

ERIGERON Dwarf fleabane

E. karvinskianus (syn. *E. mucronatus*). Long-flowering, self-seeding, dwarf perennial with masses of small, daisy-like pink flowers for months. H15-20cm/6-8in, W30cm/1ft. F6-10. Z5-7. ☼ ■

GENTIANA Gentian

Classic alpines flowering in summer or autumn. Acid soil for autumn-flowering types, slightly alkaline for spring-flowering. ☼ ✹ ◩ ■ ★
G. acaulis. Trumpet gentian. Large, deep blue flowers nestling above green mats. H10cm/4in, W30-45cm/12-18in. F3-5. Z4-7.
G. verna. Spring gentian. Small, deep azure blue flowers. H8cm/3in, W15cm/6in. F3-5. Z4-7.

G. x *macaulayi* 'Kingfisher'. Brilliant deep blue tumpets in autumn on bright green mats. H10cm/4in, W20cm/8in. F8-10. Z5-7.
G. sino-ornata. Deep sky blue flowers in autumn. 'Alba', white. 'Angel's Wings', bright blue, striped white. H10cm/4in, W20cm/8in. F8-10. Z5-7.

GERANIUM

Some forms repeat bloom in autumn until frosts arrive. See also Perennials Directory, page 123. Most ☼ ☆
G. cinereum. 'Ballerina' and 'Laurence Flatman', lilac-pink flowers veined with darker colour; the latter is much deeper, at times crimson. H15cm/6in, W30cm/1ft. F5-10. Z5-8.

IBERIS Candytuft

Sub-shrubby, glossy, evergreen foliage. Brilliant white flowers in early summer. Good for banks and walls. ☼ ■
I. 'Little Gem' (syn. 'Weisser Zwerg'). Compact shrub for alpine scree, not always long-lived. H15cm/6in, W30cm/1ft. F5-7. Z3-9.

Iberis sempervirens 'Snowflake'

I. sempervirens (syn. *I. commutata*). Vigorous, ground cover. H15cm/6in, W60cm/2ft. F4-6. Z3-9. 'Snowflake' is less spreading.

LYSIMACHIA Loosestrife

L nummularia 'Aurea'. Golden form of creeping Jenny. Spreading mat of yellow foliage, attractive from early spring to late autumn. Yellow, buttercup flowers are hardly noticeable. H5cm/2in, W60cm/2ft. F6-7. Z3-8. ☼ ✹ ◩ ■

POLYGONUM

P. vacciniifolium. Rapidly spreading mats, masses of short spikes bearing light pink flowers in autumn. Good for hanging over walls. H10cm/4in, W60cm/2ft. F9-10. Z4-8. ☼ ✹ ◩ ■

PRIMULA See Perennials Directory, page 126.

RANUNCULUS

R. ficaria. Lesser celandine. Comes into leaf in spring, followed by bright yellow flowers, dies back in mid-summer. Several selections. 'Alba', white. 'Aurantiacus', coppery orange. 'Brazen Hussey', brightest of all, coppery leaves, golden flowers. All H10cm/4in, W20cm/8in. F3-5. Z4-8. ☼ ✹ ◩ ■

RAOULIA

Carpeting evergreens grown for their tiny leaves rather than their miniature flowers. Peaty soil; good drainage in winter. ☼ ✹ ◩ ■
R. australis. Silver leaves, insignificant, yellow flowers. H1cm/½in, W30cm/1ft. F6-7. Z7-8.

SAGINA

S. subulata 'Aurea'. Bright, evergreen carpeter. Creamy yellow foliage in winter, bright yellow in summer, white flowers. Good for screes or paving. H1cm/½in, W20cm/8in. F6-7. Z6-8. ☼ ◩ ■

SATUREJA **Winter savory**
S. montana **'Pygmaea'.** Pretty semi-
evergreen bush, deep blue autumn
flowers. H20cm/8in, W15cm/6in.
F9-10. Z6-9. ☼ ■

SAXIFRAGA **Saxifrage**
Indispensable genus for evergreen
foliage and early flowers. The range
and variety is immense.
Kabschia or cushion group. Rosettes
of lime-encrusted, grey-green or
silvery foliage, often large, saucer-
shaped pink, white or yellow flowers,
generally in early spring. Excellent

Saxifraga 'Pixie'

for troughs. H5-25cm/2-10in,
W8-25cm/3-10in. F2-4. Z4-6.
☼ ◨ ■
Aizoon or encrusted group. Similar
to the Kabschia types, but much
larger leaves, often evergreen, and
flowering in late spring. H5-30cm/
2-12in, W 13-40cm/5-16in. F5-6.
Z4-7. ☼ ■ ⊕
Mossy group. Moss-like, green or
coloured foliage, masses of white,
pink, crimson, even yellow flowers
on slender stems. **'Cloth of Gold'**,
bright golden leaves. **'Hi-Ace'**,
delicately variegated foliage. **'Pixie'**,
compact, bright pink flowers. H10-
25cm/4-10in. W15-30cm/6-12in.
F3-5. Z5-6. ☼ ◨
S. juniperifolia. One of the earliest
to flower. Green hummocks
festooned with clusters of bright
yellow flowers. H5cm/2in,
W15cm/6in. F3-4. Z5-7. ◨ ■
S. oppositifolia. Showy, small, lilac-
like flowers then dark green mats –
early in spring. **'Florissa'**, bright
rose-pink. All H5cm/2in,
W45cm/18in. F3-4. Z2-6. ☼

Sedum spathulifolium 'Purpureum'

Sedum lidakense

SEDUM **Stonecrop**
There are some good evergreen
foliage types among these succulents
and a few late-flowering species.
☼ ■ ☆
S. kamtschaticum **'Variegatum'.**
Attractive, pink-tinged, yellow and
green leaves give a long period of
interest. Deciduous. Golden flowers.
H15cm/6in, W20cm/8in. F6-8.
Z3-8.
S. lidakense. Bluish grey leaves, a
good show of bright, rosy red
flowers. Deciduous. H10cm/4in,
W15cm/6in. F8-10. Z4-8.
S. spathulifolium. Dwarf, mat-
forming. Silvery grey spathe-like
leaves, yellow flowers. **'Capo
Blanco'**, dwarfer, powdery white
leaves. **'Purpureum'**, larger, purple-
tinged leaves. All H5cm/2in,
W25cm/10in. F6-7. Z4-7.

SEMPERVIVUM **Houseleek**
Rosette-forming succulents offering
wide range of size and colour.
Foliage can be red, purple, grey or
green with colourful leaf tips.
Flowers are often spasmodic,
curious, sometimes spectacular.
Gritty soil. The plants vary in size,
but all F6-7, Z5-9. ☼ ■

S. arachnoideum **'Laggeri'.** One of
the best silvered, "cobwebby" types.
Dense cushion webbed with silver
threads. H2.5-8cm/1-3in,
W20-30cm/8-12in. F6-7. Z5-9.

THYMUS **Thyme**
Popular aromatic plants, some
creeping, some more shrubby.
Carpeters, good for paving. ☼ ◨ ■
T. **'Bressingham Pink'.** Grey-green
carpet, pink flowers. H2.5cm/1in,
W15cm/6in. F5-6. Z4-7.
T. **x** *citriodorus.* Bushy, lemon-
scented, evergreen. **'Silver Posie'** and
'Silver Queen', prettily variegated
forms. Similar is the hybrid
'Anderson's Gold', bright, golden
foliage all year round. All 15cm/6in,
W30cm/1ft. F5-6. Z6-8.
T. **'Doone Valley'.** Deep green foliage
flecked with gold. H15cm/6in,
W30cm/1ft. F5-6. Z6-8.
T. nitidus. Erect, twiggy bush, grey-
green foliage, clear pink flowers.
'Peter Davis', perhaps the best form.
Both H20cm/8in, W30cm/1ft.
F5-6. Z7-8.
T. serpyllum. Grey-green carpet,
white, pink and red flowers.
H2.5cm/1in, W10-25cm/4-10in.
F5-7. Z4-8.

BULBS DIRECTORY

To most gardeners bulbs are the true harbingers of spring, starting with snowdrops and aconites which appear in late winter according to region and season. As with most other groups of plants, once you investigate you realize that the variety available is greater than you originally thought. The selection below concentrates on some of the best plants for autumn, winter and early spring interest, but there are lots of later spring-flowering bulbs that fall just beyond the scope of this book. The majority of bulbs are sold dry in late summer and autumn and most, crocus, narcissus and tulips in particular, can be planted up until early winter if thay are stored in a dry atmosphere meanwhile. Most bulbs prefer a reasonably well-drained soil. Plant them at a depth twice that of their height.

Some bulbs – snowdrops (Galanthus) *and aconites* (Eranthis) *– are best planted "in the green", just after flowering, if you can obtain them like this. More bulbs are now being offered in pots at their time of flowering in winter or early spring. These are more expensive but are a good way of acquiring some choice or well-grown plants; it is by far the best way to buy hardy cyclamens, for example, as these seldom grow satisfactorily from older, dry corms.*

Spring-flowering bulbs bring early colour

Colchicum agrippinum

CHIONODOXA Glory-of-the-snow
Late winter- and spring-flowering bulbs related to scilla. Naturalize freely, even in grass. ☼ ❋ ■
C. luciliae. Brilliant show of white-centred, bright blue, star-like flowers in early spring. Similar are *C.* 'Pink Giant', slightly taller, and *C. sardensis*, almost gentian-blue flowers but a little later. H10-15cm/4-6in, W10-15cm/4-6in. F3-4. Z4.

COLCHICUM
Open, trumpet-shaped flowers on naked stems in late summer and autumn. Use as frontal groups among shrubs, but not where their large leaves will smother smaller plants. ☼ ❋ ■
C. agrippinum. Star-shaped, lilac-purple flowers spotted with white. H10-15cm/4-6in, W30cm/1ft. F 9-10. Z6.
C. autumnale. Mauve-lilac flowers in early autumn. The form *roseum plenum*, with showy double, reddish violet trumpets is later. Both H10-15cm/4-6in, W30cm/1ft. Z5.
C. speciosium. Probably the most showy of the genus. Large lily-like flowers, shades of mauve, purple and lilac with creamy centres and golden anthers. The form *album* is white. Both H15-20cm/6-9in, W30cm/1ft. F 9-10. Z5.
Hybrids between *C. speciosium* and *C. autumnale* are equally showy, including the double '**Waterlily**', pinkish lilac flowers, and '**Atrorubens**', single, crimson-lilac.

Crocus sieberi

CROCUS
Many autumn-, winter- and early spring-flowering species but only a few can be selected here. Field mice and voles enjoy the bulbs as winter food. Like high shade under trees. ☼ ■
C. ancyrensis. Small, orange-yellow flowers rising above needle-like, deep green foliage in winter. H5-8cm/2-3in, W5-8in/2-3in. F1-2. Z5.
C. chrysanthus. Indispensable for early spring flowers. Mostly represented by named varieties from light blue to purple, white to striped, yellow to bronze. Small-flowered, they are better for naturalizing than the equally showy large-flowered, so-called Dutch crocus. Similar are selections of *C. sieberi* and *C. etruscus* and *C. tommasimianus.* All H9-12cm/3-4in, W3-4cm/9-12in. F2-3. Z5.
C. speciosus. Excellent autumn-flowering species with many variants from violet-blue to mauve to lilac and white. Naturalizes freely. H15cm/6in, W15cm/6in. F8-10. Z4.

CYCLAMEN
Worthy garden plants for flower, foliage and some for fragrance, during autumn, winter and early spring. Some naturalize very freely, self-seeding on surface mulch or undisturbed leaf mould. Apply a light mulch of composted bark or leaf mould when dormant. ☼ ❋ ■
C. coum. Brightest crimson to pink and white mid-winter flowers, unfurl

Cyclamen coum

from rounded, kidney-shaped leaves. Many selections with silver or marbled foliage. H9-12cm/3-4in, W15cm/6in. F11-3. Z6.

C. hederifolium. Pink or white flowers from late summer into autumn as marbled leaves appear, these making a total ground cover which once established lasts through winter. H10-15cm/4-6in, W15cm/6in. F8-1. Z6.

ERANTHIS
E. hyemalis. Winter aconite. The easiest and most popular of the genus. Early, cheery, golden-yellow, buttercup flowers followed by fresh green foliage. More a tuber than a bulb but can be treated in the same way; when planting in late summer or early autumn, do not plant too deep, add a leafy, peaty mulch and keep moist. Self-seeds once established. Plant beneath trees or shrubs. H5-10cm/2-4in, W8-12cm/3-5in. F1-2. Z4. ☼ ☀ ◪ ■

ERYTHRONIUM **Dog's tooth violet**
Pretty woodland plants with trumpet-shaped flowers, some with mottled leaves. Resent disturbance so plant in autumn as dry bulbs. ☼ ◪ ■ ★

E. californicum. Californian fawn lily. Clusters of creamy yellow flowers, purple-mottled leaves. H25-30/10-12in, W15cm/6in. F4-5. Z4.

E. 'Pagoda'. Pale yellow flowers. H30-45/12-18, W20cm/8in. F4-5. Z5.

GALANTHUS **Snowdrop**
Larger family than many realize,

Galanthus nivalis

with more than a hundred species and varieties in cultivation, available only from specialists. All have pendulous, white flowers some in autumn but most in winter. Best moved and planted immediately after flowering whilst leaves are still green. ☼ ☀ ◪ ★

G. nivalis. Common snowdrop. Simple, single flowers, green leaves. Seems to do well anywhere and naturalizes easily in grass, woodland or gardens. 'Plenus', pretty double. 'Viridapicis', green-tipped outer petals. All H10-15cm/4-6in, W15cm/6in. F1-3. Z4.

G. reginae-olgae. Autumn-flowering, best grown in the open. H10-15cm/4-6in, W15cm/6in. F 9-11. Z6. ■

G. 'S. Arnott'. One of the best of all and one I grow widely at Foggy Bottom. Large flowers, abundant foliage and good vigour. H15-25cm/6-10in, W15in/6in. F1-3. Z4.

IRIS
Some early spring-flowering species and varieties. Useful in containers, with alpines or nestling between dwarf shrubs or conifers. ☼ ☀ ■ ■

I. danfordiae. Beautiful early species with deep yellow flowers on sturdy stems. Best planted 2.5cm/5in deep. H10-12.5cm/4-5in, W10cm/4in. F2-3. Z4.

I. histrioides 'Major'. Best form of the species. Deep blue flowers speckled white. H8-10cm/3-4in, W10cm/4in. F1-2. Z4.

I. reticulata. Early, mostly fragrant flowers on sturdy stems. Blue to purple, the falls marked with yellow. 'Cantab', pale blue and yellow.

Eranthis hyemalis

Erythronium californicum

'Harmony', sky blue, yellow markings. 'J.S. Dijt', reddish purple. All H12-15cm/5-6ins, W10cm/4in. F2-3. Z4.

LEUCOJUM Snowflake

L. vernum. Spring snowflake. Larger flowers than snowdrops, with overlapping, green-tipped white petals, in late winter and early spring. Good for naturalizing in grass. Plant 10cm/4in deep. H10-15cm/4-6in, W15cm/6in. F2-3. Z5. ☼ ◪ ■

MUSCARI Grape hyacinth

Showy plants adding blue, poker-like flowers to the predominant yellows of mid-spring and mixing well with conifers and heathers. Plant 8cm/3in deep. Colours range from pale blue to azure and deep indigo as well as white. All 15-20cm/6-8in. Z4. ☼ ☀ ◪ ■

NARCISSUS

Large genus with just a few early flowering types suitable for rock gardens, naturalizing or general planting. ☼ ☀ ■

N. asturiensis. Perfect miniature for rock or alpine garden with small, pendent, golden-yellow trumpets. H8-10cm/3-4in, W8cm/3in. F2-3. Z4 .

N. bulbocodium. Distinctive species with nodding, petticoat-shaped flowers from pale lemon to golden-yellow, and grassy leaves. Naturalizes well in grass. H15-30cm/6-12in, W15cm/6in. F3-4. Z5. ◪

N. cyclamineus. Golden-yellow, swept back or recurved petals, the corona long and tubular. H10-20cm/4-8in, W8cm/3in. F2-3. Z3. ☼ or ☀ ◪

Hybrids. Early flowering, smaller types worth obtaining are as follows. 'February Gold', nodding, deep yellow trumpets. 'February Silver', yellow trumpets, white petals or perianth. Both H20-25cm/8-10in, W15cm/6in. F2-3. Z3. 'Peeping Tom', bright green foliage enhancing nodding, deep yellow, tubular corona and swept back perianth. H30cm/1ft, W15cm/6in. F3. Z3. 'Tête-à-Tête', early, deep yellow trumpet, lighter perianth, usually two or more flowers per

Narcissus 'Tête-à-Tête'

stem. H15cm/6in, W10cm/4in. F2-3. Z3.

NERINE

Strap-like leaves for most of the year. showy terminal flower clusters on leafless stems in autumn. Plant bulbs shallowly, against a wall or as edging. Easy and reasonably hardy, except in cold regions. Light, sandy soil. ☼ ☀ ■

N. bowdenii. Late-autumn display of clear pink, lily-like trumpets. H35cm/14in, W23cm/9in. F9-11.

Z8-10. 'Fenwick's Variety', taller and larger-flowered. H40cm/16in, W23cm/9in. F9-11. Z8-10.

PUSCHKINIA

P. scilloides. Striped squill. Early white flowers striped pale blue, closely allied to *Chionodoxa* and *Scilla*. The form *alba* is white. Plant 8cm/3in deep. Both H10cm/4in, W8cm/3in. F3. Z4. ☼ ☀ ◪ ■ ★

SCILLA

The early spring-flowering squills or wild hyacinths grow happily among shrubs, on alpine or rock gardens. Plant 8cm/3in deep. ☼ ☀ ◪ ■

S bifolia. Often variable but mostly turquoise, star-like flowers. H5-8cm/2-3in, W8cm/3in. F3-4. Z4.

S. sibirica. Siberian squill. Brilliant deep blue flowers. 'Spring Beauty', similar blue flowers but more vigorous, good for naturalizing in grass. H10-15cm/4-6in, W10cm/4in. F3-4. Z4.

S. tubergeniana. Very early, pale blue, star-like flowers with darker blue veins on backs of petals. H10cm/4in, W10cm/4in. F1-2. Z4.

Muscari armeniacum

Nerine bowdenii

BIBLIOGRAPHY

The books listed below have been helpful in expanding my knowledge about plants that have interest in autumn, winter and early spring and as general reference. Although some may be out of print, no doubt they can be found in libraries and specialist secondhand bookshops.

Bloom, Adrian, *Conifers for your Garden*. Burrall/Floraprint, 1972.

Bloom, Adrian, *Making the Most of Conifers and Heathers*. Burrall/Floraprint, 1986. (Previously published as *A Year Round Garden*, 1979.)

Bloom, Alan and Adrian, *Blooms of Bressingham Garden Plants*. HarperCollins Publishers, 1992.

Davis, Brian, *The Gardener's Encyclopedia of Trees and Shrubs*. Viking 1987.

Foster, Raymond, *The Garden in Autumn and Winter*. David and Charles, 1983.

Hillier Manual of Trees and Shrubs, The. Hillier/David and Charles, 1991.

Lacey, Stephen, *Scent in the Garden*. Frances Lincoln, 1991.

Thomas, Graham Stuart, *Colour in the Winter Garden*. JM Dent, 1957, 1984.

Thomas, Graham Stuart, *Perennial Garden Plants, or the Modern Florilegium*. JM Dent, 1990.

Verey, Rosemary, *The Garden in Winter*. Windward/Frances Lincoln, 1988.

INDEX

Page numbers in *italics* indicate illustrations

Abelia 92
Abeliophyllum distichum 80, *80*, 92, *92*
Abies 110
  procera:
    'Glauca' *32*
    'Glauca Prostrata' *53*, *110*
Acaena 136
Acer (Maple):
  capillipes 13, 20, 47-9, 54, 76, 79, 89, 92
  palmatum:
    'Garnet' *92*
    'Osakazuki' *92*
    'Senkaki' *79*
    'Shishigashira' *64*
  platanoides 'Princeton Gold' *52*
Aconite, winter *see Eranthis hyemalis*
Aconitum 119
  carmichaelii 'Arendsii' *119*
Acorus gramineus 51, 65, 130
Adiantum pedatum 129
Adonis 38, 52, 119
  amurensis *119*
Agapanthus 34, 119
  'Lilliput' *74*
Ajuga 136
  reptans 'Braunherz' *136*
Alnus 40, 89
  glutinosa 89
alpines 68, 76, 88, *136*
  directory 136-8
Alyssum saxatile 136
Amelanchier lamarckii 89
Anaphalis 119
Andropogon scoparius 130
Anemone japonica (*A.* x *hybrida*) 24, 119-20

'Alba' *24*
'Lady Gilmour' *120*
Arabis 136
Arbutus 93
  unedo 'Rubra' *93*
architectural plants 62
Arisaema candidissimum 28
Armeria 136
Aronia 20, 93
  arbutifolia 'Erecta' *20*
Artemisia:
  canescens 120
  'Powys Castle' *93*, *93*
  stelleriana 27, 120
Arum italicum pictum 82, *82*
Asarum europaeum 120
Asplenium 129
Aster 23, 84, 120-1
  amellus: 'King George' *120*
  × *frikartii* 22
Astilbe chinensis 25
Aubrieta 137
  'Bressingham Pink' *137*
Aucuba 42-3, 65, 93
Aurinia saxitalis see Alyssum saxatile
autumn 18-29
  leaf colour 21
  scent 57
Azaleas 20, 105
Azobella trifurcata 137

bark 46-9, 83-4, *83*, *84*
Berberis 20, 93
  × *media* 'Red Jewel' *93*
  thunbergii 'Dart's Red Lady' *93*
Bergenia 56, 65, 82, 83, 121
  'Baby Doll' *82*
  'Bressingham Ruby' *36*, *79*, *83*, *121*
  'Wintermärchen' *53*
berries 22-3

Betula 21, 47, 78, 83, 89-90
  costata 36
  jacquemontii 89
  nigra 'Heritage' *47*, *89*
  pendula 90
  silver *8*
  utilis 'Jacquemontii' *83*
Bidens atrosanguinea see Cosmos atrosanguineus
Birch *see Betula*
birds: berries and 22, 23
Blechnum 129
  tabulare 129
Bolax glebaria see Azobella trifurcata
Bouteloua gracilis (*B. oligostachya*) 130, *130*
Briza media 130
Buddleia 26, 93-4
  'Pink Delight' *94*
bulbs *75*, 88, *139*
  directory 139-41
Buxus sempervirens 94

Calamagrostis 50, 130
Callicarpa 94
Calluna vulgaris 65, 133-4, *134*
  'Anne Marie' *133*
  'Boskoop' *133*
  'Roma' *28*
Calocedrus decurrens 'Aureovariegata' 110, *110*
Camellia 54, 64, 79, 94
  × *williamsii* 'Donation' *56*, *79*, *94*
Carex 49, 50, 130
  comans 'Bronze Form' *36*, *74*, *79*, *79*
Caryopteris 26, 94
  × *clandonensis* 'Heavenly Blue' *26*
Cautleya 34
Cedrus (Cedar) 78, 110-11
Ceratostigma 94

willmottianum 23, *26*
Chaenomeles 94
Chamaecyparis:
  lawsoniana 78, 111
  'Pygmy' *28*
  obtusa 111
  'Graciosa' *43*
  'Nana Gracilis' *37*
  pisifera 111
  'Filifera Nana' *79*, 111
  thyoides 111
Chimonanthus 51
  praecox 38, 82, *82*, 94
Chionochloa rubra 130
Chionodoxa 85, 139
  luciliae 85
Choisya 94-5
  ternata 'Sundance' *36*, 79, *79*
Chrysanthemopsis hosmariense 75
Chrysanthemum:
  hosmariense see Chrysanthemopsis hosmariense
  rubellum see Dendranthema rubella
Cimicifuga 121
  simplex 'Elstead' *121*
Clematis 82, 95
  cirrhosa 'Freckles' *82*
  tangutica 28, *95*
climbers: for autumn 20
Colchicum 139
  agrippinum 139
Commelina coelestis 34, *34*, 121
conifers *8*, *13*, 40, 43-5, *44*, *75*, *110*
  deciduous 45-6
  directory 110-18
  dwarf *8*, 12, 65, *67*
  planting 88
  in small garden 66-9
  in snow 36
  year-round interest *19*

containers 64-5
plant associations 79, *79*
planting 65
Coreopsis 121
Cornus (dogwood) *8*, 36, 65, 72
alba 48, 65, 95
'Kesselringii' 20, 84, *84*, 95
'Sibirica' 20, 35, *48*, *49*, *61*, 95
kelseyi 49
mas 95
'Aurea' *95*
sanguinea 48, 65
'Winter Flame ('Winter Beauty') 20,
35, 48, *78*, *79*, 81, *81*, 95
stolonifera 48, 95
'Flaviramea' *48*, 95, *95*
Cortaderia:
selloana 30, 50, 130-1
'Pumila' 35, 50, *78*, *131*
Corylopsis 95
Corylus avellana 'Contorta' 40, 46, *47*,
95
Cosmos atrosanguineus 34, *34*, 121
Cotinus 95-6
'Grace' *96*
Cotoneaster 23, 90, 96
franchetii 96
Crataegus 90
Crocosmia 27, 34, 76, 121
Crocus 54, 139
sieberi *139*
Cryptomeria 45, 111-12
japonica 'Elegans' *111*
× *Cupressocyparis* 16-17, 112
Cupressus glabra 112
Cyclamen 139-40
coum 54, *55*, 139-40, *140*
hederifolium 22, *83*, 140
Cyrtomium falcatum 129

Daboecia 134
Daphne 96
mezereum *96*
Dell garden *7*, 15
Dendranthema 23-4, 121-2
rubella 'Apricot' *25*
Dentaria 54
Deschampsia 50, 131
caespitosa 'Golden Dew' ('Goldtau')
131
design 57
Dianthus 137
Diascia 76
Dicentra 'Snowflakes' 85, *85*
Dogwood *see Cornus*
Draba 137
drought-resistant plants 74-7
Dryopteris 129
borreri (*D. affinis*, *D. pseudomas*)
'Pinderi' *33*, *129*
erythrosora 82, *82*

Echinacea purpurea 122
Elaeagnus:
× ebbingei 42, 65, 75, 96-7

pungens 'Maculata' *42*
Elsholtzia stauntonii 97
Epimedium 54, 83, 122
pinnatum colchicum *54*, *83*, *122*
Eranthis hyemalis (Winter aconite) 38,
52, *81*, 84, *84*, 88, 140, *140*
Erica 26, 40, 45, 53, 65, 81, 88, 134-5
arborea 'Albert's Gold' *135*
carnea (*E. herbacea*) 79
'Aurea' *28*
'Pink Spangles' *40*, *134*, *135*
'Springwood White' *53*
'Vivellii' *53*, *81*
× darleyensis 79
'Ghost Hills' *134*
Erigeron karvinskianus (*E. mucronatus*)
137
Erythronium 140
californicum *55*, *140*
Eucalyptus 13, 43
niphophila 90, *90*
Euonymus 15, 20, 22, 40-2, 65, 79, 97
alatus: 'Compactus' 20, 97
fortunei 'Emerald 'n' Gold' *56*, *79*
planipes (*E. sachalinensis*) 97
Eupatorium 122
purpureum 'Glutball' *122*
Euphorbia 54, 83, 122-3
myrsinites *83*
wulfenii 'Humpty Dumpty' *123*
evergreens 22, 36, 40-3

Fatsia 43
ferns:
directory 129
planting 88
fertilizers 88
Festuca 50, 81, 131
glauca 'Blue Glow' *81*, *131*
flowers:
autumn 23-8
spring 53-4
winter 37-40
Foggy Bottom *7*, 8, *8*, *9*, 12-17, *13-17*,
36, *44*, *52*, 54, *56*, *61*
foliage:
autumn colour 21
winter associations 83, *83*
Forsythia 97
'Weekend' *52*
Fothergilla 20, 21, 97-8
gardenii (*F. alnifolia*) *21*, *97*
Fragaria 'Pink Panda' 84, *84*
front gardens 63-4
frost 30, 54-6
visual effects *32-3*, 35, *44-5*
frost-tender plants 34
fruit 22-3
Fuchsia 26, 98

Galanthus (Snowdrop) 52, 78, 81, 84,
85, 88, 140
nivalis *81*, *83*, *84*, *85*, 140
Garrya elliptica 40, 80, 98
'James Roof' *40*, *80*, *98*

Gaultheria 98
Gaura lindheimeri 27, 123
Gentiana 123, 137
sino-ornata 24, *24*
Geranium 76, 81, 123, 137
× riversleaianum 'Russell Prichard' *74*,
123
Ginkgo 45
grasses, ornamental 35, *44*, 49-51, 64,
75
directory 130-2
planting 88
ground cover 15, 67

Hacquetia epipactis 123
Hakonechloa macra 'Alboaurea' *36*, 50,
79
Hamamelis 20, 21, 38, 51, 54, 85, 98
× intermedia:
'Diane' *21*
'Jelena' ('Copper Beauty') *38*
'Orange Beauty' *39*
'Primavera' *98*
mollis 'Pallida' *85*
hardiness zones 34-5, 88
Heaths and heathers *8*, 8, 12, 13, *44*,
65, *133*
autumn-flowering 26
directory 133-5
planting 88
in small garden 66-9, *67*
summer-flowering 53, 68, 88
tree 135
winter-flowering 40, 53, 88
Hebe 26, 43, 65, 98-9
'Great Orme' *25*
Hedera 42, 79, 80, 82, 99
colchica:
'Dentata Variegata' *79*, *82*
'Sulphur Heart' ('Paddy's Pride') *99*
helix:
'Glacier' *83*
'Gold Heart' *80*
Helianthus salicifolius (*H. orygalis*) 123,
123
Helleborus 38, 54, 65, 78, 84, 85, 123-4
foetidus *124*
'Wester Flisk' *38*
niger *84*
orientalis *55*
'Winter Cheer' *85*
Hemerocallis 15
Heuchera 124
Hibiscus 26
Hosta 15, 56, 85, 124
Hydrangea 20, 26, 99
arborescens 'Annabelle' *99*
quercifolia 'Snow Queen' *20*, *33*
Hypericum androsaemum 99-100

Iberis 137
sempervirens 'Snowflake' *137*
Ilex (Holly) 23, 42, 65, 100
aquifolium 'Fructu Luteo'
('Bacciflava') *42*

crenata 'Golden Gem' *100*
Imperata cylindrica 'Rubra' *36*
Iris:
danfordiae 38, 54, 65, 80, 83, 124,
140-1
foetidissima 'Variegata' *83*, *124*
stylosa (*I. unguicularis*) *80*, *124*

Jasminum 38, 100
Juniperus 15, 112-13
chinensis:
'Aurea' *112*
'Kaizuka' *112*
communis:
'Green Carpet' *37*
'Horstmann' *113*
horizontalis 'Glauca' *37*
× media:
'Gold Sovereign' *7*, *37*
'Sulphur Spray' *37*, *79*

Kerria japonica 100
Kniphofia 24, 34, 76, 124-5
rooperi (*K.* 'C.M. Prichard') *125*

Lamium 83, 125
maculatum 'White Nancy' *83*, *125*
Larix (Larch) 45, 46, 113
kaempferi 'Diana' *19*, *47*, *113*
Laurus nobilis 100-1
Lavandula 26
Leucojum vernum 141
Leucothoe 101
Ligustrum 43
Liquidambar 21, 90
styraciflua 'Worplesdon' *90*
Liriope muscari (*L. macrophylla*) 24, 81,
81, 125
Lonicera 51, 101
fragrantissima *101*
Luzula sylvatica 131
Lysimachia 137

Magnolia 13, 54, 101
stellata 55
'Royal Star' *101*
Mahonia 26-8, 40, 51, 82, 101-2
aquifolium 'Atropurpurea' *101*
× media:
'Charity' *82*
'Underway' *41*
Malus 90-1
'Evereste' *91*
Maple *see Acer*
Matteuccia struthiopteris 129
Melianthus major 34
Metasequoia glyptostroboides 114
Microbiota decussata 43, 44, 114
microclimate 13
Miscanthus 49, 50, 131-2
sinensis 50
'Cascade' ('Kaskade') *131*
'Morning Light' *35*
'Purpureus' *22*
Molinia 132

altissima (M. litoralis) 'Transparent' *132*
mulches 12, 30, 66, 67, 88
Muscari 141
   armeniacum 55, 84, *141*
Myrica gale 102

Nandina domestica 20, 102
   'Firepower' *102*
Narcissus 54, 85, 141
   'February Silver' *85*
   'Jack Snipe' *53*
   'Mrs R. O. Backhouse' *52*
   'Tête-à-tête' *141*
Nerine 26, 34, 141
   bowdenii 25, 80, *80*, 141, *141*

Omphalodes 125
Ophiopogon planiscapus 'Nigrescens' 51, 65, *81*, 83, *83*
Origanum 125
Osmanthus 43, 102
   × *burkwoodii* 102
Osmarea burkwoodii see Osmanthus ×
   burkwoodii
Oxydendrum arboreum 20, *102*, 103

Panicum virgatum 'Rubrum' 132
Parthenocissus 20, 103
   henryana *103*
Pennisetum 132
Penstemon 34, 125
perennials:
   autumn-flowering 23-6
   directory 119-28
   planting 88
   winter protection 34
Perovskia atriplicifolia 103
Persicaria see Polygonum
Phormium 13, 15, 34, 43
Photinia 103
Phyllitis see Asplenium
Physalis franchetii 125, *125*
Physostegia 125-6
Picea:
   abies 63, 114-15
   glauca 'Coerulea' *114*
   pungens:
     'Globosa' ('Glauca Globosa') *114*
     'Hoopsii' *115*
     'Prostrata' ('Glauca Prostrata',
     'Procumbens') *115*
     'Thomsen' *43*
Pieris 64, 103-4
   japonica 'Pink Delight' *103*
Pinus 43, 115-17
   leucodermis (P. heldreichii leucodermis)
   43
   mugo:
     'Ophir' *19*
     Winter Gold' *48*, 116
   parviflora 'Glauca' *45, 51*, 116
   sylvestris:
     'Aurea' *43*
     'Gold Coin' *55*

Pittosporum 43, 104
plant associations 78-85
   planting 88
Podocarpus 117
pollarding 48
Polygala 104
   chamaebuxus 'Grandiflora' *(P.
   rhodoptera)* 104
Polygonum 126, 137
   amplexicaule 'Taurus' *126*
Polypodium 129
Polystichum 129
   setiferum 'Herrenhausen' *32*, 129
ponds 15, *22*
Populus alba 'Richardii' 91, *91*
Potentilla 15, 26, 84, 104, 126
   'Red Robin' *26*
Primula 54, 126
pruning 63
Prunus 20, 43, 46, 79, 80, 91, 104-5
   incisa 'Kojo-no-mai' *62, 79, 104*
   mume 'Beni-shidare' *80*
   serrula 47, *91*
Pseudolarix 45
Pulmonaria 22, 54, *75*, 81, 82, 84, 85,
   126-7
   'Highdown' ('Lewis Palmer') *54, 81*
   longifolia 'Roy Davidson' *53*
   officinalis 'Sissinghurst White' *82, 126*
   saccharata 'Leopard' *85*
Puschkinia scilloides 141
Pyracantha 23, 37, 80, 105
   'Orange Glow' *7, 23, 37, 80*

Ranunculus ficaria 54, 137
Raoulia 137
Rhododendron 20, 43, 54, 64, 105
   'Olive' *105*
Rhus 20, 105-6
   glabra 'Laciniata' *105*
Ribes 106
   sanguineum:
     'Red Pimpernel' *106*
     'White Icicle' *56*
Rosa 26, 106
   rugosa 23
   virginiana 33, *106*
Rosmarinus 106-7
   'Sissinghurst' 80, *80*
Rubus:
   biflorus 48, 78, 84, 107
   cockburnianus 'Golden Vale' *84*
Rudbeckia 127
   deamii 22
Ruscus aculeatus 107

Sagina 137
Salix (Willow) 36, 45, 46, 48, 84, 107
   irrorata 48
   × *sepulcralis* 'Erythroflexuosa'
     (S.erythroflexuosa) 46, *79*, 84
Salvia 34, 107, 127
   officinalis 'Berggarten' *107*
   uliginosa *127*
Santolina 80, 107

chamaecyparissus (S. incana) 80
Sarcococca 51, 57, 79, 82, 107
   confusa 79
   humilis 82
Satureja 138
Saxifraga 54, 127, 138
   fortunei 'Rubrifolia' *127*
   'Pixie' *32, 138*
Scabiosa 127
scented plants 51, 57, 80, *80*
Schizostylis 24, 34, 127
Scilla 54, 141
Scolopendrium see Asplenium
scree bed 70, 72
Sedum 24-6, 127-8, 138
   'Autumn Joy' ('Herbstfreude') *27, 50*
   lidakense *138*
   spathulifolium 'Purpureum' *138*
   spectabile 'Brilliant' *128*
Sempervivum 138
Serratula 128
shrubs:
   for autumn 20
   autumn-flowering 26-8
   coloured bark and stems 46-9
   directory 92-109
   evergreen 40-3
   planting 88
   in small garden 66-9, *75*
   twisting branches 45-6
   winter-flowering 38-40
Skimmia 65, 79, 107-8
   reevesiana 79, *108*
small gardens:
   choosing plants for 63
   drought-resistant 74-7, *74-7*
   low-maintenance 66-9, *66-9*
   winter colour in 60-3, 70-3, *70-3*
snow 36
soil:
   improving 12
   variations across garden 13-15
Solidago 128
Sorbus 23, 91, 108
   koehneana 108
specimen plants 62-3
Spiraea 20, 108
spring 52-7
   planting for semi-shade 85, *85*
   scent 57
Stachyurus 54
Stephanandra tanakae 108, *108*
Stewartia 54
Stipa:
   arundinacea 132
   calamagrostis 50, *78*, 132
   gigantea 132, *132*
   tenuifolia 44, 50, *51*, 132
Stranvaesia davidiana see Photinia
Symphoricarpos 108

Taxodium distichum 45-6, 117, *117*
Taxus (Yew) *29*, 117-18
   baccata 'Standishii' *117*
tender plants:

planting 88
   winter protection 34
Thuja 118
   orientalis:
     'Aurea Nana' *37*
     'Elegantissima' *118*
   plicata 118
Thymus 138
Tradescantia 128
trees:
   coloured bark and stems 46-9
   directory 89-91
   grown as shrubs 76
   planting 88
   twisting branches 45-6
Tricyrtis 128
Tsuga canadensis 118

Ulex europaeus 108

Vaccineum 20, 23, 108-9
Verbena bonariensis 128
Viburnum 28, 38-40, 51, 65, 79, 109
   × *bodnantense* 'Dawn' *109*
   tinus 'Eve Price' *79*
Vinca 128
Viola 54
Vitis 109
   coignetiae 109
   *inconstans see Parthenocissus
   tricuspidata*

wall:
   semi-shady 82, *82*
   sunny: scented plants for 80, *80*
weeding 67
Weigela 15
window boxes 30, 65, *65*
winter 30-51
   flowers for 37-40
   plant associations for 78-85
   protecting plants in 34
   scent 51, 57
Winter aconite *see Eranthis hyemalis*
Wisteria 54

Yew *see Taxus*
Yucca 43
   filamentosa 128, *128*
   'Variegata' *27, 50*

Zauschneria 34, 128